THE MIND AND ITS EDUCATION

THE MIND AND ITS EDUCATION

BY

GEORGE HERBERT BETTS, Ph.D.

PROFESSOR OF PSYCHOLOGY IN CORNELL COLLEGE

2008

Kaveri Books

New Delhi - 110 002

First Indian Edition 2008

ISBN-10 : 81-7479- 085-3
ISBN-13 : 978-81-7479-085-9

Published by
Kaveri Books
4697/ 5-21 A, Ansari Road,
New Delhi - 110 002 (India).

Ph.: 011-2328 8140, 2324 5799
E-mail: kaveribooks@vsnl.com

Laser Typesetting by
Aarati Computers, Delhi - 110 009.

Printed at
Chawla Offset Printers, Delhi-110052.

PRINTED IN INDIA

PREFACE

Authors, no doubt, are always gratified when their works find favorable acceptance. The writer of this text has been doubly gratified, however, at the cordial reception and widespread use accorded to the present volume. This feeling does not arise from any narrow personal pride or selfish interest, but rather from the fact that the warm approval of the educational public has proved an important point; namely, that the fundamental truths of psychology, when put simply and concretely, can be made of interest and value to students of all ages from high school juniors up, and to the general public as well. More encouraging still, it has been demonstrated that the teachings of psychology can become immediately helpful, not only in study or teaching, but also in business or profession, in the control and guidance of the personal life, and in the problems met in the routine of the day's work or its play.

In effecting the present revision, the salient features of the original edition have been kept. The truths presented are the most fundamental and important in the field of psychology. Disputed theories and unsettled opinions are excluded. The subject matter is made concrete and practical by the use of many illustrations and through application to real problems. The style has been kept easy and familiar to facilitate the reading. In short, there has been, while seeking to improve the volume, a conscious purpose to omit none of the characteristics which secured acceptance for the former edition.

On the other hand, certain changes and additions have been made which, it is believed, will add to the strength of the work. First of all, the later psychological studies and investigations have been drawn upon to insure that the matter shall at all points be abreast of the times in scientific accuracy. Because of the wide use of the text in the training of teachers, a more specific educational application to schoolroom problems has been made in various chapters. Exercises for the guidance of observation work and personal introspection are freely used. The chapter on Sensation and Perception has been separated into two chapters, and each subject given more extensive treatment. A new chapter has been added on Association. The various chapters have been subdivided into numbered sections, and cut-in paragraph topics have been used to facilitate the study and teaching of the text. Minor changes and additions occur throughout the volume, thus adding some forty pages to the number in the original edition.

Many of the modifications made in the revision are due to valuable suggestions and kindly criticisms received from many teachers of the text in various types of schools. To all who have thus helped so generously by freely giving the author the fruits of their judgment and experience he gladly renders grateful thanks.

CORNELL COLLEGE,
IOWA.

CONTENTS

CHAPTER I
THE MIND, OR CONSCIOUSNESS

CHAPTER II
ATTENTION

CHAPTER III

THE BRAIN AND NERVOUS SYSTEM

CHAPTER IV

MENTAL DEVELOPMENT AND MOTOR TRAINING

CHAPTER XI
MEMORY

CHAPTER XII
THINKING

CHAPTER XIII
INSTINCT

CHAPTER XIV
FEELING AND ITS FUNCTIONS

CHAPTER XV
THE EMOTIONS

CHAPTER XVI
INTEREST

CHAPTER XVIII
SELF-EXPRESSION AND DEVELOPMENT

CHAPTER I
THE MIND, OR CONSCIOUSNESS

We are to study the mind and its education; but how? It is easy to understand how we may investigate the great world of material things about us; for we can see it, touch it, weigh it, or measure it. But how are we to discover the nature of the mind, or come to know the processes by which consciousness works? For mind is intangible; we cannot see it, feel it, taste it, or handle it. Mind belongs not to the realm of matter which is known to the senses, but to the realm of *spirit*, which the senses can never grasp. And yet the mind can be known and studied as truly and as scientifically as can the world of matter. Let us first of all see how this can be done.

1. HOW MIND IS TO BE KNOWN

The Personal Character of Consciousness: Mind can be observed and known. But each one can know directly only his own mind, and not another's. You and I may look into each other's face and there guess the meaning that lies back of the smile or frown or flash of the eye, and so read something of the mind's activity. But neither directly meets the other's mind. I may learn to recognize your features, know your voice, respond to the clasp of your hand; but the mind, the consciousness, which does your thinking and feels your joys and sorrows, I can never know completely. Indeed I can never know your mind at all except through your bodily acts and expressions. Nor is there any way in which you can reveal your mind, your spiritual self, to me except through these means.

It follows therefore that only *you* can ever know *you* and only *I* can ever know *I* in any first-hand and immediate way. Between your consciousness and mine there exists a wide gap that cannot be bridged. Each of us lives apart. We are like ships that pass and hail each other in passing but do not touch. We may work together, live together, come to love or hate each other, and yet our inmost selves forever stand alone. They must live their own lives, think their own thoughts, and arrive at their own destiny.

Introspection the Only Means of Discovering Nature of Consciousness: What, then, is mind? What is the thing that we call consciousness? No mere definition can ever make it clearer than it is at this moment to each of us. The only way to know what mind is, is to look in upon our own consciousness and observe what is transpiring there. In the language of the psychologist, we must *introspect.* For one can never come to understand the nature of mind and its laws of working by listening to lectures or reading text books alone. There is no *psychology* in the text, but only in your living, flowing stream of thought and mine. True, the lecture and the book may tell us what to look for when we introspect, and how to understand what we find. But the statements and descriptions about our minds must be verified by our own observation and experience before they become vital truth to us.

How We Introspect: Introspection is something of an art; it has to be learned. Some master it easily, some with more difficulty, and some, it is to be feared, never become skilled in its use. In order to introspect one must catch himself unawares, so to speak, in the very act of thinking, remembering, deciding, loving, hating, and all the rest. These fleeting phases of consciousness are ever on the wing; they never pause in their restless flight and we must catch them as they go. This is not so easy as it appears; for the moment we turn to look in upon the mind, that moment consciousness changes. The thing we meant to examine is gone, and something else has taken its place. All that is left us then is to view the mental object while it is still fresh in the memory, or to catch it again when it returns.

Studying Mental States of Others through Expression: Although I can meet only my own mind face to face, I am, nevertheless, under the necessity of judging your mental states and knowing what is taking place in your consciousness. For in order to work successfully with you, in order to teach you, understand you, control you or obey you, be your friend or enemy, or associate with you in any other way, I must *know* you. But the real you that I must know is hidden behind the physical mask that we call the body. I must, therefore, be able to understand your states of consciousness as they are reflected in your bodily expressions. Your face, form, gesture, speech, the tone of voice, laughter and tears, the poise of attention, the droop of grief, the tenseness of anger and start of fear,—all these tell the story of the mental state that lies behind the senses. These various expressions are the pictures on the screen by which your mind reveals itself to others; they are the language by which the inner self speaks to the world without.

Learning to Interpret Expression: If I would understand the workings of your mind I must therefore learn to read the language of physical expression. I must study human nature and learn to observe others. I must apply the information found in the texts to an interpretation of those about me. This study of others may be *uncritical*, as in the mere intelligent observation of those I meet; or it may be *scientific*, as when I conduct carefully planned psychological experiments. But in either case it consists in judging the inner states of consciousness by their physical manifestations.

The three methods by which mind may be studied are, then: (1) text-book *description and explanation*; (2) *introspection* of my own conscious processes; and (3) *observation* of others, either uncritical or scientific.

2. THE NATURE OF CONSCIOUSNESS

Inner Nature of the Mind Not Revealed by Introspection: We are not to be too greatly discouraged if, even by introspection, we cannot discover exactly *what* the mind is. No one knows what electricity is, though nearly everyone uses it in one form or another. We study the dynamo, the motor, and the conductors through which electricity manifests itself. We observe its effects in light, heat, and mechanical power, and so learn the laws which govern its operations. But we are almost as far from understanding its true nature as were the ancients who knew nothing of its uses. The dynamo does not create the electricity, but only furnishes the conditions which make it possible for electricity to manifest itself in doing the world's work. Likewise the brain or nervous system does not create the mind, but it furnishes the machine through which the mind works. We may study the nervous system and learn something of the conditions and limitations under which the mind operates, but this is not studying the mind itself. As in the case of electricity, what we know about the mind we must learn through the activities in which it manifests itself—these we can know, for they are in the experience of all. It is, then, only by studying these processes of consciousness that we come to know the laws which govern the mind and its development. *What* it is that thinks and feels and wills in us is too hard a problem for us here—indeed, has been too hard a problem for the philosophers through the ages. But the thinking and feeling and willing we can watch as they occur, and hence come to know.

Consciousness as a Process or Stream: In looking in upon the mind we must expect to discover, then, not a *thing*, but a *process*. The *thing* forever eludes us, but the process is always present. Consciousness is like a stream, which, so far as we are concerned with it in a psychological discussion, has its rise at the cradle and its end at the grave. It begins with the babe's first faint groping after light in his new world as he enters it, and ends with the man's last blind groping after light in his old world as he leaves it. The stream is very narrow at first, only as wide as the few sensations which come to the babe when it sees the light or hears the sound; it grows wider as the mind develops, and is at last measured by the grand sum total of life's experience.

This mental stream is irresistible. No power outside of us can stop it while life lasts. We cannot stop it ourselves. When we try to stop thinking, the stream but changes its direction and flows on. While we wake and while we sleep, while we are unconscious under an anesthetic, even, some sort of mental process continues. Sometimes the stream flows slowly, and our thoughts lag—we "feel slow"; again the stream flows faster, and we are lively and our thoughts come with a rush; or a fever seizes us and delirium comes on; then the stream runs wildly onward, defying our control, and a mad jargon of thoughts takes the place of our usual orderly array. In different persons, also, the mental stream moves at different rates, some minds being naturally slow-moving and some naturally quick in their operations.

Consciousness resembles a stream also in other particulars. A stream is an unbroken whole from its source to its mouth, and an observer stationed at one point cannot see all of it at once. He sees but the one little section which happens to be passing his station point at the time. The current may look much the same from moment to moment, but the component particles which constitute the stream are constantly changing. So it is with our thought. Its stream is continuous from birth till death, but we cannot see any considerable portion of it at one time. When we turn about quickly and look in upon our minds, we see but the little present moment. That of a few seconds ago is gone and will never return. The thought which occupied us a moment since can no more be recalled, just as it was, than can the particles composing a stream be re-collected and made to pass a given point in its course in precisely the same order and relation to one another as before. This means, then, that we can never have precisely the same mental state twice; that the thought of the moment cannot have the same associates that it had the first time; that the thought of this moment will never be ours again; that all we can know of our minds at any one time is the part of the process present in consciousness at that moment.

The Wave in the Stream of Consciousness.—The surface of our mental stream is not level, but is broken by a wave which stands above the rest; which is but another way of saying that some one thing is always more prominent in our thought than the rest. Only when we are in a sleepy reverie, or not thinking about much of anything, does the stream approximate a level. At all other times some one object occupies the highest point in our thought, to the more or less complete exclusion of other things which we might think about. A thousand and one objects are possible to our thought at any moment, but all except one thing occupy a secondary place, or are not present to our consciousness at all. They exist on the margin, or else are clear off the8 edge of consciousness, while the one thing occupies the center. We may be reading a fascinating book late at night in a cold room. The charm of the writer, the beauty of the heroine, or the bravery of the hero so occupies the mind that the weary eyes and chattering teeth are unnoticed. Consciousness has piled up in a high wave on the points of interest in the book, and the bodily sensations are for the moment on a much lower level. But let the book grow dull for a moment, and the make-up of the stream changes in a flash. Hero, heroine, or literary style no longer occupies the wave. They forfeit their place, the wave is taken by the bodily sensations, and we are conscious of the smarting eyes and shivering body, while these in turn give way to the next object which occupies the wave. Figs. 1-3 illustrate these changes.

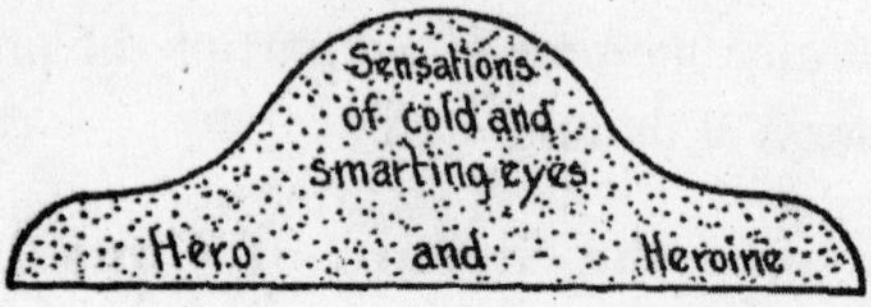

FIG. 1

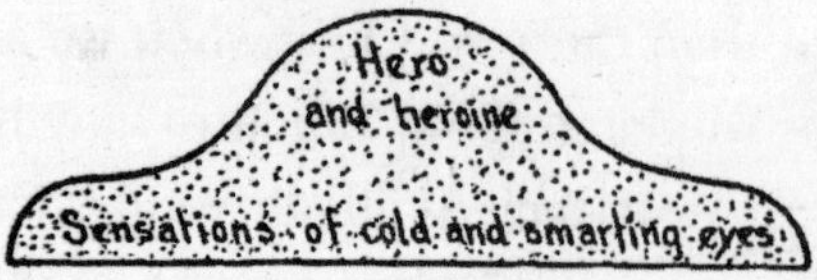

FIG. 2

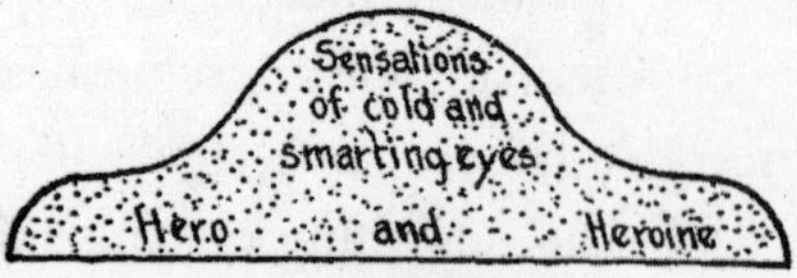

FIG. 3

Consciousness Likened to a Field—The consciousness of any moment has been less happily likened to a field, in the center of which there is an elevation higher than the surrounding level. This center is where consciousness is piled up on the object which is for the moment foremost in our thought. The other objects of our consciousness are on the margin of the field for the time being, but any of them may the next moment claim the center and drive the former object to the margin, or it may drop entirely out of consciousness. This moment a noble resolve may occupy the center of the field, while a troublesome tooth begets sensations of discomfort which linger dimly on the outskirts of our consciousness; but a shooting pain from the tooth or a random thought crossing the mind, and lo! the tooth holds sway, and the resolve dimly fades to the margin of our consciousness and is gone.

The "Piling Up" of Consciousness is Attention: This figure is not so true as the one which likens our mind to a stream with its ever onward current answering to the flow of our thought; but whichever figure we employ, the truth remains the same. Our mental energy is always piled up higher at one point than at others. Either because our interest leads us, or because the will dictates, the mind is withdrawn from the thousand and one things we might think about, and directed to this one thing, which for the time occupies chief place. In other words, we *attend*; for this piling up of consciousness is nothing, after all, but attention.

3. CONTENT OF THE MENTAL STREAM

We have seen that our mental life may be likened to a stream flowing now faster, now slower, ever shifting, never ceasing. We have yet to inquire what constitutes the material of the stream, or what is the stuff that makes up the current of our thought—what is the *content* of consciousness? The question cannot be fully answered at this point, but a general notion can be gained which will be of service.

Why We Need Minds: Let us first of all ask what mind is for, why do animals, including men, have minds? The biologist would say, in order that they may *adapt* themselves to their environment. Each individual from mollusk to man needs the amount and type of mind that serves to fit its possessor into its particular world of activity. Too little mind leaves the animal helpless in the struggle for existence. On the other hand a mind far above its possessor's station would prove useless if not a handicap; a mollusk could not use the mind of a man.

Content of Consciousness Determined by Function: How much mind does man need? What range and type of consciousness will best serve to adjust us to our world of opportunity and responsibility? First of all we must *know* our world, hence, our mind must be capable of gathering knowledge. Second, we must be able to *feel* its values and respond to the great motives for action arising from the emotions. Third, we must have the power to exert self-compulsion, which is to say that we possess a *will* to control our acts. These three sets of processes, *knowing*, *feeling*, and *willing*, we shall, therefore, expect to find making up the content of our mental stream.

Let us proceed at once to test our conclusion by introspection. If we are sitting at our study table puzzling over a difficult problem in geometry, *reasoning* forms the wave in the stream of consciousness—the center of the field. It is the chief thing in our thinking. The fringe of our consciousness is made up of various sensations of the light from the lamp, the contact of our clothing, the sounds going on in the next room, some bit of memory seeking recognition, a "tramp" thought which comes along, and a dozen other experiences not strong enough to occupy the center of the field.

But instead of the study table and the problem, give us a bright fireside, an easy-chair, and nothing to do. If we are aged, *memories*—images from out the past—will probably come thronging in and occupy the field to such extent that the fire burns low and the room grows cold, but still the forms from the past hold sway. If we are young, visions of the future may crowd everything else to the margin of the field, while the "castles in Spain" occupy the center.

Our memories may also be accompanied by emotions—sorrow, love, anger, hate, envy, joy. And, indeed, these emotions may so completely occupy the field that the images themselves are for the time driven to the margin, and the mind is occupied with its sorrow, its love, or its joy.

Once more, instead of the problem or the memories or the "castles in Spain," give us the necessity of making some decision, great or small, where contending motives are pulling us now in this direction, now in that, so that the question finally has to be settled by a supreme effort summed up in the words, *I will.* This is the struggle of the will which each one knows for himself; for who has not had a raging battle of motives occupy the center of the field while all else, even the sense of time, place and existence, gave way in the face of this conflict! This struggle continues until the decision is made, when suddenly all the stress and strain drop out and other objects may again have place in consciousness.

The Three Fundamental Phases of Consciousness: Thus we see that if we could cut the stream of consciousness across as we might cut a stream of water from bank to bank with a huge knife, and then look at the cut-off section, we should find very different constituents in the stream at different times. We should at one time find the mind manifesting itself in *perceiving*, *remembering*, *imagining*, *discriminating*, *comparing*, *judging*, *reasoning*, or the acts by which we gain our knowledge; at another in *fearing*, *loving*, *hating*, *sorrowing*, *enjoying*, or the acts of feeling; at still another in *choosing*, or the act of the will. These processes would make up the stream, or, in other words, these are the acts which the mind performs in doing its work. We should never find a time when the stream consists of but one of the processes, or when all these modes of mental activity are not represented. They will be found in varying proportions, now more of knowing, now of feeling, and now of willing, but some of each is always present in our consciousness. The nature of these different elements in our mental stream, their relation to each other, and the manner in which they all work together in amazing perplexity yet in perfect harmony to produce the wonderful *mind*, will constitute the subject-matter we shall consider together in the pages which follow.

4. WHERE CONSCIOUSNESS RESIDES

I—the conscious self—dwell somewhere in this body, but where? When my finger tips touch the object I wish to examine, I seem to be in them. When the brain grows weary from over study, I seem to be in it. When the heart throbs, the breath comes quick, and the muscles grow tense from noble resolve or strong emotion, I seem to be in them all. When, filled with the buoyant life of vigorous youth, every fiber and nerve is a-tingle with health and enthusiasm, I live in every part of my marvelous body. Small wonder that the ancients located the soul at one time in the heart, at another in the pineal gland of the brain, and at another made it coextensive with the body!

Consciousness Works through the Nervous System: Later13 science has taught that the *mind resides in and works through the nervous system, which has its central office in the brain.* And the reason why *I* seem to be in every part of my body is because the nervous system extends to every part, carrying messages of sight or sound or touch to the brain, and bearing in return orders for movements, which set the feet a-dancing or the fingers a-tingling. But more of this later.

This partnership between mind and body is very close. Just how it happens that spirit may inhabit matter we may not know. But certain it is that they interact on each other. What will hinder the growth of one will handicap the other, and what favors the development of either will help both. The methods of their cooperation and the laws that govern their relationship will develop as our study goes on.

5. PROBLEMS IN OBSERVATION AND INTROSPECTION

One should always keep in mind that psychology is essentially a laboratory science, and not a text-book subject. The laboratory material is to be found in ourselves and in those about us. While the text should be thoroughly mastered, its statements should always be verified by reference to one's own experience, and observation of others. Especially should prospective teachers constantly correlate the lessons of the book with the observation of children at work in the school. The problems suggested for observation and introspection will, if mastered, do much to render practical and helpful the truths of psychology.

1. Think of your home as you last left it. Can you see vividly just how it looked, the color of the paint on the outside, with the familiar form of the roof and all; can you recall the

perfume in some old drawer, the taste of a favorite dish, the sound of a familiar voice in farewell?

2. What illustrations have you observed where the mental content of the moment seemed chiefly *thinking* (knowledge process); chiefly *emotion* (feeling process); chiefly *choosing*, or self-compulsion (willing process)?

3. When you say that you remember a circumstance that occurred yesterday, how do you remember it? That is, do you see in your mind things just as they were, and hear again sounds which occurred, or feel again movements which you performed? Do you experience once more the emotions you then felt?

4. What forms of expression most commonly reveal *thought*; what reveal emotions? (i.e., can you tell what a child is *thinking about* by the expression on his face? Can you tell whether he is *angry*, *frightened*, *sorry*, by his face? Is speech as necessary in expressing feeling as in expressing thought?)

5. Try occasionally during the next twenty-four hours to turn quickly about mentally and see whether you can observe your thinking, feeling, or willing in the very act of taking place.

6. What becomes of our mind or consciousness while we are asleep? How are we able to wake up at a certain hour previously determined? Can a person have absolutely *nothing* in his mind?

7. Have you noticed any children especially adept in expression? Have you noticed any very backward? If so, in what form of expression in each case?

8. Have you observed any instances of expression which you were at a loss to interpret (remember that "expression" includes every form of physical action, voice, speech, face, form, hand, etc.)?

CHAPTER II
ATTENTION

How do you rank in mental ability, and how effective are your mind's grasp and power? The answer that must be given to these questions will depend not more on your native endowment than on your skill in using attention.

1. NATURE OF ATTENTION

It is by attention that we gather and mass our mental energy upon the critical and important points in our thinking. In the last chapter we saw that consciousness is not distributed evenly over the whole field, but "piled up," now on this object of thought, now on that, in obedience to interest or necessity. *The concentration of the mind's energy on one object of thought is attention.*

The Nature of Attention: Everyone knows what it is to attend. The story so fascinating that we cannot leave it, the critical points in a game, the interesting sermon or lecture, the sparkling conversation—all these compel our attention. So completely is our mind's energy centered on them and withdrawn from other things that we are scarcely aware of what is going on about us.

We are also familiar with another kind of attention. For we all have read the dull story, watched the slow game, listened to the lecture or sermon that drags, and taken part in conversation that was a bore. We gave these things our attention, but only with effort. Our mind's energy seemed to center on anything rather than the matter in hand. A thousand objects from outside enticed us away, and it required the frequent "mental jerk" to bring us to the subject in hand. And when brought back to our thought problem we felt the constant "tug" of mind to be free again.

Normal Consciousness Always in a State of Attention: But this very effort of the mind to free itself from one object of thought that it may busy itself with another is *because attention is solicited by this other*. Some object in our field of consciousness is always exerting an appeal for attention; and to attend *to* one thing is always to attend *away from* a multitude of other things upon which the thought might rest. We may therefore say that attention is constantly *selecting* in our stream of thought those aspects that are to receive emphasis and consideration. From moment to moment it determines the points at which our mental energy shall be centered.

2. THE EFFECTS OF ATTENTION

Attention Makes Its Object Clear and Definite: Whatever attention centers upon stands out sharp and clear in consciousness. Whether it be a bit of memory, an "air-castle," a sensation from an aching tooth, the reasoning on an algebraic formula, a choice which we are making, the setting of an emotion—whatever be the object to which we are attending, that object is illumined and made to stand out from its fellows as the one prominent thing in the mind's eye while the attention rests on it. It is like the one building which the searchlight picks out among a city full of buildings and lights up, while the remainder are left in the semi light or in darkness.

Attention Measures Mental Efficiency: In a state of attention the mind may be likened to the rays of the sun which have been passed through a burning glass. You may let all the rays which can pass through your window pane fall hour after hour upon the paper lying on your desk, and no marked effects follow. But let the same amount of sunlight be passed through a lens and converged to a point the size of your pencil point, and the paper will at once burst into flame. What the diffused rays could not do in hours or in ages is now accomplished in seconds. Likewise the mind, allowed to scatter over many objects, can accomplish but little. We may sit and dream away an hour or a day over a page or a problem without securing results. But let us call in our wits from their wool-gathering and "buckle down to it" with all our might, withdrawing our thoughts from everything else but this *one thing*, and concentrating our mind on it. More can now be accomplished in minutes than before in hours. Nay, *things which could not be accomplished at all before* now become possible.

Again, the mind may be compared to a steam engine which is constructed to run at a certain pressure of steam, say one hundred and fifty pounds to the square inch of boiler surface. Once I ran such an engine; and well I remember a morning during my early apprenticeship when the foreman called for power to run some of the lighter machinery, while my steam gauge registered but seventy-five pounds. "Surely," I thought, "if one hundred and fifty pounds will run all this machinery, seventy-five pounds should run half of it," so I opened the valve.

But the powerful engine could do but little more than turn its own wheels, and refused to do the required work. Not until the pressure had risen above one hundred pounds could the engine perform half the work which it could at one hundred and fifty pounds. And so with our mind. If it is meant to do its best work under a certain degree of concentration, it cannot in a given time do half the work with half the attention. Further, there will be much *which it cannot do at all* unless working under full pressure. We shall not be overstating the case if we say that as attention increases in arithmetical ratio, mental efficiency increases in geometrical ratio. It is in large measure a difference in the power of attention which makes one man a master in thought and achievement and another his humble follower. One often hears it said that "genius is but the power of sustained attention," and this statement possesses a large element of truth.

3. HOW WE ATTEND

Someone has said that if our attention is properly trained we should be able "to look at the point of a cambric needle for half an hour without winking." But this is a false idea of attention. The ability to look at the point of a cambric needle for half an hour might indicate a very laudable power of concentration; but the process, instead of enlightening us concerning the point of the needle, would result in our passing into a hypnotic state. Voluntary attention to any one object can be sustained for but a brief time—a few seconds at best. It is essential that the object change, that we turn it over and over incessantly, and consider its various aspects and relations. Sustained voluntary attention is thus a repetition of successive efforts to bring back the object to the mind. Then the subject grows and develops—it is living, not dead.

Attention a Relating Activity: When we are attending strongly to one object of thought it does not mean that consciousness sits staring vacantly at this one object, but rather that it uses it as a central core of thought, and thinks into relation with this object the things which belong with it. In working out some mathematical solution the central core is the principle upon which the solution is based, and concentration in this case consists in thinking the various conditions of the problem in relation to this underlying principle. In the accompanying diagram (Fig. 4) let A be the central core of some object of thought, say a patch of cloud in a picture, and let *a*, *b*, *c*, *d*, etc., be the related facts, or the shape, size, color, etc., of the cloud. The arrows indicate the passing of our thought from cloud to related fact, or from related fact to cloud, and from related fact to related fact. As long as these related facts lead back to the cloud each time, that long we are attending to the cloud and thinking about it. It is when our thought fails to go back that we "wander" in our attention. Then we leave *a*, *b*, *c*, *d*, etc., which are related to the cloud, and, flying off to *x*, *y*, and *z*, finally bring up heaven knows where.

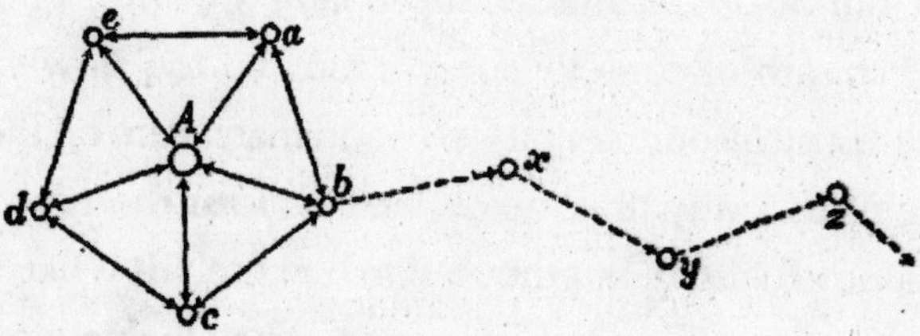

FIG. 4

The Rhythms of Attention: Attention works in rhythms. This is to say that it never maintains a constant level of concentration for any considerable length of time, but regularly ebbs and flows. The explanation of this rhythmic action would take us too far a field at this point. When we remember, however, that our entire organism works within a great system of rhythms—hunger, thirst, sleep, fatigue, and many others—it is easy to see that the same law may apply to attention. The rhythms of attention vary greatly, the fluctuations often being only a few seconds apart for certain simple sensations, and probably a much greater distance apart for the more complex process of thinking. The seeming variation in the sound of a distant waterfall, now loud and now faint, is caused by the rhythm of attention and easily allows us to measure the rhythm for this particular sensation.

4. POINTS OF FAILURE IN ATTENTION

Lack of Concentration: There are two chief types of inattention whose danger threatens every person. *First*, we may be thinking about the right things, but not thinking *hard* enough. We lack mental pressure. Outside thoughts which have no relation to the subject in hand may not trouble us much, but we do not attack our problem with vim. The current in our stream of consciousness is moving too slowly. We do not gather up all our mental forces and mass them on the subject before us in a way that means victory. Our thoughts may be sufficiently focused, but they fail to "set fire." It is like focusing the sun's rays while an eclipse is on. They lack energy. They will not kindle the paper after they have passed through the lens. This kind of attention means mental dawdling. It means inefficiency. For the individual it means defeat in life's battles; for the nation it means mediocrity and stagnation.

A college professor said to his faithful but poorly prepared class, "Judging from your worn and tired appearance, young people, you are putting in twice too many hours on study." At this commendation the class brightened up visibly. "But," he continued, "judging from your preparation, you do not study quite half hard enough."

Happy is the student who, starting in on his lesson rested and fresh, can study with such concentration that an hour of steady application will leave him mentally exhausted and limp. That is one hour of triumph for him, no matter what else he may have accomplished or failed to accomplish during the time. He can afford an occasional pause for rest, for difficulties will melt rapidly away before him. He possesses one key to successful achievement.

Mental Wandering: *Second*, we may have good mental power and be able to think hard and efficiently on any one point, but lack the power to think in a straight line. Every stray thought that comes along is a "will-o'-the-wisp" to lead us away from the subject in hand and into lines of thought not relating to it. Who has not started in to think on some problem, and, after a few moments, been surprised to find himself miles away from the topic upon which he started! Or who has not read down a page and, turning to the next, found that he did not know a word on the preceding page, his thoughts having wandered away, his eyes only going through the process of reading! Instead of sticking to the *a*, *b*, *c*, *d*, etc., of our topic and relating them all up to A, thereby reaching a solution of the problem, we often jump at once to *x*, *y*, *z*, and find ourselves far a field with all possibility of a solution gone. We may have brilliant thoughts about *x*, *y*, *z*, but they are not related to anything in particular, and so they pass from us and are gone—lost in oblivion because they are not attached to something permanent.

Such a thinker is at the mercy of circumstances, following blindly the leadings of trains of thought which are his master instead of his servant, and which lead him anywhere or nowhere without let or hindrance from him. His consciousness moves rapidly enough and with enough force, but it is like a ship without a helm. Starting for the intellectual port *A* by way of *a*, *b*, *c*, *d*, he is mentally shipwrecked at last on the rocks *x*, *y*, *z*, and never reaches harbor. Fortunate is he who can shut out intruding thoughts and think in a straight line. Even with mediocre ability he may accomplish more by his thinking than the brilliant thinker who is constantly having his mental train wrecked by stray thoughts which slip in on his right of way.

5. TYPES OF ATTENTION

The Three Types of Attention: Attention may be secured in three ways: (1) It is demanded by some sudden or intense sensory stimulus or insistent idea, or (2) it follows interest, or (3) it is compelled by the will. If it comes in the first way, as from a thunderclap or a flash of light, or from the persistent attempt of some unsought idea to secure entrance into the mind, it is called *involuntary* attention. This form of attention is of so little importance, comparatively, in our mental life that we shall not discuss it further.

If attention comes in the second way, following interest, it is called *non-voluntary* or spontaneous attention; if in the third, compelled by the will, *voluntary* or active attention. Non-voluntary attention has its motive in some object external to consciousness, or else follows a more or less uncontrolled current of thought which interests us; voluntary attention is controlled from within—*we* decide what we shall attend to instead of letting interesting objects of thought determine it for us.

Interest and Non-voluntary Attention: In non-voluntary attention the environment largely determines what we shall attend to. All that we have to do with directing this kind of attention is in developing certain lines of interest, and then the interesting things attract attention. The things we see and hear and touch and taste and smell, the things we like, the things we do and hope to do—these are the determining factors in our mental life so long as we are giving non-voluntary attention. Our attention follows the beckoning of these things as the needle the magnet. It is no effort to attend to them, but rather the effort would be to keep from attending to them. Who does not remember reading a story, perhaps a forbidden one, so interesting that when mother called up the stairs for us to come down to attend to some duty, we replied, "Yes, in a minute," and then went on reading! We simply could not stop at that place. The minute lengthens into ten, and another call startles us. "Yes, I'm coming;" we turn just one more leaf, and are lost again. At last comes a third call in tones so imperative that it cannot be longer ignored, and we lay the book down, but open to the place where we left off, and where we hope soon to begin further to unravel the delightful mystery. Was it an effort to attend to the reading? Ah, no! it took the combined force of our will and of mother's authority to drag the attention away. This is non-voluntary attention.

Left to itself, then, attention simply obeys natural laws and follows the line of least resistance. By far the larger portion of our attention is of this type. Thought often runs on hour after hour when we are not conscious of effort or struggle to compel us to cease thinking about this thing and begin thinking about that. Indeed, it may be doubted whether this is not the case with some persons for days at a time, instead of hours. The things that present themselves to the mind are the things which occupy it; the character of the thought is determined by the character of our interests. It is this fact which makes it vitally necessary that our interests shall be broad and pure if our thoughts are to be of this type. It is not enough that we have the strength to drive from our minds a wrong or impure thought which seeks entrance. To stand guard as a policeman over our thoughts to see that no unworthy one enters, requires too much time and energy. Our interests must be of such a nature as to lead us away from the field of unworthy thoughts if we are to be free from their tyranny.

The Will and Voluntary Attention: In voluntary attention there is a conflict either between the will and interest or between the will and the mental inertia or laziness, which has to be overcome before we can think with any degree of concentration. Interest says, "Follow this line, which is easy and attractive, or which requires but little effort—follow the line of least resistance." Will says, "Quit that line of dalliance and ease, and take this harder way which I direct—cease the line of least resistance and take the one of greatest resistance." When day dreams and "castles in Spain" attempt to lure you from your lessons, refuse to follow; shut out these vagabond thoughts and stick to your task. When intellectual inertia deadens your thought and clogs your mental stream, throw it off and court forceful effort. If wrong or impure thoughts seek entrance to your mind, close and lock your mental doors to them. If thoughts of desire try to drive out thoughts of duty, be heroic and insist that thoughts of duty shall have right of way. In short, see that *you* are the master of your thinking, and do not let it always be directed without your consent by influences outside of yourself.

It is just at this point that the strong will wins victory and the weak will breaks down. Between the ability to control one's thoughts and the inability to control them lies all the difference between right actions and wrong actions; between withstanding temptation and yielding to it; between an inefficient purposeless life and a life of purpose and endeavor; between success and failure. For we act in accordance with those things which our thought rests upon. Suppose two lines of thought represented by *A* and *B*, respectively, lie before you; that *A* leads to a course of action difficult or unpleasant, but necessary to success or duty, and that *B* leads to a course of action easy or pleasant, but fatal to success or duty. Which course will you follow—the rugged path of duty or the easier one of pleasure? The answer depends almost wholly, if not entirely, on your power of attention. If your will is strong enough to pull your thoughts away from the fatal but attractive *B* and hold them resolutely on the less attractive *A*, then *A* will dictate your course of action, and you will respond to the call for endeavor, self-denial, and duty; but if your thoughts break away from the domination of your will and allow the beckoning of your interests alone, then *B* will dictate your course of action, and you will follow the leading of ease and pleasure. *For our actions are finally and irrevocably dictated by the things we think about.*

Not Really Different Kinds of Attention: It is not to be understood, however, from what has been said, that there are *really* different kinds of attention. All attention denotes an active or dynamic phase of consciousness. The difference is rather *in the way we secure attention*; whether it is demanded by sudden stimulus, coaxed from us by interesting objects of thought without effort on our part, or compelled by force of will to desert the more interesting and take the direction which we dictate.

6. IMPROVING THE POWER OF ATTENTION

While attention is no doubt partly a natural gift, yet there is probably no power of the mind more susceptible to training than is attention. And with attention, as with every other power of body and mind, the secret of its development lies in its use. Stated briefly, the only way to train attention is by attending. No amount of theorizing or resolving can take the place of practice in the actual process of attending.

Making Different Kinds of Attention Reinforce Each Other: A very close relationship and interdependence exists between non-voluntary and voluntary attention. It would be impossible to hold our attention by sheer force of will on objects which were forever devoid of interest; likewise the blind following of our interests and desires would finally lead to shipwreck in all our lives. Each kind of attention must support and reinforce the other. The lessons, the sermons, the lectures, and the books in which we are most interested, and hence to which we attend non-voluntarily and with the least effort and fatigue, are the ones out of which, other things being equal, we get the most and remember the best and longest. On the other hand, there are sometimes lessons and lectures and books, and many things besides, which are not intensely interesting, but which should be attended to nevertheless. It is at this point that the will must step in and take command. If it has not the strength to do this, it is in so far a weak will, and steps should be taken to develop it. We are to "*keep the faculty of effort alive in us by a little gratuitous exercise every day*." We are to be systematically heroic in the little points of everyday life and experience. We are not to shrink from tasks because they are difficult or unpleasant. Then, when the test comes, we shall not find ourselves unnerved and untrained, but shall be able to stand in the evil day.

The Habit of Attention: Finally, one of the chief things in training the attention is *to form the habit of attending*. This habit is to be formed only by *attending* whenever and wherever the proper thing to do is to attend, whether "in work, in play, in making fishing flies, in preparing for an examination, in courting a sweetheart, in reading a book." The lesson, or the sermon, or the lecture, may not be very interesting; but if they are to be attended to at all, our rule should be to attend to them completely and absolutely. Not by fits and starts, now drifting away and now jerking ourselves back, but *all the time*. And, furthermore, the one who will deliberately do this will often find the dull and uninteresting task become more interesting; but if it never becomes interesting, he is at least forming a habit which will be invaluable to him through life. On the other hand, the one who fails to attend except when his interest is captured, who never exerts effort to compel attention, is forming a habit which will be the bane of his thinking until his stream of thought shall end.

7. PROBLEMS IN OBSERVATION AND INTROSPECTION

1. Which fatigues you more, to give attention of the non-voluntary type, or the voluntary? Which can you maintain longer? Which is the more pleasant and agreeable to give? Under which can you accomplish more? What bearing have these facts on teaching?

2. Try to follow for one or two minutes the "wave" in your consciousness, and then describe the course taken by your attention.

3. Have you observed one class alert in attention, and another lifeless and inattentive? Can you explain the causes lying back of this difference? Estimate the relative amount of work accomplished under the two conditions.

4. What distractions have you observed in the schoolroom tending to break up attention?

5. Have you seen pupils inattentive from lack of (i) change, (ii) pure air, (iii) enthusiasm on the part of the teacher, (iv) fatigue, (v) ill health?

6. Have you noticed a difference in the *habit* of attention in different pupils? Have you noticed the same thing for whole schools or rooms?

7. Do you know of children too much given to daydreaming? Are you?

8. Have you seen a teacher rap the desk for attention? What type of attention was secured? Does it pay?

9. Have you observed any instance in which pupils' lack of attention should be blamed on the teacher? If so, what was the fault? The remedy?

10. Visit a school room or a recitation, and then write an account of the types and degrees of attention you observed. Try to explain the factors responsible for any failures in attention, and also those responsible for the good attention shown.

CHAPTER III
THE BRAIN AND NERVOUS SYSTEM

A fine brain, or a good mind. These terms are often used interchangeably, as if they stood for the same thing. Yet the brain is material substance—so many cells and fibers, a pulpy protoplasmic mass weighing some three pounds and shut away from the outside world in a casket of bone. The mind is a spiritual thing—the sum of the processes by which we think and feel and will, mastering our world and accomplishing our destiny.

1. THE RELATIONS OF MIND AND BRAIN

Interaction of Mind and Brain: How, then, come these two widely different facts, mind and brain, to be so related in our speech? Why are the terms so commonly interchanged?— It is because mind and brain are so vitally related in their processes and so inseparably connected in their work. No movement of our thought, no bit of sensation, no memory, no feeling, no act of decision but is accompanied by its own particular activity in the cells of the brain. It is this that the psychologist has in mind when he says, *no psychosis without its corresponding neurosis.*

So far as our present existence is concerned, then, no mind ever works except through some brain, and a brain without a mind becomes but a mass of dead matter, so much clay. Mind and brain are perfectly adapted to each other. Nor is this mere accident. For through the ages of man's past history each has grown up and developed into its present state of efficiency by working in conjunction with the other. Each has helped form the other and determine its qualities. Not only is this true for the race in its evolution, but for every individual as he passes from infancy to maturity.

The Brain as the Mind's Machine: In the first chapter we saw that the brain does not create the mind, but that the mind works through the brain. No one can believe that the brain secretes mind as the liver secretes bile, or that it grinds it out as a mill does flour. Indeed, just what their exact relation is has not yet been settled. Yet it is easy to see that if the mind must use the brain as a machine and work through it, then the mind must be subject to the limitations of its machine, or, in other words, the mind cannot be better than the brain through which it operates. A brain and nervous system that are poorly developed or insufficiently nourished mean low grade of efficiency in our mental processes, just as a poorly constructed or wrongly adjusted motor means loss of power in applying the electric current to its work. We will, then, look upon the mind and the brain as counterparts of each other, each performing activities which correspond to activities in the other, both inextricably bound together at least so far as this life is concerned, and each getting its significance by its union with the other. This view will lend interest to a brief study of the brain and nervous system.

2. THE MIND'S DEPENDENCE ON THE EXTERNAL WORLD

But can we first see how in a general way the brain and nervous system are primarily related to our thinking? Let us go back to the beginning and consider the babe when it first opens its eyes on the scenes of its new existence. What is in its mind? What does it think about? Nothing. Imagine, if you can, a person born blind and deaf, and without the sense of touch, taste, or smell. Let such a person live on for a year, for five years, for a lifetime. What would he know? What ray of intelligence would enter his mind? What would he think about? All would be dark to his eyes, all silent to his ears, all tasteless to his mouth, all odorless to his nostrils, all touch less to his skin. His mind would be a blank. He would have no mind. He could not get started to think. He could not get started to act. He would belong to a lower scale of life than the tiny animal that floats with the waves and the tide in the ocean without power to direct its own course. He would be but an inert mass of flesh without sense or intelligence.

The Mind at Birth: Yet this is the condition of the babe at birth. It is born practically blind and deaf, without definite sense of taste or smell. Born without anything to think about, and no way to get anything to think about until the senses wake up and furnish some material from the outside world. Born with all the mechanism of muscle and nerve ready to perform the countless complex movements of arms and legs and body which characterize every child, he could not successfully start these activities without a message from the senses to set them going. At birth the child probably has only the senses of contact and temperature present with any degree of clearness; taste soon follows; vision of an imperfect sort in a few days; hearing about the same time, and smell a little later. The senses are waking up and beginning their acquaintance with the outside world.

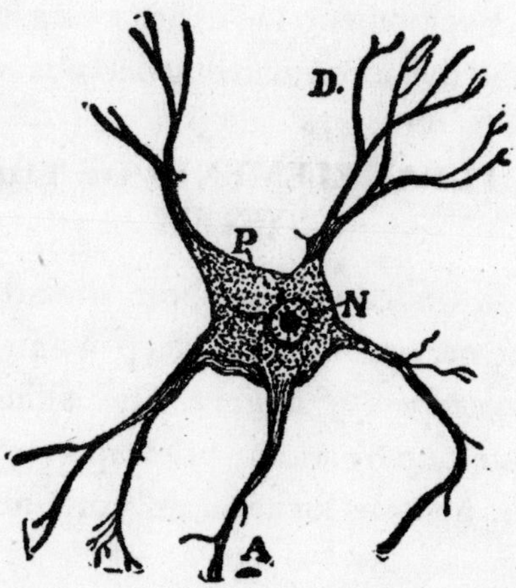

FIG. 5.—A Neuron from a Human Spinal Cord. The central portion represents the cell body. N, the nucleus; P, a pigmented or colored spot; D, a dendrite, or relatively short fiber,—which branches freely; A, an axon or long fiber, which branches but little.

The Work of the Senses: And what a problem the senses have to solve! On the one hand the great universe of sights and sounds, of tastes and smells, of contacts and temperatures, and whatever else may belong to the material world in which we live; and on the other hand the little shapeless mass of gray and white pulpy matter called the brain, incapable of sustaining its own shape, shut away in the darkness of a bony case with no possibility of contact with the outside world, and possessing no means of communicating with it except through the senses. And yet this universe of external things must be brought into communication with the seemingly insignificant but really wonderful brain, else the mind could never be. Here we discover, then, the two great factors which first require our study if we would understand the growth of the mind—*the material world without, and the brain within*. For it is the action and interaction of these which lie at the bottom of the mind's development. Let us first look a little more closely at the brain and the accompanying nervous system.

3. STRUCTURAL ELEMENTS OF THE NERVOUS SYSTEM

It will help in understanding both the structure and the working of the nervous system to keep in mind that it contains *but one fundamental unit of structure*. This is the neuron. Just as the house is built up by adding brick upon brick, so the union of numberless neurons forms brain, cord, nerves and organs of sense.

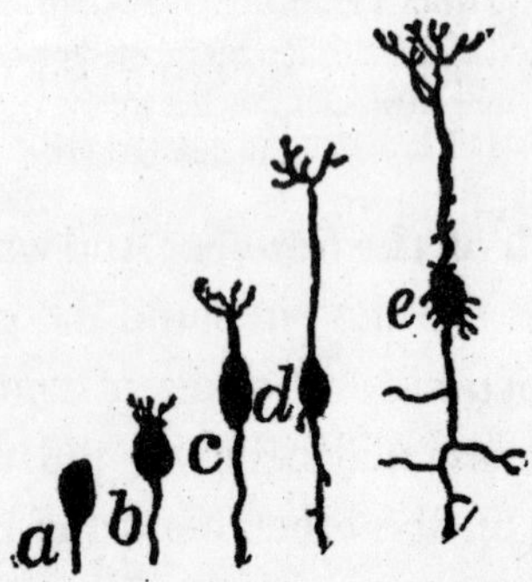

Fig. 6.—Neurons in different stages of development, from *a* to *e*. In *a*, the elementary cell body alone is present; in *c*, a dendrite is shown projecting upward and an axon downward.—After Donaldson.

The Neuron: What, then, is a neuron? What is its structure, its function, how does it act? A neurone is *a* *protoplasmic cell, with its outgrowing fibers.* The cell part of the neurone is of a variety of shapes, triangular, pyramidal, cylindrical, and irregular. The cells vary in size from 1/250 to 1/3500 of an inch in diameter. In general the function of the cell is thought to be to generate the nervous energy responsible for our consciousness—sensation, memory, reasoning, feeling and all the rest, and for our movements. The cell also provides for the nutrition of the fibers.

FIG. 7.—Longitudinal (A) and transverse (B) section of nerve fiber. The heavy border represents the medullary, or enveloping sheath, which becomes thicker in the larger fibers.—After DONALDSON.

Neuron Fibers: The neuron fibers are of two kinds, *dendrites* and *axons*. The dendrites are comparatively large in diameter, branch freely, like the branches of a tree, and extend but a relatively short distance from the parent cell. Axons are slender, and branch but little, and then approximately at right angles. They reach a much greater distance from the cell body than the dendrites. Neurons vary greatly in length. Some of those found in the spinal cord and brain are not more than 1/12 of an inch long, while others which reach from the extremities to the cord, measure several feet. Both dendrites and axons are of diameter so small as to be invisible except under the microscope.

Neuralgia: Out of this simple structural element, the neuron, the entire nervous system is built. True, the neurons are held in place, and perhaps insulated, by a kind of soft cement called *neuralgia*. But this seems to possess no strictly nervous function. The number of the microscopic neurons required to make up the mass of the brain, cord and peripheral nervous system is far beyond our mental grasp. It is computed that the brain and cord contain some 3,000 millions of them.

Complexity of the Brain: Something of the complexity of the brain structure can best be understood by an illustration. Professor Stratton estimates that if we were to make a model of the human brain, using for the neuron fibers wires so small as to be barely visible to the eye, in order to find room for all the wires the model would need to be the size of a city block on the base and correspondingly high. Imagine a telephone system of this complexity operating from one switch-board!

"Gray" and "White" Matter: The "gray matter" of the brain and cord is made up of nerve cells and their dendrites, and the terminations of axons, which enter from the adjoining white matter. A part of the mass of gray matter also consists of the neuralgia, which surrounds the nerve cells and fibers, and a network of blood vessels. The "white matter" of the central system consists chiefly of axons with their enveloping or medullary, sheath and neuralgia. The white matter contains no nerve cells or dendrites. The difference in color of the gray and the white matter is caused chiefly by the fact that in the gray masses the medullary sheath, which is white, is lacking, thus revealing the ashen gray of the nerve threads. In the white masses the medullary sheath is present.

4. GROSS STRUCTURE OF THE NERVOUS SYSTEM

Divisions of the Nervous System: The nervous system may be considered in two divisions: (1) The *central* system, which consists of the brain and spinal cord, and (2) the *peripheral* system, which comprises the sensory and motor neurons connecting the periphery and the internal organs with the central system and the specialized end-organs of the senses. The *sympathetic* system, which is found as a double chain of nerve connections joining the roots of sensory and motor nerves just outside the spinal column, does not seem to be directly related to consciousness and so will not be discussed here. A brief description of the nervous system will help us better to understand how its parts all work together in so wonderful a way to accomplish their great result.

The Central System: In the brain we easily distinguish three major divisions—the *cerebrum*, the *cerebellum* and the *medulla oblongata*. The medulla is but the enlarged upper part of the cord where it connects with the brain. It is about an inch and a quarter long, and is composed of both medullated and unmedullated fibers—that is of both "white" and "gray" matter. In the medulla, the unmedullated neurons, which comprise the center of the cord, are passing to the outside, and the medullated to the inside, thus taking the positions they occupy in the cerebrum. Here also the neurons are crossing, or changing sides, so that those which pass up the right side of the cord finally connect with the left side of the brain, and vice versa.

The Cerebellum: Lying just back of the medulla and at the rear part of the base of the cerebrum is the cerebellum, or "little brain," approximately as large as the fist, and composed of a complex arrangement of white and gray matter. Fibers from the spinal cord enter this mass, and others emerge and pass on into the cerebrum, while its two halves also are connected with each other by means of cross fibers.

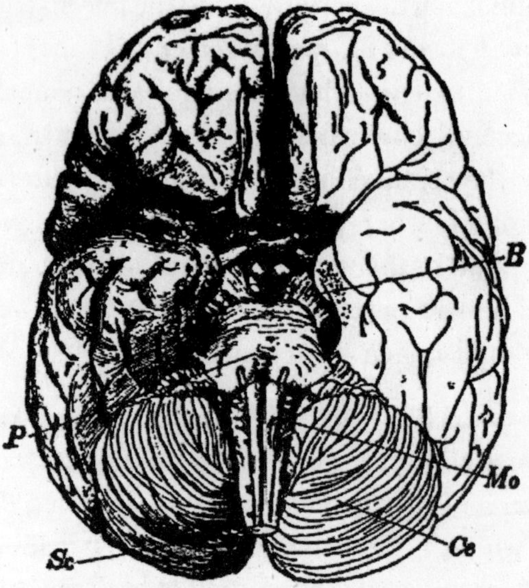

FIG. 8.—View of the under side of the brain. B, basis of the crura; P, pons; Mo, medulla oblongata; Ce, cerebellum; Sc, spinal cord.

The Cerebrum: The cerebrum occupies all the upper part of the skull from the front to the rear. It is divided symmetrically into two hemispheres, the right and the left. A small bridge of fibers called the corpus callosum connects these hemispheres with each other. Each hemisphere is furrowed and ridged with convolutions, an arrangement which allows greater surface for the distribution of the gray cellular matter over it. Besides these irregularities of surface, each hemisphere is marked also by two deep clefts or *fissures*—the fissure of Rolando, extending from the middle upper part of the hemisphere downward and forward, passing a little in front of the ear and stopping on a level with the upper part of it; and the fissure of Sylvius, beginning at the base of the brain somewhat in front of the ear and extending upward and backward at an acute angle with the base of the hemisphere.

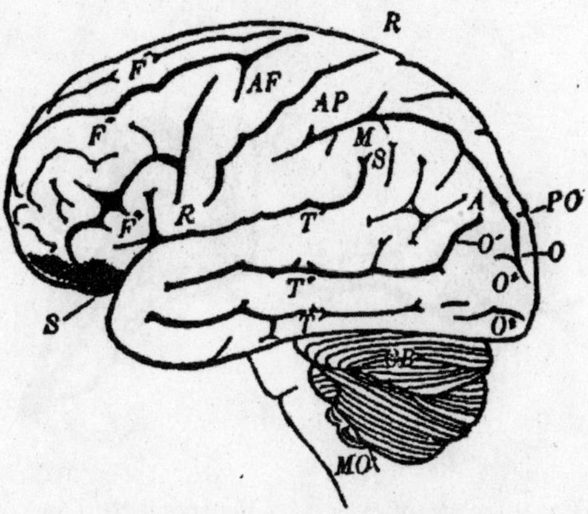

FIG. 9.—Diagrammatic side view of brain, showing cerebellum (CB) and medulla oblongata (MO). F' F'' F''' are placed on the first, second, and third frontal convolutions, respectively; AF, on the ascending frontal; AP, on the ascending parietal; M, on the marginal; A, on the angular. T' T'' T''' are placed on the first, second, and third temporal convolutions. R-R marks the fissure of Rolando; S-S, the fissure of Sylvius; PO, the parieto-occipital fissure.

The surface of each hemisphere may be thought of as mapped out into four lobes: The frontal lobe, which includes the front part of the hemisphere and extends back to the fissure of Rolando and down to the fissure of Sylvius; the parietal lobe, which lies back of the fissure of Rolando and above that of Sylvius and extends back to the occipital lobe; the occipital lobe, which includes the extreme rear portion of the hemisphere; and the temporal lobe, which lies below the fissure of Sylvius and extends back to the occipital lobe.

The Cortex: The gray matter of the hemispheres, unlike that of the cord, lies on the surface. This gray exterior portion of the cerebrum is called the *cortex*, and varies from one-twelfth to one-eighth of an inch in thickness. The cortex is the seat of all consciousness and of the control of voluntary movement.

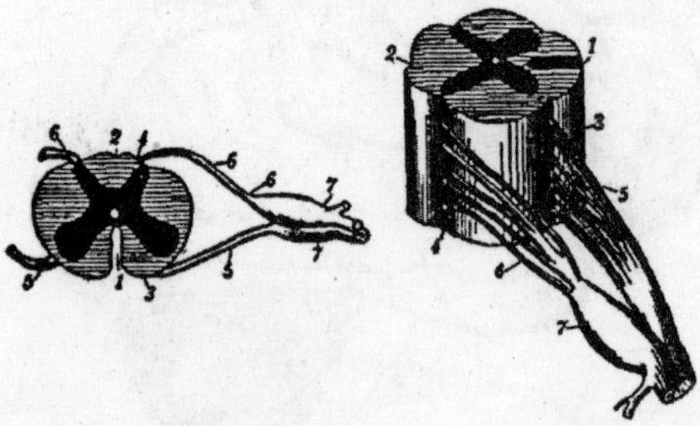

FIG. 10.—Different aspects of sections of the spinal cord and of the roots of the spinal nerves from the cervical region: 1, different views of anterior median fissure, 2, posterior fissure; 3, anterior lateral depression for anterior roots; 4, posterior lateral depression for posterior roots; 5 and 6, anterior and posterior roots, respectively; 7, complete spinal nerve, formed by the union of the anterior and posterior roots.

The Spinal Cord: The spinal cord proceeds from the base of the brain downward about eighteen inches through a canal provided for it in the vertebra of the spinal column. It is composed of white matter on the outside, and gray matter within. A deep fissure on the anterior side and another on the posterior cleave the cord nearly in twain, resembling the brain in this particular. The gray matter on the interior is in the form of two crescents connected by a narrow bar.

The *peripheral* nervous system consists of thirty-one pairs of *nerves*, with their end-organs, branching off from the cord, and twelve pairs that have their roots in the brain. Branches of these forty-three pairs of nerves reach to every part of the periphery of the body and to all the internal organs.

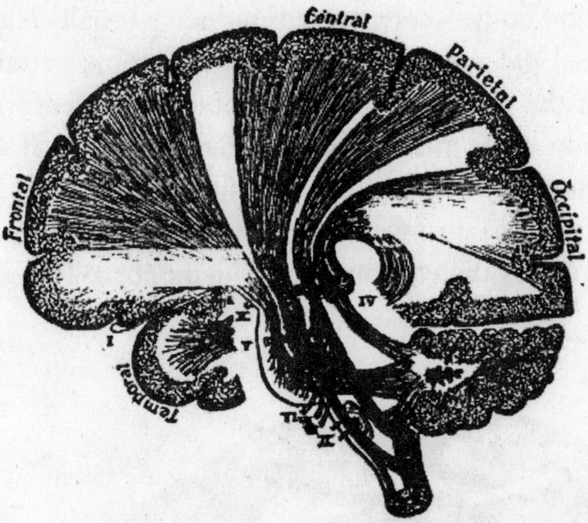

FIG. 11.—The projection fibers of the brain. I-IX, the first nine pairs of cranial nerves.

It will help in understanding the peripheral system to remember that a *nerve* consists of a bundle of neuron fibers each wrapped in its medullary sheath and sheath of Schwann. Around this bundle of neurons that is around the nerve is still another wrapping, silvery-white, called the neurilemma. The number of fibers going to make up a nerve varies from about 5,000 to 100,000. Nerves can easily be identified in a piece of lean beef, or even at the edge of a serious gash in one's own flesh!

Bundles of sensory fibers constituting a sensory nerve root enter the spinal cord on the posterior side through holes in the vertebra. Similar bundles of motor fibers in the form of a motor nerve root emerge from the cord at the same level. Soon after their emergence from the cord, these two nerves are wrapped together in the same sheath and proceed in this way to the periphery of the body, where the sensory nerve usually ends in a specialized *end-organ* fitted to respond to some certain stimulus from the outside world. The motor nerve ends in minute filaments in the muscular organ which it governs. Both sensory and motor nerves connect with fibers of like kind in the cord and these in turn with the cortex, thus giving every part of the periphery direct connection with the cortex.

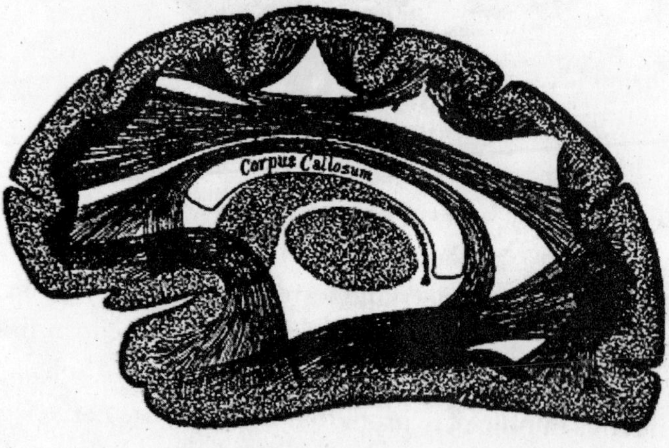

FIG. 12.—Schematic diagram showing association fibers connecting cortical centers with each other.—After JAMES and STARR.

The *end-organs* of the sensory nerves are nerve masses, some of them, as the taste buds of the tongue, relatively simple; and others, as the eye or ear, very complex. They are all alike in one particular; namely, that each is fitted for its own particular work and can do no other. Thus the eye is the end-organ of sight, and is a wonderfully complex arrangement of nerve structure combined with refracting media, and arranged to respond to the rapid ether waves of light. The ear has for its essential part the specialized endings of the auditory nerve, and is fitted to respond to the waves carried to it in the air, giving the sensation of sound. The end-organs of touch, found in greatest perfection in the finger tips, are of several kinds, all very complicated in structure. And so on with each of the senses. Each particular sense has some form of end-organ specially adapted to respond to the kind of stimulus upon which its sensation depends, and each is insensible to the stimuli of the others, much as the receiver of a telephone will respond to the tones of our voice, but not to the touch of our fingers as will the telegraph instrument, and *vice versa*. Thus the eye is not affected by sounds, nor touch by light. Yet by means of all the senses together we are able to come in contact with the material world in a variety of ways.

5. LOCALIZATION OF FUNCTION IN THE NERVOUS SYSTEM

Division of Labor: Division of labor is the law in the organic world as in the industrial. Animals of the lowest type, such as the ameba, do not have separate organs for respiration, digestion, assimilation, elimination, etc., the one tissue performing all of these functions. But in the higher forms each organ not only has its own specific work, but even within the same organ each part has its own particular function assigned. Thus we have seen that the two parts of the neuron probably perform different functions, the cells generating energy and the fibers transmitting it.

It will not seem strange, then, that there is also a division of labor in the cellular matter itself in the nervous system. For example, the little masses of ganglia which are distributed at intervals along the nerves are probably for the purpose of reinforcing the nerve current, much as the battery cells in the local telegraph office reinforce the current from the central office. The cellular matter in the spinal cord and lower parts of the brain has a very important work to perform in receiving messages from the senses and responding to them in directing the simpler reflex acts and movements which we learn to execute without our consciousness being called upon, thus leaving the mind free from these petty things to busy itself in higher ways. The cellular matter of the cortex performs the highest functions of all, for through its activity we have consciousness.

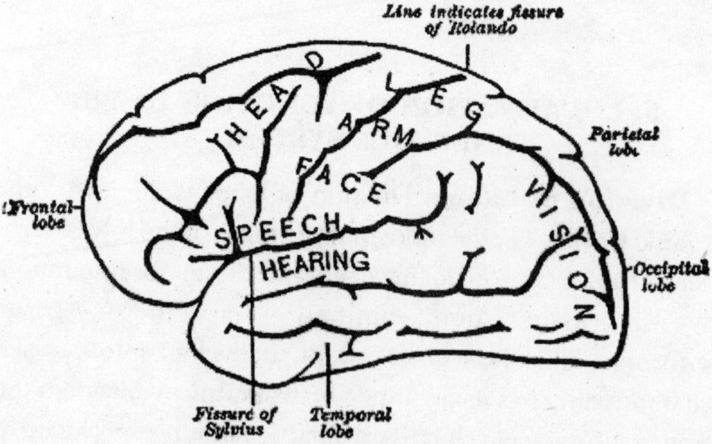

FIG. 13.—Side view of left hemisphere of human brain, showing the principal localized areas.

The gray matter of the cerebellum, the medulla, and the cord may receive impressions from the senses and respond to them with movements, but their response is in all cases wholly automatic and unconscious. A person whose hemispheres had been injured in such a way as to interfere with the activity of the cortex might still continue to perform most if not all of the habitual movements of his life, but they would be mechanical and not intelligent. He would lack all higher consciousness. It is through the activity of this thin covering of cellular matter of the cerebrum, the *cortex*, that our minds operate; here are received stimuli from the different senses, and here sensations are experienced. Here all our movements which are consciously directed have their origin. And here all our thinking, feeling, and willing are done.

Division of Labor in the Cortex: Nor does the division of labor in the nervous system end with this assignment of work. The cortex itself probably works essentially as a unit, yet it is through a shifting of tensions from one area to another that it acts, now giving us a sensation, now directing a movement, and now thinking a thought or feeling an emotion. Localization of function is the rule here also. Certain areas of the cortex are devoted chiefly to sensations, others to motor impulses, and others to higher thought activities, yet in such a way that all work together in perfect harmony, each reinforcing the other and making its work significant. Thus the front portion of the cortex seems to be devoted to the higher thought activities; the region on both sides of the fissure of Rolando, to motor activities; and the rear and lower parts to sensory activities; and all are bound together and made to work together by the association fibers of the brain.

In the case of the higher thought activities, it is not probable that one section of the frontal lobes of the cortex is set apart for thinking, one for feeling, and one for willing, etc., but rather that the whole frontal part of the cortex is concerned in each. In the motor and sensory areas, however, the case is different; for here a still further division of labor occurs. For example, in the motor region one small area seems connected with movements of the head, one with the arm, one with the leg, one with the face, and another with the organs of speech; likewise in the sensory region, one area is devoted to vision, one to hearing, one to taste and smell, and one to touch, etc. We must bear in mind, however, that these regions are not mapped out as accurately as are the boundaries of our states—that no part of the brain is restricted wholly to either sensory or motor nerves, and that no part works by itself independently of the rest of the brain. We name a tract from the predominance of nerves which end there, or from the chief functions which the area performs. The motor localization seems to be the most perfect. Indeed, experimentation on the brains of monkeys has been successful in mapping out motor areas so accurately that such small centers as those connected with the bending of one particular leg or the flexing of a thumb have been located. Yet each area of the cortex is so connected with every other area by the millions of association fibers that the whole brain is capable of working together as a unit, thus unifying and harmonizing our thoughts, emotions, and acts.

6. FORMS OF SENSORY STIMULI

Let us next inquire how this mechanism of the nervous system is acted upon in such a way as to give us sensations. In order to understand this, we must first know that all forms of matter are composed of minute atoms which are in constant motion, and by imparting this motion to the air or the ether which surrounds them, are constantly radiating energy in the form of minute waves throughout space. These waves, or radiations, are incredibly rapid in some instances and rather slow in others. In sending out its energy in the form of these waves, the physical world is doing its part to permit us to form its acquaintance. The end-organs of the sensory nerves must meet this advance half-way, and be so constructed as to be affected by the different forms of energy which are constantly beating upon them.

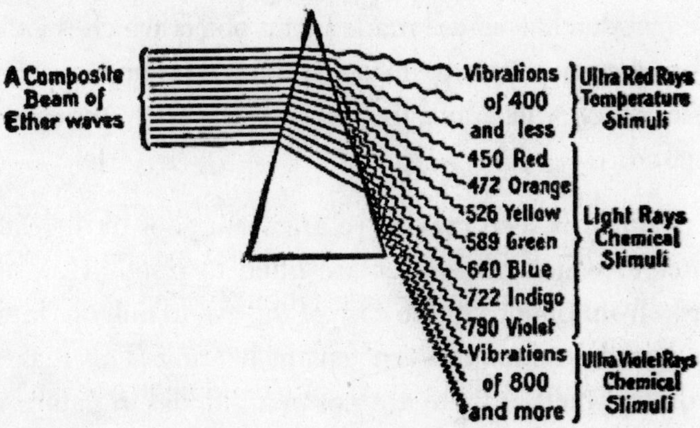

FIG. 14.—The prism's analysis of a bundle of light rays. On the right are shown the relation of vibration rates to temperature stimuli, to light and to chemical stimuli. The rates are given in billions per second.—After WITMER.

The End-organs and Their Response to Stimuli: Thus the radiations of ether from the sun, our chief source of light, are so rapid that billions of them enter the eye in a second of time, and the retina is of such a nature that its nerve cells are thrown into activity by these waves; the impulse is carried over the optic nerve to the occipital lobe of the cortex, and the sensation of sight is the result. The different colors also, from the red of the spectrum to the violet, are the result of different vibration rates in the waves of ether which strike the retina; and in order to perceive color, the retina must be able to respond to the particular vibration rate which represents each color. Likewise in the sense of touch the end-organs are fitted to respond to very rapid vibrations, and it is possible that the different qualities of touch are produced by different vibration rates in the atoms of the object we are touching. When we reach the ear, we have the organ which responds to the lowest vibration rate of all, for we can detect a sound made by an object which is vibrating from twenty to thirty times a second. The highest vibration rate which will affect the ear is some forty thousand per second.

Thus it is seen that there are great gaps in the different rates to which our senses are fitted to respond—a sudden drop from billions in the case of the eye to millions in touch, and to thousands or even tens in hearing. This makes one wonder whether there are not many things in nature which man has never discovered simply because he has not the sense mechanism enabling him to become conscious of their existence. There are undoubtedly "more things in heaven and earth than are dreamt of in our philosophy."

Dependence of the Mind on the Senses: Only as the senses bring in the material, has the mind anything with which to build. Thus have the senses to act as messengers between the great outside world and the brain; to be the servants who shall stand at the doorways of the body—the eyes, the ears, the finger tips—each ready to receive its particular kind of impulse from nature and send it along the right path to the part of the cortex where it belongs, so that the mind can say, "A sight," "A sound," or "A touch." Thus does the49 mind come to know the universe of the senses. Thus does it get the material out of which memory, imagination, and thought begin. Thus and only thus does the mind secure the crude material from which the finished superstructure is finally built.

CHAPTER IV
MENTAL DEVELOPMENT AND MOTOR TRAINING

Education was long looked upon as affecting the mind only; the body was either left out of account or neglected. Later science has shown, however, that the mind cannot be trained *except as the nervous system is trained and developed.* For not sensation and the simpler mental processes alone, but memory, imagination, judgment, reasoning and every other act of the mind are dependent on the nervous system finally for their efficiency. The little child gets its first mental experiences in connection with certain movements or acts set up reflex by the pre-organized nervous system. From this time on movement and idea are so inextricably bound together that they cannot be separated. The mind and the brain are so vitally related that it is impossible to educate one without performing a like office for the other; and it is likewise impossible to neglect the one without causing the other to suffer in its development.

1. FACTORS DETERMINING THE EFFICIENCY OF THE NERVOUS SYSTEM

Development and Nutrition: Ignoring the native differences in nervous systems through the influence of heredity, the efficiency of a nervous system is largely dependent on two factors: (1) The development of the cells and fibers of which it is composed, and (2) its general tone of health and vigor. The actual number of cells in the nervous system increases but little if at all after birth. Indeed, it is doubtful whether Edison's brain and nervous system has a greater number of cells in it than yours or mine. The difference between the brain of a genius and that of an ordinary man is not in the *number* of cells which it contains, but rather in the development of the cells and fibers which are present, potentially, at least, in every nervous system. The histologist tells us that in the nervous system of every child there are tens of thousands of cells which are so immature and undeveloped that they are useless; indeed, this is the case to some degree in every adult person's nervous system as well. Thus each individual has inherent in his nervous system potentialities of which he has never taken advantage, the utilizing of which may make him a genius and the neglecting of which will certainly leave him on the plane of mediocrity. The first problem in education, then, is to take the unripe and inefficient nervous system and so develop it in connection with the growing mind that the possibilities which nature has stored in it shall become actualities.

Undeveloped Cells: Professor Donaldson tells us on this point that: "At birth, and for a long time after, many [nervous] systems contain cell elements which are more or less immature, not forming a functional part of the tissue, and yet under some conditions capable of further development.... For the cells which are continually appearing in the developing cortex no other source is known than the nuclei or granules found there in its earliest stages. These elements are metamorphosed neuroblasts—that is, elementary cells out of which the nervous matter is developed—which have shrunken to a volume less than that which they had at first, and which remain small until, in the subsequent process of enlargement necessary for their full development, they expand into well-marked cells. Elements intermediate between these granules and the fully developed cells are always found, even in mature brains, and therefore it is inferred that the latter are derived from the former. The appearances there also lead to the conclusion that many elements which might possibly develop in any given case are far beyond the number that actually does so.... The possible number of cells latent and functional in the central system is early fixed. At any age this number is accordingly represented by the granules as well as by the cells which have already undergone further development. During growth the proportion of developed cells increases, and sometimes, owing to the failure to recognize potential nerve cells in the granules, the impression is carried away that this increase implies the formation of new elements. As has been shown, such is not the case."[1]

Development of Nerve Fibers: The nerve *fibers*, no less than the cells, must go through a process of development. It has already been shown that the fibers are the result of a branching of cells. At birth many of the cells have not yet thrown out branches, and hence the fibers are lacking; while many of those which are already grown out are not sufficiently developed to transmit impulses accurately. Thus it has been found that most children at birth are able to support the weight of the body for several seconds by clasping the fingers around a small rod, but it takes about a year for the child to become able to stand. It is evident that it requires more actual strength to cling to a rod than to stand; hence the conclusion is that the difference is in the earlier development of the nerve centers which have to do with clasping than of those concerned in standing. Likewise the child's first attempts to feed himself or do any one of the thousand little things about which he is so awkward, are partial failures not so much because he has not had practice as because his nervous machinery connected with those movements is not yet developed sufficiently to enable him to be accurate. His brain is in a condition which Flechsig calls "unripe." How, then, shall the undeveloped cells and system ripen? How shall the undeveloped cells and fibers grow to full maturity and efficiency?

2. DEVELOPMENT OF NERVOUS SYSTEM THROUGH USE

Importance of Stimulus and Response: Like all other tissues of the body, the nerve cells and fibers are developed by judicious use. The sensory and association centers require the constant stimulus of nerve currents running in from the various end-organs, and the motor centers require the constant stimulus of currents running from them out to the muscles. In other words, the conditions upon which both motor and sensory development depend are: (1) A rich environment of sights and sounds and tastes and smells, and everything else which serves as proper stimulus to the sense organs, and to every form of intellectual and social interest; and (2) no less important, an opportunity for the freest and most complete forms of response and motor activity.

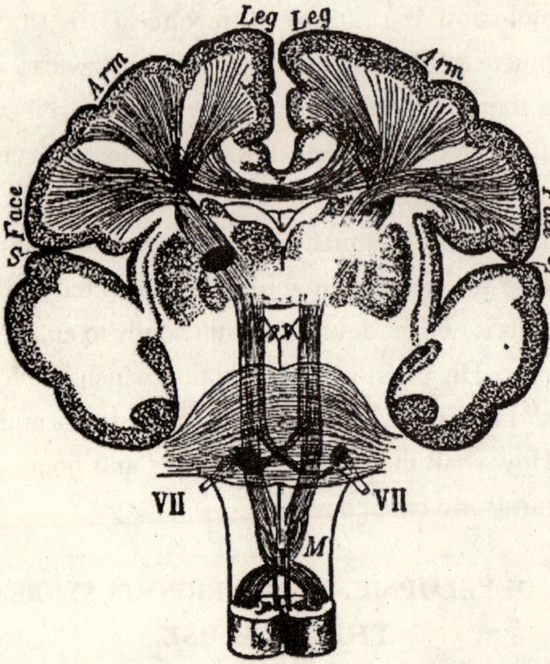

Fig. 15.—Schematic transverse section of the human brain showing the projection of the motor fibers, their crossing in the neighborhood of the medulla, and their termination in the different areas of localized function in the cortex. S, fissure of Sylvius; M, the medulla; VII, the roots of the facial nerves.

An illustration of the effects of the lack of sensory stimuli on the cortex is well shown in the case of Laura Bridgman, whose brain was studied by Professor Donaldson after her death. Laura Bridgman was born a normal child, and developed as other children do up to the age of nearly three years. At this time, through an attack of scarlet fever, she lost her hearing completely and also the sight of her left eye. Her right eye was so badly affected that she could see but little; and it, too, became entirely blind when she was eight.

She lived in this condition until she was sixty years old, when she died. Professor Donaldson submitted the cortex of her brain to a most careful examination, also comparing the corresponding areas on the two hemispheres with each other. He found that as a whole the cortex was thinner than in the case of normal individuals. He found also that the cortical area connected with the left eye—namely, the right occipital region—was much thinner than that for the right eye, which had retained its sight longer than the other. He says: "It is interesting to notice that those parts of the cortex which, according to the current view, were associated with the defective sense organs were also particularly thin. The cause of this thinness was found to be due, at least in part, to the small size of the nerve cells there present. Not only were the large and medium-sized cells smaller, but the impression made on the observer was that they were also less numerous than in the normal cortex."

Effect of Sensory Stimuli: No doubt if we could examine the brain of a person who has grown up in an environment rich in stimuli to the eye, where nature, earth, and sky have presented a changing panorama of color and form to attract the eye; where all the sounds of nature, from the chirp of the insect to the roar of the waves and the murmur of the breeze, and from the softest tones of the voice to the mightiest sweep of the great orchestra, have challenged the ear; where many and varied odors and perfumes have assailed the nostrils; where a great range of tastes have tempted the palate; where many varieties of touch and temperature sensations have been experienced—no doubt if we could examine such a brain we should find the sensory areas of the cortex excelling in thickness because its cells were well developed and full sized from the currents which had been pouring into them from the outside world. On the other hand, if we could examine a cortex which had lacked any one of these stimuli, we should find some area in it undeveloped because of this deficiency. Its owner therefore possesses but the fraction of a brain, and would in a corresponding degree find his mind incomplete.

Necessity for Motor Activity: Likewise in the case of the motor areas. Pity the boy or girl who has been deprived of the opportunity to use every muscle to the fullest extent in the unrestricted plays and games of childhood. For where such activities are not wide in their scope, there some areas of the cortex will remain undeveloped, because unused, and the person will be handicapped later in his life from lack of skill in the activities depending on these centers. Halleck says in this connection: "If we could examine the developing motor region with a microscope of sufficient magnifying power, it is conceivable that we might learn wherein the modification due to exercise consists. We might also, under such conditions, be able to say, 'This is the motor region of a piano player; the modifications here correspond precisely to those necessary for controlling such movements of the hand.' Or, 'This is the motor tract of a blacksmith; this, of an engraver; and these must be the cells which govern the vocal organs of an orator.'" Whether or not the microscope will ever reveal such things to us, there is no doubt that the conditions suggested exist, and that back of every inefficient and awkward attempt at physical control lies a motor area with its cells undeveloped by use. No wonder that our processes of learning physical adjustment and control are slow, for they are a growth in the brain rather than a simple "learning how."

The training of the nervous system consists finally, then, in the development and coordination of the neurons of which it is composed. We have seen that the sensory cells are to be developed by the sensory stimuli pouring in upon them, and the motor cells by the motor impulses which they send out to the muscles. The sensory and the motor fibers likewise, being an outgrowth of their respective cells, find their development in carrying the impulses which result in sensation and movement. Thus it is seen that the neuron is, in its development as in its work, a unit.

Development of the Association Centers: To this simpler type of sensory and motor development which we have been considering, we must add that which comes from the more complex mental processes, such as memory, thought, and imagination. For it is in connection with these that the association fibers are developed, and the brain areas so connected that they can work together as a unit. A simple illustration will enable us to see more clearly how the nervous mechanism acts to bring this about.

Suppose that I am walking along a country road deeply engaged in meditation, and that I come to a puddle of water in my pathway. I may turn aside and avoid the obstruction without my attention being called to it, and without interruption of my train of thought. The act has been automatic. In this case the nerve current has passed from the eye (*S*) over an afferent fiber to a sensory center (*s*) in the nervous system below the cortex; from there it has been forwarded to a motor center (*m*) in the same region, and on out over a motor fiber to the proper muscles (*M*), which are to execute the required act. The act having been completed, the sensory nerves connected with the muscles employed report the fact back that the work is done, thus completing the circuit. This event may be taken as an illustration of literally thousands of acts which we perform daily without the intervention of consciousness, and hence without involving the hemispheres.

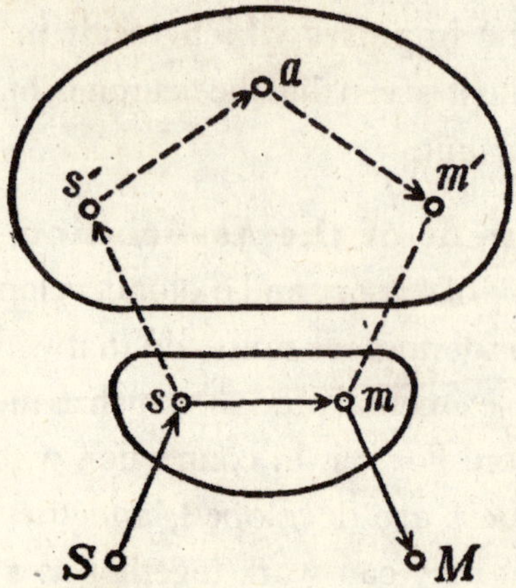

FIG. 16.—Diagram illustrating the paths of association.

If, however, instead of avoiding the puddle unconsciously, I do so from consideration of the danger of wet feet and the disagreeableness of soiled shoes and the ridiculous appearance I shall make, then the current cannot take the short circuit, but must pass on up to the cortex. Here it awakens consciousness to take notice of the obstruction, and calls forth the images which aid in directing the necessary movements. This simple illustration may be greatly complicated, substituting for it one of the more complex problems which are continually presenting themselves to us for solution, or the associated trains of thought that are constantly occupying our minds. But the truth of the illustration still holds. Whether in the simple or the complex act, there is always a forward passing of the nerve current through the sensory and thought centers, and on out through the motor centers to the organs which are to be concerned in the motor response.

The Factors Involved in a Simple Action: Thus it will be seen that in the simplest act which can be considered there are the following factors: (1) The stimulus which acts on the end-organ; (2) the ingoing current over an afferent nerve; (3) the sensory or interpreting cells; (4) the fibers connecting the sensory with a motor center; (5) the motor cells; (6) the efferent nerve to carry the direction for the movement outward to the muscle; (7) the motor response; and, finally, (8) the report back that the act has been performed. With this in mind it fairly bewilders one to think of the marvelous complexity of the work that is going on in our nervous mechanism every moment of our life, even without considering the higher thought processes at all. How, with these added, the resulting complexity all works out into beautiful harmony is indeed beyond comprehension.

3. EDUCATION AND THE TRAINING OF THE NERVOUS SYSTEM

Fortunately, many of the best opportunities for sensory and motor training do not depend on schools or courses of study. The world is full of stimuli to our senses and to our social natures; and our common lives are made up of the responses we make to these stimuli,—the movements, acts and deeds by which we fit ourselves into our world of environment. Undoubtedly the most rapid and vital progress we make in our development is accomplished in the years before we have reached the age to go to school. Yet it is the business of education to see that we do not lack any essential opportunity, to make sure that necessary lines of stimuli or of motor training have not been omitted from our development.

Education to Supply Opportunities for Stimulus and Response: The great problem of education is, on the physical side, it would seem, then, to provide for ourselves and those we seek to educate as rich an environment of sensory and social stimuli as possible; one whose impressions will be full of suggestions to response in motor activity and the higher thought processes; and then to give opportunity for thought and for expression in acts and deeds in the largest possible number of lines. And added to this must be frequent and clear sensory and motor recall, a living over again of the sights and sounds and odors and the motor activities we have once experienced. There must also be the opportunity for the forming of worthy plans and ideals. For in this way the brain centers which were concerned in the original sensation or thought or movement are again brought into exercise, and their development continued. Through recall and imagination we are able not only greatly to multiply the effects of the immediate sensory and motor stimuli which come to us, but also to improve our power of thinking by getting a fund of material upon which the mind can draw.

Order of Development in the Nervous System: Nature has set the order in which the powers of the nervous system shall develop. And we must follow this order if we would obtain the best results. Stated in technical terms, the order is *from fundamental to accessory*. This is to say that the nerve centers controlling the larger and more general movements of the body ripen first, and those governing the finer motor adjustments later. For example, the larger body muscles of the child which are concerned with sitting up come under control earlier than those connected with walking. The arm muscles develop control earlier than the finger muscles, and the head and neck muscles earlier than the eye muscles. So also the more general and less highly specialized powers of the mind ripen sooner than the more highly specialized. Perception and observation precede powers of critical judgment and association. Memory and imagination ripen earlier than reasoning and the logical ability.

This all means that our educational system must be planned to follow the order of nature. Children of the primary grades should not be required to write with fine pencils or pens, which demand delicate finger adjustments, since the brain centers for these finer coordinations are not yet developed. Young children should not be set at work necessitating difficult eye control, such as stitching through perforated cardboard, reading fine print and the like, as their eyes are not yet ready for such tasks. The more difficult analytical problems of arithmetic and relations of grammar should not be required of pupils at a time when the association areas of the brain are not yet ready for this type of thinking. For such methods violate the law of nature, and the child is sure to suffer the penalty.

4. IMPORTANCE OF HEALTH AND VIGOR OF THE NERVOUS SYSTEM

Parallel with opportunities for proper stimuli and response the nervous system must possess good *tonicity*, or vigor. This depends in large degree on general health and nutrition, with freedom from over fatigue. No favorableness of environment nor excellence of training can result in an efficient brain if the nerve energy has run low from depleted health, want of proper nourishment, or exhaustion.

The Influence of Fatigue: Histologists find that the nuclei of nerve cells are shrunk as much as fifty per cent by extreme fatigue. Reasonable fatigue followed by proper recuperation is not harmful, but even necessary if the best development is to be attained; but fatigue without proper nourishment and rest is fatal to all mental operations, and indeed finally to the nervous system itself, leaving it permanently in a condition of low tone, and incapable of rallying to strong effort. For rapid and complete recuperation the cells must have not only the best of nourishment but opportunity for rest as well.

Extreme and long-continued fatigue is hostile to the development and welfare of any nervous system, and especially to that of children. Not only does over fatigue hinder growth, but it also results in the formation of certain *toxins*, or poisons, in the organism, which are particularly harmful to nervous tissue. It is these fatigue toxins that account for many of the nervous and mental disorders which accompany breakdowns from overwork. On the whole, the evil effects from mental overstrain are more to be feared than from physical overstrain.

The Effects of Worry: There is, perhaps, no greater foe to brain growth and efficiency than the nervous and worn-out condition which comes from loss of sleep or from worry. Experiments in the psychological laboratories have shown that nerve cells shrivel up and lose their vitality under loss of sleep. Let this go on for any considerable length of time, and the loss is irreparable; for the cells can never recuperate. This is especially true in the case of children or young people. Many school boys and girls, indeed many college students, are making slow progress in their studies not because they are mentally slow or inefficient, not even chiefly because they lose time that should be put on their lessons, but because they are incapacitating their brains for good service through late hours and the consequent loss of sleep. Add to this condition that of worry, which often accompanies it from the fact of failure in lessons, and a naturally good and well-organized nervous system is sure to fail. Worry, from whatever cause, should be avoided as one would avoid poison, if we would bring ourselves to the highest degree of efficiency. Not only does worry temporarily unfit the mind for its best work, but its evil results are permanent, since the mind is left with a poorly developed or undone nervous system through which to work, even after the cause for worry has been removed and the worry itself has ceased.

Not only should each individual seek to control the causes of worry in his own life, but the home and the school should force upon childhood as few causes for worry as may be. Children's worry over fears of the dark, over sickness and death, over prospective but delayed punishment, over the thousand and one real or imaginary troubles of childhood, should be eliminated so far as possible. School examinations that prey on the peace of mind, threats of failure of promotion, all nagging and sarcasm, and whatever else may cause continued pain or worry to sensitive minds should be barred from our schoolroom methods and practice. The price we force the child to pay for results through their use is too great for them to be tolerated. We must seek a better way.

The Factors in Good Nutrition: For the best nutrition there is necessity first of all plenty of nourishing and healthful food. Science and experience have both disproved the supposition that students should be scantily fed. O'Shea claims that many brain workers are far short of their highest grade of efficiency because of starving their brains from poor diet. And not only must the food be of the right quality, but the body must be in good health. Little good to eat the best of food unless it is being properly digested and assimilated. And little good if all the rest is as it should be, and the right amount of oxidation does not go on in the brain so as to remove the worn-out cells and make place for new ones. This warns us that pure air and a strong circulation are indispensable to the best working of our brains. No doubt many students who find their work too hard for them might locate the trouble in their stomachs or their lungs or the food they eat, rather than in their minds.

5. PROBLEMS FOR INTROSPECTION AND OBSERVATION

1. Estimate the mental progress made by the child during the first five years and compare with that made during the second five years of its life. To do this make a list, so far as you are able, of the acquisitions of each period. What do you conclude as to the importance of play and freedom in early education? Why not continue this method instead of sending the child to school?

2. Which has the better opportunity for sensory training, the city child or the country child? For social training? For motor development through play? It is said by specialists that country children are not as good players as city children. Why should this be the case?

3. Observe carefully some group of children for evidences of lack of sensory training (Interest in sensory objects, skill in observation, etc.). For lack of motor training (Failure in motor control, awkwardness, lack of skill in play, etc.). Do you find that general mental ability seems to be correlated with sensory and motor ability, or not?

4. What sensory training can be had from (1) geography, (2) agriculture, (3) arithmetic, (4) drawing? What lines of motor training ought the school to afford, (1) in general, (2) for the hand, (3) in the grace and poise of carriage or bearing, (4) in any other line? Make observation tests of these points in one or more school rooms and report the results.

5. Describe what you think must be the type of mental life of Helen Keller. (Read "The World I Live In," by Helen Keller.)

6. Study groups of children for signs of deficiency in brain power from lack of nutrition. From fatigue. From worry. From lack of sleep.

CHAPTER V
HABIT

Habit is our "best friend or worst enemy." We are "walking bundles of habits." Habit is the "fly-wheel of society," keeping men patient and docile in the hard or disagreeable lot which some must fill. Habit is a "cable which we cannot break." So say the wise men. Let me know your habits of life and you have revealed your moral standards and conduct. Let me discover your intellectual habits, and I understand your type of mind and methods of thought. In short, our lives are largely a daily round of activities dictated by our habits in this line or that. Most of our movements and acts are habitual; we think as we have formed the habit of thinking; we decide as we are in the habit of deciding; we sleep, or eat, or speak as we have grown into the habit of doing these things; we may even say our prayers or perform other religious exercises as matters of habit. But while habit is the veriest tyrant, yet its good offices far exceed the bad even in the most fruitless or depraved life.

1. THE NATURE OF HABIT

Many people when they speak or think of habit give the term a very narrow or limited meaning. They have in mind only certain moral or personal tendencies usually spoken of as one's "habits." But in order to understand habit in any thorough and complete way we must, as suggested by the preceding paragraph, broaden our concept to include every possible line of physical and mental activity. Habit may be defined as *the tendency of the nervous system to repeat any act that has been performed once or many times.*

The Physical Basis of Habit: Habit is to be explained from the standpoint of its physical basis. Habits are formed because the tissues of our brains are capable of being modified by use, and of so retaining the effects of this modification that the same act is easier of performance each succeeding time. This results in the old act being repeated instead of a new one being selected, and hence the old act is perpetuated.

Even dead and inert matter obeys the same principles in this regard as does living matter. Says M. Leon Dumont: "Everyone knows how a garment, having been worn a certain time, clings to the shape of the body better than when it was new; there has been a change in the tissue, and this change is a new habit of cohesion; a lock works better after having been used some time; at the outset more force was required to overcome certain roughness in the mechanism. The overcoming of this resistance is a phenomenon of habituation. It costs less trouble to fold a paper when it has been folded already. This saving of trouble is due to the essential nature of habit, which brings it about that, to reproduce the effect, a less amount of the outward cause is required. The sounds of a violin improve by use in the hands of an able artist, because the fibers of the wood at last contract habits of vibration conformed to harmonic relations. This is what gives such inestimable value to instruments that have belonged to great masters. Water, in flowing, hollows out for itself a channel, which grows broader and deeper; and, after having ceased to flow, it resumes when it flows again the path traced for itself before. Just so, the impressions of outer objects fashion for themselves in the nervous system more and more appropriate paths, and these vital phenomena recur under similar excitements from without, when they have been interrupted for a certain time."[2]

All Living Tissue Plastic: What is true of inanimate matter is doubly true of living tissue. The tissues of the human body can be molded into almost any form you choose if taken in time. A child may be placed on his feet at too early an age, and the bones of his legs form the habit of remaining bent. The Flathead Indian binds a board on the skull of his child, and its head forms the habit of remaining flat on the top. Wrong bodily postures produce curvature of the spine, and pernicious modes of dress deform the bones of the chest. The muscles may be trained into the habit of keeping the shoulders straight or letting them droop; those of the back, to keep the body well up on the hips, or to let it sag; those of locomotion, to give us a light, springy step, or to allow a shuffling carriage; those of speech, to give us a clear-cut, accurate articulation, or a careless, halting one; and those of the face, to give us a cheerful cast of countenance, or a glum and morose expression.

Habit a Modification of Brain Tissue: But the nervous tissue is the most sensitive and easily molded of all bodily tissues. In fact, it is probable that the real *habit* of our characteristic walk, gesture, or speech resides in the brain, rather than in the muscles which it controls. So delicate is the organization of the brain structure and so unstable its molecules, that even the perfume of the flower, which assails the nose of a child, the song of a bird, which strikes his ear, or the fleeting dream, which lingers but for a second in his sleep, has so modified his brain that it will never again be as if these things had not been experienced. Every sensory current which runs in from the outside world; every motor current which runs out to command a muscle; every thought that we think, has so modified the nerve structure through which it acts, that a tendency remains for a like act to be repeated. Our brain and nervous system is daily being molded into fixed habits of acting by our thoughts and deeds, and thus becomes the automatic register of all we do.

The old Chinese fairy story hits upon a fundamental and vital truth. These celestials tell their children that each child is accompanied by day and by night, every moment of his life, by an invisible fairy, who is provided with a pencil and tablet. It is the duty of this fairy to put down every deed of the child, both good and evil, in an indelible record which will one day rise as a witness against him. So it is in very truth with our brains. The wrong act may have been performed in secret, no living being may ever know that we performed it, and a merciful Providence may forgive it; but the inexorable monitor of our deeds was all the time beside us writing the record, and the history of that act is inscribed forever in the tissues of our brain. It may be repented of bitterly in sackcloth and ashes and be discontinued, but its effects can never be quite effaced; they will remain with us a handicap till our dying day, and in some critical moment in a great emergency we shall be in danger of defeat from that long past and forgotten act.

We Must Form Habits: We *must*, then, form habits. It is not at all in our power to say whether we will form habits or not; for, once started, they go on forming themselves by day and night, steadily and relentlessly. Habit is, therefore, one of the great factors to be reckoned with in our lives, and the question becomes not, Shall we form habits? but *What habits we shall form.* And we have the determining of this question largely in our own power, for habits do not just happen, nor do they come to us ready made. We ourselves make them from day to day through the acts we perform, and in so far as we have control over our acts, in that far we can determine our habits.

2. THE PLACE OF HABIT IN THE ECONOMY OF OUR LIVES

Habit is one of nature's methods of economizing time and effort, while at the same time securing greater skill and efficiency. This is easily seen when it is remembered that habit tends towards *automatic* action; that is, towards action governed by the lower nerve centers and taking care of itself, so to speak, without the interference of consciousness. Everyone has observed how much easier in the performance and more skillful in its execution is the act, be it playing a piano, painting a picture, or driving a nail, when the movements involved have ceased to be consciously directed and become automatic.

Habit Increases Skill and Efficiency: Practically all increase in skill, whether physical or mental, depends on our ability to form habits. Habit holds fast to the skill already attained while practice or intelligence makes ready for the next step in advance. Could we not form habits we should improve but little in our way of doing things, no matter how many times we did them over. We should now be obliged to go through the same bungling process of dressing ourselves as when we first learned it as children. Our writing would proceed as awkwardly in the high school as the primary, our eating as adults would be as messy and wide of the mark as when we were infants, and we should miss in a thousand ways the motor skill that now seems so easy and natural. All highly skilled occupations, and those demanding great manual dexterity, likewise depend on our habit-forming power for the accurate and automatic movements required.

So with mental skill. A great portion of the fundamentals of our education must be made automatic—must become matters of habit. We set out to learn the symbols of speech. We hear words and see them on the printed page; associated with these words are meanings, or ideas. Habit binds the word and the idea together, so that to think of the one is to call up the other—and language is learned. We must learn numbers, so we practice the "combinations," and with 4×6, or 3×8 we associate 24. Habit secures this association in our minds, and lo! we soon know our "tables." And so on throughout the whole range of our learning. We learn certain symbols, or facts, or processes, and habit takes hold and renders these automatic so that we can use them freely, easily, and with skill, leaving our thought free for matters that cannot be made automatic. One of our greatest dangers is that we shall not make sufficiently automatic, enough of the necessary foundation material of education. Failing in this, we shall at best be but blunderers intellectually, handicapped because we failed to make proper use of habit in our development.

For, as we have seen in an earlier chapter, there is a limit to our mental energy and also to the number of objects to which we are able to attend. It is only when attention has been freed from the many things that can always be thought or done *in the same way*, that the mind can devote itself to the real problems that require judgment, imagination or reasoning. The writer whose spelling and punctuation do not take care of themselves will hardly make a success of writing. The mathematician whose number combinations, processes and formula are not automatic in his mind can never hope to make progress in mathematical thinking. The speaker who, while speaking, has to think of his gestures, his voice or his enunciation will never sway audiences by his logic or his eloquence.

Habit Saves Effort and Fatigue: We do most easily and with least fatigue that which we are accustomed to do. It is the new act or the strange task that tires us. The horse that is used to the farm wearies if put on the road, while the roadster tires easily when hitched to the plow. The experienced penman works all day at his desk without undue fatigue, while the man more accustomed to the pick and the shovel than to the pen, is exhausted by a half hour's writing at a letter. Those who follow a sedentary and inactive occupation do not tire by much sitting, while children or others used to freedom and action may find it a wearisome task merely to remain still for an hour or two.

Not only would the skill and speed demanded by modern industry be impossible without the aid of habit, but without its help none could stand the fatigue and strain. The new workman placed at a high-speed machine is ready to fall from weariness at the end of his first day. But little by little he learns to omit the unnecessary movements, the necessary movements become easier and more automatic through habit, and he finds the work easier. We may conclude, then, that not only do consciously directed movements show less skill than the same movements made automatic by habit, but they also require more effort and produce greater fatigue.

Habit Economizes Moral Effort: To have to decide each time the question comes up whether we will attend to this lecture or sermon or lesson; whether we will persevere and go through this piece of disagreeable work which we have begun; whether we will go to the trouble of being courteous and kind to this or that poor or unlovely or dirty fellow-mortal; whether we will take this road because it looks easy, or that one because we know it to be the one we ought to take; whether we will be strictly fair and honest when we might just as well be the opposite; whether we will resist the temptation which dares us; whether we will do this duty, hard though it is, which confronts us—to have to decide each of these questions every time it presents itself is to put too large a proportion of our thought and energy on things which should take care of themselves. For all these things should early become so nearly habitual that they can be settled with the very minimum of expenditure of energy when they arise.

The Habit of Attention: It is a noble thing to be able to attend by sheer force of will when the interest lags, or some more attractive thing appears, but far better is it so to have formed the habit of attention that we naturally fall into that attitude when this is the desirable thing. To understand what I mean, you only have to look over a class or an audience and note the different ways which people have of finally settling down to listening. Some with an attitude which says, "Now here I am, ready to listen to you if you will interest me, otherwise not." Others with a manner which says, "I did not really come here expecting to listen, and you will have a large task if you interest me; I never listen unless I am compelled to, and the responsibility rests on you." Others plainly say, "I really mean to listen, but I have hard work to control my thoughts, and if I wander I shall not blame you altogether; it is just my way." And still others say, "When I am expected to listen, I always listen whether there is anything much to listen to or not. I have formed that habit, and so have no quarrel with myself about it. You can depend on me to be attentive, for I cannot afford to weaken my habit of attention whether you do well or not." Every speaker will clasp these last listeners to his heart and feed them on the choicest thoughts of his soul; they are the ones to whom he speaks and to whom his address will appeal.

Habit Enables Us to Meet the Disagreeable: To be able to persevere in the face of difficulties and hardships and carry through the disagreeable thing in spite of the protests of our natures against the sacrifice which it requires, is a creditable thing; but it is more creditable to have so formed the habit of perseverance that the disagreeable duty shall be done without a struggle, or protest, or question. Horace Mann testifies of himself that whatever success he was able to attain was made possible through the early habit which he formed of never stopping to inquire whether he *liked* to do a thing which needed doing, but of doing everything equally well and without question, both the pleasant and the unpleasant.

The youth who can fight out a moral battle and win against the allurements of some attractive temptation is worthy the highest honor and praise; but so long as he has to fight the same battle over and over again, he is on dangerous ground morally. For good morals must finally become habits, so ingrained in us that the right decision comes largely without effort and without struggle. Otherwise the strain is too great, and defeat will occasionally come; and defeat means weakness and at last disaster, after the spirit has tired of the constant conflict. And so on in a hundred lines. Good habits are more to be coveted than individual victories in special cases, much as these are to be desired. For good habits mean victories all along the line.

Habit the Foundation of Personality: The biologist tells us that it is the *constant* and not the *occasional* in the environment that impresses itself on an organism. So also it is the *habitual* in our lives that builds itself into our character and personality. In a very real sense we *are* what we are in the habit of doing and thinking.

Without habit, personality could not exist; for we could never do a thing twice alike, and hence would be a new person each succeeding moment. The acts which give us our own peculiar individuality are our habitual acts—the little things that do themselves moment by moment without care or attention, and are the truest and best expression of our real selves. Probably no one of us could be very sure which arm he puts into the sleeve, or which foot he puts into the shoe, first; and yet each of us certainly formed the habit long ago of doing these things in a certain way. We might not be able to describe just how we hold knife and fork and spoon, and yet each has his own characteristic and habitual way of handling them. We sit down and get up in some characteristic way, and the very poise of our heads and attitudes of our bodies are the result of habit. We get sleepy and wake up, become hungry and thirsty at certain hours, through force of habit. We form the habit of liking a certain chair, or nook, or corner, or path, or desk, and then seek this to the exclusion of all others. We habitually use a particular pitch of voice and type of enunciation in speaking, and this becomes one of our characteristic marks; or we form the habit of using barbarisms or solecisms of language in youth, and these cling to us and become an inseparable part of us later in life.

On the mental side the case is no different. Our thinking is as characteristic as our physical acts. We may form the habit of thinking things out logically, or of jumping to conclusions; of thinking critically and independently, or of taking things unquestioningly on the authority of others. We may form the habit of carefully reading good, sensible books, or of skimming sentimental and trashy ones; of choosing elevating, ennobling companions, or the opposite; of being a good conversationalist and doing our part in a social group, or of being a drag on the conversation, and needing to be "entertained." We may form the habit of observing the things about us and enjoying the beautiful in our environment, or of failing to observe or to enjoy. We may form the habit of obeying the voice of conscience or of weakly yielding to temptation without a struggle; of taking a reverent attitude of prayer in our devotions, or of merely saying our prayers.

Habit Saves Worry and Rebellion: Habit has been called the "balance wheel" of society. This is because men readily become habituated to the hard, the disagreeable, or the inevitable, and cease to battle against it. A lot that at first seems unendurable after a time causes less revolt. A sorrow that seems too poignant to be borne in the course of time loses some of its sharpness. Oppression or injustice that arouses the fiercest resentment and hate may finally come to be accepted with resignation. Habit helps us learn that "what cannot be cured must be endured."

3. THE TYRANNY OF HABIT

Even Good Habits Need to Be Modified: But even in good habits there is danger. Habit is the opposite of attention. Habit relieves attention of unnecessary strain. Every habitual act was at one time, either in the history of the race or of the individual, a voluntary act; that is, it was performed under active attention. As the habit grew, attention was gradually rendered unnecessary, until finally it dropped entirely out. And herein lies the danger. Habit once formed has no way of being modified unless in some way attention is called to it, for a habit left to itself becomes more and more firmly fixed. The rut grows deeper. In very few, if any, of our actions can we afford to have this the case. Our habits need to be progressive, they need to grow, to be modified, to be improved. Otherwise they will become an incrusting shell, fixed and unyielding, which will limit our growth.

It is necessary, then, to keep our habitual acts under some surveillance of attention, to pass them in review for inspection every now and then, that we may discover possible modifications which will make them more serviceable. We need to be inventive, constantly to find out better ways of doing things. Habit takes care of our standing, walking, sitting; but how many of us could not improve his poise and carriage if he would? Our speech has become largely automatic, but no doubt all of us might remove faults of enunciation, pronunciation or stress from our speaking. So also we might better our habits of study and thinking, our methods of memorizing, or our manner of attending.

The Tendency of "Ruts.": But this will require something of heroism. For to follow the well-beaten path of custom is easy and pleasant, while to break out of the rut of habit and start a new line of action is difficult and disturbing. Most people prefer to keep doing things as they always have done them, to continue reading and thinking and believing as they have long been in the habit of doing, not so much because they feel that their way is best, but because it is easier than to change. Hence the great mass of us settle down on the plane of mediocrity, and become "old fogy." We learn to do things passably well, cease to think about improving our ways of doing them, and so fall into a rut. Only the few go on. They make use of habit as the rest do, but they also continue to attend at critical points of action, and so make habit an *ally* in place of accepting it as a *tyrant*.

4. HABIT-FORMING A PART OF EDUCATION

It follows from the importance of habit in our lives that no small part of education should be concerned with the development of serviceable habits. Says James, "Could the young but realize how soon they will become mere walking bundles of habits, they would give more heed to their conduct while in the plastic state. We are spinning our own fates, good or evil, and never to be undone. Every smallest stroke of virtue or of vice leaves its never-so-little scar." Any youth who is forming a large number of useful habits is receiving no mean education, no matter if his knowledge of books may be limited;

on the other hand, no one who is forming a large number of bad habits is being well educated, no matter how brilliant his knowledge may be.

Youth the Time for Habit-forming: Childhood and youth is the great time for habit-forming. Then the brain is plastic and easily molded, and it retains its impressions more indelibly; later it is hard to modify, and the impressions made are less permanent. It is hard to teach an old dog new tricks; nor would he remember them if you could teach them to him, nor be able to perform them well even if he could remember them. The young child will, within the first few weeks of its life, form habits of sleeping and feeding. It may in a few days be led into the habit of sleeping in the dark, or requiring a light; of going to sleep lying quietly, or of insisting upon being rocked; of getting hungry by the clock, or of wanting its food at all times when it finds nothing else to do, and so on. It is wholly outside the power of the mother or the nurse to determine whether the child shall form habits, but largely within their power to say what habits shall be formed, since they control his acts.

As the child grows older, the range of his habits increases; and by the time he has reached his middle teens, the greater number of his personal habits are formed. It is very doubtful whether a boy who has not formed habits of punctuality before the age of fifteen will ever be entirely trustworthy in matters requiring precision in this line. The girl who has not, before this age, formed habits of neatness and order will hardly make a tidy housekeeper later in her life. Those who in youth have no opportunity to habituate themselves to the usages of society may study books on etiquette and employ private instructors in the art of polite behavior all they please later in life, but they will never cease to be awkward and ill at ease. None are at a greater disadvantage than the suddenly-grown-rich who attempt late in life to surround themselves with articles of art and luxury, though their habits were all formed amid barrenness and want during their earlier years.

The Habit of Achievement: What youth does not dream of being great, or noble, or a celebrated scholar! And how few there are who finally achieve their ideals! Where does the cause of failure lie? Surely not in the lack of high ideals. Multitudes of young people have "Excelsior!" as their motto, and yet never get started up the mountain slope, let alone toiling on to its top. They have put in hours dreaming of the glory farther up, *and have never begun to climb*. The difficulty comes in not realizing that the only way to become what we wish or dream that we may become is *to form the habit of being that thing*. To form the habit of achievement, of effort, of self-sacrifice, if need be. To form the habit of deeds along with dreams; to form the habit of *doing*.

Who of us has not at this moment lying in wait for his convenience in the dim future a number of things which he means to do just as soon as this term of school is finished, or this job of work is completed, or when he is not so busy as now? And how seldom does he ever get at these things at all! Darwin tells that in his youth he loved poetry, art, and music, but was so busy with his scientific work that he could ill spare the time to indulge these tastes. So he promised himself that he would devote his time to scientific work and make his mark in this. Then he would have time for the things that he loved, and would cultivate his taste for the fine arts. He made his mark in the field of science, and then turned again to poetry, to music, to art. But alas! they were all dead and dry bones to him, without life or interest. He had passed the time when he could ever form the taste for them. He had formed his habits in another direction, and now it was forever too late to form new habits. His own conclusion is, that if he had his life to live over again, he would each week listen to some musical concert and visit some art gallery, and that each day he would read some poetry, and thereby keep alive and active the love for them.

So every school and home should be a species of habit-factory—a place where children develop habits of neatness, punctuality, obedience, politeness, dependability and the other graces of character.

5. RULES FOR HABIT-FORMING

James's Three Maxims for Habit-forming: On the forming of new habits and the leaving off of old ones, I know of no better statement than that of James, based on Bain's chapter on "Moral Habits." I quote this statement at some length: "In the acquisition of a new habit, or the leaving off of an old one, we must take care to *launch ourselves with as strong and decided an initiative as possible.* Accumulate all the possible circumstances which shall reinforce right motives; put yourself assiduously in conditions that encourage the new way; make engagements incompatible with the old; take a public pledge, if the case allows; in short, develop your resolution with every aid you know. This will give your new beginning such a momentum that the temptation to break down will not occur as soon as it otherwise might; and every day during which a breakdown is postponed adds to the chances of its not occurring at all.

"The second maxim is: *Never suffer an exception to occur until the new habit is securely rooted in your life.* Each lapse is like letting fall a ball of string which one is carefully winding up; a single slip undoes more than a great many turns will wind again. *Continuity* of training is the great means of making the nervous system act infallibly right.... The need of securing success nerves one to future vigor.

"A third maxim may be added to the preceding pair: *Seize the very first possible opportunity to act on every resolution you make, and on every emotional prompting you may experience in the direction of the habits you aspire to gain.* It is not in the moment of their forming, but in the moment of their producing *motor effects*, that resolves and aspirations communicate the new 'set' to the brain."[3]

The Preponderance of Good Habits Over Bad: And finally, let no one be disturbed or afraid because in a little time you become a "walking bundle of habits." For in so far as your good actions predominate over your bad ones, that much will your good habits outweigh your bad habits. Silently, moment by moment, efficiency is growing out of all worthy acts well done. Every bit of heroic self-sacrifice, every battle fought and won, every good deed performed, is being irreducibly credited to you in your nervous system, and will finally add its mite toward achieving the success of your ambitions.

6. PROBLEMS IN OBSERVATION AND INTROSPECTION

1. Select some act which you have recently begun to perform and watch it grow more and more habitual. Notice

carefully for a week and see whether you do not discover some habits which you did not know you had. Make a catalog of your bad habits; of the most important of your good ones.

2. Set out to form some new habits which you desire to possess; also to break some undesirable habit, watching carefully what takes place in both cases, and how long it requires.

3. Try the following experiment and relate the results to the matter of automatic control brought about by habit: Draw a star on a sheet of cardboard. Place this on a table before you, with a hand-mirror so arranged that you can see the star in the mirror. Now trace the outline of the star with a pencil, looking steadily in the mirror to guide your hand. Do not lift the pencil from the paper from the time you start until you finish. Have others try this experiment.

4. Study some group of pupils for their habits (1) of attention, (2) of speech, (3) of standing, sitting, and walking, (4) of study. Report on your observations and suggest methods of curing bad habits observed.

5. Make a list of "mannerisms" you have observed, and suggest how they may be cured.

6. Make a list of from ten to twenty habits which you think the school and its work should especially cultivate. What ones of these are the schools you know least successful in cultivating? Where does the trouble lie?

CHAPTER VI
SENSATION

We can best understand the problems of sensation and perception if we first think of the existence of two great worlds—the world of physical nature without and the world of mind within. On the one hand is our material environment, the things we see and hear and touch and taste and handle; and on the other hand our consciousness, the means by which we come to know this outer world and adjust ourselves to it. These two worlds seem in a sense to belong to and require each other. For what would be the meaning or use of the physical world with no mind to know or use it; and what would be the use of a mind with nothing to be known or thought about?

1. HOW WE COME TO KNOW THE EXTERNAL WORLD

There is a marvel about our coming to know the external world which we shall never be able fully to understand. We have come by this knowledge so gradually and unconsciously that it now appears to us as commonplace, and we take for granted many things that it would puzzle us to explain.

Knowledge through the Senses: For example, we say, "Of course I see yonder green tree: it is about ten rods distant." But why "of course"? Why should objects at a distance from us and with no evident connection between us and them be known to us at all merely by turning our eyes in their direction when there is light? Why not rather say with the blind son of Professor Puiseaux of Paris, who, when asked if he would like to be restored to sight, answered: "If it were not for curiosity I would rather have long arms. It seems to me that my hands would teach me better what is passing in the moon than your eyes or telescopes."

We listen and then say, "Yes, that is a certain bell ringing in the neighboring village," as if this were the most simple thing in the world. But why should one piece of metal striking against another a mile or two away make us aware that there is a bell there at all, let alone that it is a certain bell whose tone we recognize? Or we pass our fingers over a piece of cloth and decide, "That is silk." But why, merely by placing our skin in contact with a bit of material, should we be able to know its quality, much less that it is cloth and that its threads were originally spun by an insect? Or we take a sip of liquid and say, "This milk is sour." But why should we be able by taking the liquid into the mouth and bringing it into contact with the mucous membrane to tell that it is milk, and that it possesses the quality which we call *sour*? Or, once more, we get a whiff of air through the open window in the springtime and say, "There is a lilac bush in bloom on the lawn." Yet why, from inhaling air containing particles of lilac, should we be able to know that there is anything outside, much less that it is a flower and of a particular variety which we call lilac? Or, finally, we hold a heated flatiron up near the cheek and say, "This is too hot! it will burn the cloth." But why by holding this object a foot away from the face do we know that it is there, let alone knowing its temperature?

The Unity of Sensory Experience: Further, our senses come through experience to have the power of fusing, or combining their knowledge, so to speak, by which each expresses its knowledge in terms of the others. Thus we take a glance out of the window and say that the day looks cold, although we well know that we cannot see *cold*. Or we say that the melon sounds green, or the bell sounds cracked, although a *crack* or *greenness* cannot be heard. Or we say that the box feels empty, although *emptiness* cannot be felt. We have come to associate cold, originally experienced with days which look like the one we now see, with this particular appearance, and so we say we see the cold; sounds like the one coming from the bell we have come to associate with cracked bells, and that coming from the melon with green melons, until we say unhesitatingly that the bell sounds cracked and the melon sounds green. And so with the various senses. Each gleans from the world its own particular bit of knowledge, but all are finally in a partnership and what is each one's knowledge belongs to every other one in so far as the other can use it.

The Sensory Processes to Be Explained: The explanation of the ultimate nature of knowledge, and how we reach it through contact with our material environment, we will leave to the philosophers. And battles enough they have over the question, and still others they will have before the matter is settled. The easier and more important problem for us is to describe the *processes* by which the mind comes to know its environment, and to see how it uses this knowledge in thinking. This much we shall be able to do, for it is often possible to describe a process and discover its laws even when we cannot fully explain its nature and origin. We know the process of digestion and assimilation, and the laws which govern them, although we do not understand the ultimate nature and origin of *life* which makes these possible.

The Qualities of Objects Exist in the Mind: Yet even in the relatively simple description which we have proposed many puzzles confront us, and one of them appears at the very outset. This is that the qualities which we usually ascribe to objects really exist in our own minds and not in the objects at all. Take, for instance, the common qualities of light and color. The physicist tells us that what we see as light is occasioned by an incredibly rapid beating of ether waves on the retina of the eye. All space is filled with this ether; and when it is light—that is, when some object like the sun or other light-giving body is present—the ether is set in motion by the vibrating molecules of the body which is the source of light, its waves strike the retina, a current is produced and carried to the brain, and we see light. This means, then, that space, the medium in which we see objects, is not filled with light (the sensation), but with very rapid waves of ether, and that the light which we see really occurs in our own minds as the mental response to the physical stimulus of ether waves. Likewise with color. Color is produced by ether waves of different lengths and degrees of rapidity.

Thus ether waves at the rate of 450 billions a second give us the sensation of red; of 472 billions a second, orange; of 526 billions a second, yellow; of 589 billions a second, green; of 640 billions a second, blue; of 722 billions a second, indigo; of 790 billions a second, violet. What exists outside of us, then, is these ether waves of different rates, and not the colors (as sensations) themselves. The beautiful yellow and crimson of a sunset, the variegated colors of a landscape, the delicate pink in the cheek of a child, the blush of a rose, the shimmering green of the lake—these reside not in the objects themselves, but in the consciousness of the one who sees them. The objects possess but the quality of reflecting back to the eye ether waves of the particular rate corresponding to the color which we ascribe to them. Thus "red" objects, and no others, reflect back ether waves of a rate of 450 billions a second: "white" objects reflect all rates; "black" objects reflect none.

The case is no different with regard to sound. When we speak of a sound coming from a bell, what we really mean is that the vibrations of the bell have set up waves in the air between it and our ear, which have produced corresponding vibrations in the ear; that a nerve current was thereby produced; and that a sound was heard. But the sound (i.e., sensation) is a mental thing, and exists only in our own consciousness. What passed between the sounding object and ourselves was waves in the intervening air, ready to be translated through the machinery of nerves and brain into the beautiful tones and melodies and harmonies of the mind. And so with all other sensations.

The Three Sets of Factors: What exists outside of us therefore is a *stimulus*, some form of physical energy, of a kind suitable to excite to activity a certain end-organ of taste, or touch, or smell, or sight, or hearing; what exists within us is the *nervous machinery* capable of converting this stimulus into a nerve current which shall produce an activity in the cortex of the brain; what results is the *mental object* which we call a *sensation* of taste, smell, touch, sight, or hearing.

2. THE NATURE OF SENSATION

Sensation Gives Us Our World of Qualities: In actual experience sensations are never known apart from the objects to which they belong. This is to say that when we see *yellow* or *red* it is always in connection with some surface, or object; when we taste *sour*, this quality belongs to some substance, and so on with all the senses. Yet by sensation we mean only *the simple qualities of objects known in consciousness as the result of appropriate stimuli applied to end-organs.* We shall later see how by perception these qualities fuse or combine to form objects, but in the present chapter we shall be concerned with the qualities only. Sensations are, then, the simplest and most elementary knowledge we may get from the physical world,—the red, the blue, the bitter, the cold, the fragrant, and whatever other qualities may belong to the external world. We shall not for the present be concerned with the objects or sources from which the qualities may come.

To quote James on the meaning of sensation: "All we can say on this point is that *what we mean by sensations are first things in the way of consciousness.* They are the *immediate* results upon consciousness of nerve currents as they enter the brain, and before they have awakened any suggestions or associations with past experience. But it is obvious that *such immediate sensations can be realized only in the earliest days of life.*"

The Attributes of Sensation: Sensations differ from each other in at least four respects; namely, *quality*, *intensity*, *extensity*, and *duration.*

It is a difference in *quality* that makes us say, "This paper is red, and that, blue; this liquid is sweet, and that, sour."

Differences in quality are therefore fundamental differences in *kind.* Besides the quality-differences that exist within the same general field, as of taste or vision, it is evident that there is a still more fundamental difference existing between the various fields. One can, for example, compare red with blue or sweet with sour, and tell which quality he prefers. But let him try to compare red with sweet, or blue with sour, and the quality-difference is so profound that there seems to be no basis for comparison.

Differences in *intensity* of sensation are familiar to every person who prefers two lumps of sugar rather than one lump in his coffee; the sweet is of the same quality in either case, but differs in intensity. In every field of sensation, the intensity may proceed from the smallest amount to the greatest amount discernible. In general, the intensity of the sensation depends on the intensity of the stimulus, though the condition of the sense-organ as regards fatigue or adaptation to the stimulus has its effect. It is obvious that a stimulus may be too weak to produce any sensation; as, for example, a few grains of sugar in a cup of coffee or a few drops of lemon in a quart of water could not be detected. It is also true that the intensity of the stimulus may be so great that an increase in intensity produces no effect on the sensation; as, for example, the addition of sugar to a solution of saccharine would not noticeably increase its sweetness. The lowest and highest intensity points of sensation are called the lower and upper *limen*, or threshold, respectively.

By *extensity* is meant the space-differences of sensations. The touch of the point of a toothpick on the skin has a different space quality from the touch of the flat end of a pencil. Low tones seem to have more volume than high tones. Some pains feel sharp and others dull and diffuse. The warmth felt from spreading the palms of the hands out to the fire has a "bigness" not felt from heating one solitary finger. The extensity of a sensation depends on the number of nerve endings stimulated.

The *duration* of a sensation refers to the time it lasts. This must not be confused with the duration of the stimulus, which may be either longer or shorter than the duration of the sensation. Every sensation must exist for some space of time, long or short, or it would have no part in consciousness.

3. SENSORY QUALITIES AND THEIR END-ORGANS

All are familiar with the "five senses" of our elementary physiologies, sight, hearing, taste, smell, and touch. A more complete study of sensation reveals nearly three times this number, however. This is to say that the body is equipped with more than a dozen different kinds of end-organs, each prepared to receive its own particular type of stimulus. It must also be understood that some of the end-organs yield more than one sense. The eye, for example, gives not only visual but muscular sensations; the ear not only auditory, but tactual; the tongue not only gustatory, but tactual and cold and warmth sensations.

Sight: Vision is a *distance* sense; we can see afar off. The stimulus is *chemical* in its action; this means that the ether waves, on striking the retina, cause a chemical change which sets up the nerve current responsible for the sensation.

The eye, whose general structure is sufficiently described in all standard physiologies, consists of a visual apparatus designed to bring the images of objects to a clear focus on the retina at the *fovea*, or area of clearest vision, near the point of entrance of the optic nerve.

The sensation of sight coming from this retinal image unaided by other sensations gives us but two qualities, *light and color*. The eye can distinguish many different grades of light from purest white on through the various grays to densest black. The range is greater still in color. We speak of the seven colors of the spectrum, violet, indigo, blue, green, yellow, orange, and red. But this is not a very serviceable classification, since the average eye can distinguish about 35,000 color effects. It is also somewhat bewildering to find that all these colors seem to be produced from the four fundamental hues, red, green, yellow, and blue, plus the various tints. These four, combined in varying proportions and with different degrees of light (i.e., different shades of gray), yield all the color effects known to the human eye. Herschel estimates that the workers on the mosaics at Rome must have distinguished 30,000 different color tones. The *hue* of a color refers to its fundamental quality, as red or yellow; the *chroma*, to its saturation, or the strength of the color; and the *tint*, to the amount of brightness (i.e., white) it contains.

Hearing: Hearing is also a distance sense. The action of its stimulus is mechanical, which is to say that the vibrations produced in the air by the sounding body are finally transmitted by the mechanism of the middle ear to the inner ear. Here the impulse is conveyed through the liquid of the internal ear to the nerve endings as so many tiny blows, which produce the nerve current carried to the brain by the auditory nerve.

The sensation of hearing, like that of sight, gives us two qualities: namely, *tones* with their accompanying pitch and timbre, and *noises*. Tones, or musical sounds, are produced by isochroous or equal-timed vibrations; thus *C* of the first octave is produced by 256 vibrations a second, and if this tone is prolonged the vibration rate will continue uniformly the same. Noises, on the other hand, are produced by vibrations which have no uniformity of vibration rate. The ear's sensibility to pitch extends over about seven octaves. The seven-octave piano goes down to 27-1/2 vibrations and reaches up to 3,500 vibrations. Notes of nearly 50,000 vibrations can be heard by an average ear, however, though these are too painfully shrill to be musical. Taking into account this upper limit, the range of the ear is about eleven octaves. The ear, having given us *loudness* of tones, which depends on the amplitude of the vibrations, *pitch*, which depends on the rapidity of the vibrations, and *timbre*, or *quality*, which depends on the complexity of the vibrations, has no further qualities of sound to reveal.

Taste: The sense of taste is located chiefly in the tongue, over the surface of which are scattered many minute *taste-bulbs*. These can be seen as small red specks, most plentifully distributed along the edges and at the tip of the tongue. The substance tasted must be in *solution*, and come in contact with the nerve endings. The action of the stimulus is *chemical*.

The sense of taste recognizes the four qualities of *sour*, *sweet*, *salt*, and *bitter*. Many of the qualities which we improperly call tastes are in reality a complex of taste, smell, touch, and temperature. Smell contributes so largely to the sense of taste that many articles of food become "tasteless" when we have a catarrh, and many nauseating doses of medicine can be taken without discomfort if the nose is held. Probably none of us, if we are careful to exclude all odors by plugging the nostrils with cotton, can by taste distinguish between scraped apple, potato, turnip, or beet, or can tell hot milk from tea or coffee of the same temperature.

Smell: In the upper part of the nasal cavity lies a small brownish patch of mucous membrane. It is here that the olfactory nerve endings are located. The substance smelled must be volatile, that is, must exist in gaseous form, and come in direct contact with the nerve endings. Chemical action results in a nerve current.

The sensations of smell have not been classified so well as those of taste, and we have no distinct names for them. Neither do we know how many olfactory qualities the sense of smell is capable of revealing. The only definite classification of smell qualities is that based on their pleasantness or the opposite. We also borrow a few terms and speak of *sweet* or *fragrant* odors and *fresh* or *close* smells. There is some evidence when we observe animals, or even primitive men, that the human race has been evolving greater sensibility to certain odors, while at the same time there has been a loss of keenness of what we call scent.

Various Sensations from the Skin: The skin, besides being a protective and excretory organ, affords a lodging-place for the end-organs giving us our sense of pressure, pain, cold, warmth, tickle, and itch. *Pressure* seems to have for its end-organ the *hair-bulbs* of the skin; on hairless regions small bulbs called the *corpuscles of Meissner* serve this purpose. *Pain* is thought to be mediated by free nerve endings. *Cold* depends on end-organs called the *bulbs of Krause*; and *warmth* on the *Ruffinian corpuscles*.

Coetaneous or skin sensation may arise from either *mechanical* stimulation, such as pressure, a blow, or tickling, from *thermal* stimulation from hot or cold objects, from *electrical* stimulation, or from the action of certain *chemicals*, such as acids and the like. Stimulated mechanically, the skin gives us but two sensation qualities, *pressure* and *pain*. Many of the qualities, which we commonly ascribe to the skin sensations, are really a complex of coetaneous and muscular sensations. *Contact* is light pressure. *Hardness* and *softness* depend on the intensity of the pressure. *Roughness* and *smoothness* arise from interrupted and continuous pressure, respectively, and require movement over the rough or smooth surface. *Touch* depends on pressure accompanied by the muscular sensations involved in the movements connected with the act. Pain is clearly a different sensation from pressure; but any of the coetaneous or muscular sensations may, by excessive stimulation, be made to pass over into pain. All parts of the skin are sensitive to pressure and pain; but certain parts, like the finger tips, and the tip of the tongue, are more highly sensitive than others. The skin varies also in its sensitivity to *heat* and *cold*. If we take a hot or a very cold pencil point and pass it rather lightly and slowly over the skin, it is easy to discover certain spots from which a sensation of warmth or of cold flashes out. In this way it is possible to locate the end-organs of temperature very accurately.

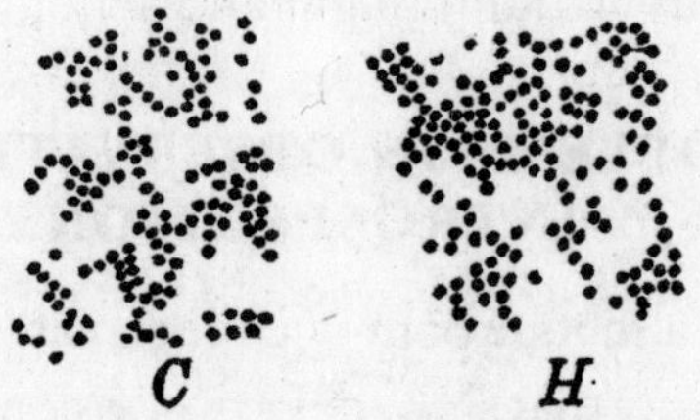

Fig. 17.—Diagram showing distribution of hot and cold spots on the back of the hand. C, cold spots; H, hot spots.

The Kinesthetic Senses: The muscles, tendons, and joints also give rise to perfectly definite sensations, but they have not been named as have the sensations from most of the other end-organs. *Weight* is the most clearly marked of these sensations. It is through the sensations connected with movements of muscles, tendons, and joints that we come to judge *form*, *size*, and *distance*.

The Organic Senses: Finally, to the sensations mentioned so far must be added those which come from the internal organs of the body. From the alimentary canal we get the sensations of *hunger*, *thirst*, and *nausea*; from the heart, lungs, and organs of sex come numerous well-defined but unnamed sensations which play an important part in making up the feeling-tone of our daily lives.

Thus we see that the senses may be looked upon as the sentries of the body, standing at the outposts where nature and ourselves meet. They discover the qualities of the various objects with which we come in contact and hand them over to the mind in the form of sensations. And these sensations are the raw material out of which we begin to construct our material environment. Only as we are equipped with good organs of sense, especially good eyes and ears, therefore, are we able to enter fully into the wonderful world about us and receive the stimuli necessary to our thought and action.

4. PROBLEMS IN OBSERVATION AND INTROSPECTION

1. Observe a schoolroom of children at work with the aim of discovering any that show defects of vision or hearing. What are the symptoms? What is the effect of inability to hear or see well upon interest and attention?

2. Talk with your teacher about testing the eyes and ears of the children of some school. The simpler tests for vision and hearing are easily applied, and the expense for material almost nothing. What tests should be used? Does your school have the test card for vision?

3. Use a rotator or color tops for mixing discs of white and black to produce different shades of gray. Fix in mind the gray made of half white and half black; three-fourths white and one-fourth black; one-fourth-white and three-fourths black.

4. In the same way mix the two complementariness yellow and blue to produce a gray; mix red and green in the same way. Try various combinations of the four fundamental colors, and discover how different colors are produced. Seek for these same colors in nature—sky, leaves, flowers, etc.

5. Take a large wire nail and push it through a cork so that it can be handled without touching the metal with the fingers. Now cool it in ice or very cold water, then dry it and move the point slowly across the back of the hand. Do you feel occasional thrills of cold as the point passes over a bulb of Krause? Heat the nail with a match flame or over a lamp, and perform the same experiment. Do you feel the thrills of heat from the corpuscles of Ruffini?

6. Try stopping the nostrils with cotton and having someone give you scraped apple, potato, onion, etc., and see whether, by taste alone, you can distinguish the difference. Why cannot sulphur be tasted?

CHAPTER VII
PERCEPTION

No young child at first sees objects as we see them, or hears sounds as we hear them. This power, the power of perception, is a gradual development. It grows day by day out of the learner's experience in his world of sights and sounds, and whatever other fields his senses respond to.

1. THE FUNCTION OF PERCEPTION

Need of Knowing the Material World: It is the business of perception to give us knowledge of our world of material *objects* and their relations in *space* and *time*. The material world which we enter through the gateways of the senses is more marvelous by far than any fairy world created by the fancy of story-tellers; for it contains the elements of all they have conceived and much more besides. It is more marvelous than any structure planned and executed by the mind of man; for all the wonders and beauties of the Coliseum or of St. Peter's existed in nature before they were discovered by the architect and thrown together in those magnificent structures. The material advancement of civilization has been but the discovery of the objects, forces, and laws of nature, and their use in inventions serviceable to men. And these forces and laws of nature were discovered only as they were made manifest through objects in the material world.

The problem lying before each individual who would enter fully into this rich world of environment, then, is to discover at first hand just as large a part of the material world about him as possible. In the most humble environment of the most uneventful life is to be found the material for discoveries and inventions yet undreamed of. Lying in the shade of an apple tree under the open sky, Newton read from a falling apple the fundamental principles of the law of gravitation which has revolutionized science; sitting at a humble tea table Watt watched the gurgling of the steam escaping from the kettle, and evolved the steam engine there from; with his simple kite, Franklin drew down the lightning from the clouds, and started the science of electricity; through studying a ball, the ancient scholars conceived the earth to be a sphere, and Columbus discovered America.

The Problem Which Confronts the Child.— Well it is that the child, starting his life's journey, cannot see the magnitude of the task before him. Cast amid a world of objects of whose very existence he is ignorant, and whose meaning and uses have to be learned by slow and often painful experience, he proceeds step by step through the senses in his discovery of the objects about him. Yet, considered again, we ourselves are after all but a step in advance of the child. Though we are somewhat more familiar with the use of our senses than he, and know a few more objects about us, yet the knowledge of the wisest of us is at best pitifully meager compared with the richness of nature. So impossible is it for us to know all our material environment, that men have taken to becoming specialists. One man will spend his life in the study of a certain variety of plants, while there are hundreds of thousands of varieties all about him; another will study a particular kind of animal life, perhaps too minute to be seen with the naked eye, while the world is teeming with animal forms which he has not time in his short day of life to stop to examine; another will study the land forms and read the earth's history from the rocks and geological strata, but here again nature's volume is so large that he has time to read but a small fraction of the whole. Another studies the human body and learns to read from its expressions the signs of health and sickness, and to prescribe remedies for its ills; but in this field also he has found it necessary to divide the work, and so we have specialists for almost every organ of the body.

2. THE NATURE OF PERCEPTION

How a Percept is Formed.—How, then, do we proceed to the discovery of this world of objects? Let us watch the child and learn the secret from him. Give the babe a ball, and he applies every sense to it to discover its qualities. He stares at it, he takes it in his hands and turns it over and around, he lifts it, he strokes it, he punches it and jabs it, he puts it to his mouth and bites it, he drops it, he throws it and creeps after it. He leaves no stone unturned to find out what that thing really is. By means of the *qualities* which come to him through the avenues of sense, he constructs the *object*. And not only does he come to know the ball as a material object, but he comes to know also its uses. He is forming his own best definition of a ball in terms of the sensations which he gets from it and the uses to which he puts it, and all this even before he can name it or is able to recognize its name when he hears it. How much better his method than the one he will have to follow a little later when he goes to school and learns that "A ball is a spherical body of any substance or size, used to play with, as by throwing, kicking, or knocking, etc.!"

The Percept Involves All Relations of the Object.—Nor is the case in the least different with ourselves. When we wish to learn about a new object or discover new facts about an old one, we do precisely as the child does if we are wise. We apply to it every sense to which it will afford a stimulus, and finally arrive at the object through its various qualities. And just in so far as we have failed to use in connection with it every sense to which it can minister, just in that degree will we have an incomplete perception of it. Indeed, just so far as we have failed finally to perceive it in terms of its functions or uses, in that far also have we failed to know it completely. Tomatoes were for many years grown as ornamental garden plants before it was discovered that the tomatoes could minister to the taste as well as to the sight. The clothing of civilized man gives the same sensation of texture and color to the savage that it does to its owner, but he is so far from perceiving it in the same way that he packs it away and continues to go naked. The Orientals, who disdain the use of chairs and prefer to sit cross-legged on the floor, can never perceive a chair just as we do who use chairs daily, and to whom chairs are so saturated with social suggestions and associations.

The Content of the Percept.—The percept, then, always contains a basis of *sensation*. The eye, the ear, the skin or some other sense organ must turn in its supply of sensory material or there can be no percept. But the percept contains more than just sensations. Consider, for example, your percept of an automobile flashing past your windows. You really *see* but very little of it, yet you *perceive* it as a very familiar vehicle. All that your sense organs furnish is a more or less blurred patch of black of certain size and contour, one or more objects of somewhat different color whom you know to be passengers, and various sounds of a whizzing, chugging or roaring nature. Your former experience with automobiles enables you to associate with these meager sensory details the upholstered seats, the whirling wheels, the swaying movement and whatever else belongs to the full meaning of a motor car.

The percept that contained only sensory material, and lacked all memory elements, ideas and meanings, would be no percept at all. And this is the reason why a young child cannot see or hear like ourselves. It lacks the associative material to give significance and meaning to the sensory elements supplied by the end-organs. The dependence of the percept on material from past experience is also illustrated in the common statement that what one gets from an art exhibit or a concert depends on what he brings to it. He who brings no knowledge, no memory, no images from other pictures or music will secure but relatively barren percepts, consisting of little besides the mere sensory elements. Truly, "to him that hath shall be given" in the realm of perception.

The Accuracy of Percepts Depends on Experience.— We must perceive objects through our motor response to them as well as in terms of sensations. The boy who has his knowledge of a tennis racket from looking at one in a store window, or indeed from handling one and looking it over in his room, can never know a tennis racket as does the boy who plays with it on the court. Objects get their significance not alone from their qualities, but even more from their use as related to our own activities.

Like the child, we must get our knowledge of objects, if we are to get it well, from the objects themselves at first hand, and not second hand through descriptions of them by others. The fact that there is so much of the material world about us that we can never hope to learn it all, has made it necessary to put down in books many of the things which have been discovered concerning nature. This necessity has, I fear, led many away from nature itself to books—away from the living reality of things to the dead embalming cases of words, in whose empty forms we see so little of the significance which resides in the things themselves. We are in danger of being satisfied with the *forms* of knowledge without its *substance*—with definitions contained in words instead of in qualities and uses.

Not Definitions, But First-hand Contact.—In like manner we come to know distance, form and size. If we have never become acquainted with a mile by actually walking a mile, running a mile, riding a bicycle a mile, driving a horse a mile, or traveling a mile on a train, we might listen for a long time to someone tell how far a mile is, or state the distance from Chicago to Denver, without knowing much about it in any way except word definitions. In order to understand a mile, we must come to know it in as many ways as possible through sense activities of our own. Although many children have learned that it is 25,000 miles around the earth, probably no one who has not encircled the globe has any reasonably accurate notion just how far this is. For words cannot take the place of perceptions in giving us knowledge. In the case of shorter distances, the same rule holds. The eye must be assisted by experience of the muscles and tendons and joints in actually covering distance, and learn to associate these sensations with those of the eye before the eye alone can be able to say, "That tree is ten rods distant." Form and size are to be learned in the same way. The hands must actually touch and handle the object, experiencing its hardness or smoothness, the way this curve and that angle feels, the amount of muscular energy it takes to pass the hand over this surface and along that line, the eye taking note all the while, before the eye can tell at a glance that yonder object is a sphere and that this surface is two feet on the edge.

3. THE PERCEPTION OF SPACE

Many have been the philosophical controversies over the nature of space and our perception of it. The psychologists have even quarreled concerning whether we possess an *innate* sense of space, or whether it is a product of experience and training. Fortunately, for our present purpose we shall not need to concern ourselves with either of these controversies. For our discussion we may accept space for what common sense understands it to be. As to our sense of space, whatever of this we may possess at birth, it certainly has to be developed by use and experience to become of practical value. In the perception of space we must come to perceive *distance*, *direction*, *size*, and *form*. As a matter of fact, however, size is but so much distance, and form is but so much distance in this, that, or the other direction.

The Perceiving of Distance.—Unquestionably the eye comes to be our chief dependence in determining distance. Yet the muscle and joint senses give us our earliest knowledge of distance. The babe reaches for the moon simply because the eye does not tell it that the moon is out of reach. Only as the child reaches for its playthings, creeps or walks after them, and in a thousand ways uses its muscles and joints in measuring distance, does the perception of distance become dependable.

At the same time the eye is slowly developing its power of judging distance. But not for several years does visual perception of distance become in any degree accurate. The eye's perception of distance depends in part on the sensations arising from the muscles controlling the eye, probably in part from the adjustment of the lens, and in part from the retinal image. If one tries to look at the tip of his nose he easily feels the muscle strain caused by the required angle of adjustment. We come unconsciously to associate distance with the muscle sensations arising from the different angles of vision. The part played by the retinal image in judging distance is easily understood in looking at two trees, one thirty feet and the other three hundred feet distant. We note that the nearer tree shows the *detail* of the bark and leaves, while the more distant one lacks this detail. The nearer tree also reflects more *light*, and *color* than the one farther away. These minute differences, registered as they are on the retinal image, come to stand for so much of distance.

The ear also learns to perceive distance through differences in the quality and the intensity of sound. Auditory perception of distance is, however, never very accurate.

The Perceiving of Direction.—The motor senses probably give us our first perception of direction, as they do of distance. The child has to reach this way or that way for his rattle; turn the eyes or head so far in order to see an interesting object; twist the body, crawl or walk to one side or the other to secure his bottle. In these experiences he is gaining his first knowledge of direction.

Along with these muscle-joint experiences, the eye is also being trained. The position of the image on the retina comes to stand for direction, and the eye finally develops so remarkable a power of perceiving direction that a picture hung a half inch out of plumb is a source of annoyance. The ear develops some skill in the perception of direction, but is less dependable than the eye.

4. THE PERCEPTION OF TIME

The philosophers and psychologists agree little better about our sense of time than they do about our sense of space. Of this much, however, we may be certain, our perception of time is subject to development and training.

Nature of the Time Sense.—How we perceive time is not so well understood as our perception of space. It is evident, however, that our idea of time is simpler than our idea of space—it has less of content, less that we can describe. Probably the most fundamental part of our idea of time is *progression*, or change, without which it is difficult to think of time at all. The question then becomes, how do we perceive change, or succession?

If one looks in upon his thought stream he finds that the movement of consciousness is not uniformly continuous, but that his thought moves in pulses, or short rushes, so to speak. When we are seeking for some fact or conclusion, there is a moment of expectancy, or poising, and then the leap forward to the desired point, or conclusion, from which an immediate start is taken for the next objective point of our thinking. It is probable that our sense of the few seconds of passing time that we call the *immediate present* consists of the recognition of the succession of these pulsations of consciousness, together with certain organic rhythms, such as heart beat and breathing.

No Perception of Empty time.—Our perception does not therefore act upon empty time. Time must be filled with a procession of events, whether these be within our own consciousness or in the objective world without. All longer periods of time, such as hours, days, or years, are measured by the events which they contain. Time filled with happenings that interest and attract us seems short while passing, but longer when looked back upon. On the other hand, time relatively empty of interesting experience hangs heavy on our hands in passing, but, viewed in retrospect, seems short. A fortnight of travel passes more quickly than a fortnight of illness, but yields many more events for the memory to review as the "filling" for time.

Probably no one has any very accurate feeling of the length, that is, the actual *duration* of a year—or even of a month! We therefore divide time into convenient units, as weeks, months, years and centuries. This allows us to think of time in mathematical terms where immediate perception fails in its grasp.

5. THE TRAINING OF PERCEPTION

In the physical world as in the spiritual there are many people who, "having eyes, see not and ears, hear not." For the ability to perceive accurately and richly in the world of physical objects depends not alone on good sense organs, but also on *interest* and the habit of *observation*. It is easy if we are indifferent or untrained to look at a beautiful landscape, a picture or a cathedral without *seeing* it; it is easy if we lack interest or skill to listen to an orchestra or the myriad sounds of nature without *hearing* them.

Perception Needs to Be Trained.—Training in perception does not depend entirely on the work of the school. For the world about us exerts a constant appeal to our senses. A thousand sights, sounds, contacts, tastes, smells or other sensations, hourly throng in upon us, and the appeal is irresistible. We must in some degree attend. We must observe.

Yet it cannot be denied that most of us are relatively unskilled in perception; we do not know how, or take the trouble to observe. For example, a stranger was brought into the classroom and introduced by the instructor to a class of fifty college students in psychology. The class thought the stranger was to address them, and looked at him with mild curiosity. But, after standing before them for a few moments, he suddenly withdrew, as had been arranged by the instructor. The class were then asked to write such a description of the stranger as would enable a person who had never seen him to identify him. But so poor had been the observation of the class that they ascribed to him clothes of four different colors, eyes and hair each of three different colors, a tie of many different hues, height ranging from five feet and four inches to over six feet, age from twenty-eight to forty-five years, and many other details as wide of the mark. Nor is it probable that this particular class was below the average in the power of perception.

School Training in Perception.—The school can do much in training the perception. But to accomplish this, the child must constantly be brought into immediate contact with the physical world about him and taught to observe. Books must not be substituted for things. Definitions must not take the place of experiment or discovery. Geography and nature study should be taught largely out of doors, and the lessons assigned should take the child into the open for observation and investigation. All things that live and grow, the sky and clouds, the sunset colors, the brown of upturned soil, the smell of the clover field, or the new mown hay, the sounds of a summer night, the distinguishing marks by which to identify each family of common birds or breed of cattle—these and a thousand other things that appeal to us from the simplest environment afford a rich opportunity for training the perception. And he who has learned to observe, and who is alert to the appeal of nature, has no small part of his education already assured.

6. PROBLEMS IN OBSERVATION AND INTROSPECTION

1. Test your power of observation by walking rapidly past a well-filled store window and then seeing how many of the objects you can name.

2. Suppose a tailor, a bootblack, a physician, and a detective are standing on the street corner as you pass by. What will each one be most likely to observe about you? *Why?*

3. Observe carefully green trees at a distance of a few rods; a quarter of a mile; a mile; several miles. Describe differences (1) in color, (2) in brightness, or light, and (3) in detail.

4. How many common birds can you identify? How many kinds of trees? Of wild flowers? Of weeds?

5. Observe the work of an elementary school for the purpose of determining:

a. Whether the instruction in geography, nature study, agriculture, etc., calls for the use of the eyes, ears and fingers.

b. Whether definitions are used in place of first-hand information in any subjects.

c. Whether the assignment of lessons to pupils includes work that would require the use of the senses, especially out of doors.

d. Whether the work offered in arithmetic demands the use of the senses as well as the reason.

e. Whether the language lessons make use of the power of observation.

CHAPTER VIII
MENTAL IMAGES AND IDEAS

As you sit thinking, a company of you together, your thoughts run in many diverse lines. Yet with all this diversity, your minds possess this common characteristic: *Though your thinking all takes place in what we call the present moment, it goes on largely in terms of past experiences.*

1. THE PART PLAYED BY PAST EXPERIENCE

Present Thinking Depends on Past Experience: Images or ideas of things you have seen or heard or felt; of things you have thought of before and which now recur to you; of things you remember, such as names, dates, places, events; of things that you do not remember as a part of your past at all, but that belong to it nevertheless—these are the things which form a large part of your mental stream, and which give content to your thinking. You may think of a thing that is going on now, or of one that is to occur in the future; but, after all, you are dependent on your past experience for the material which you put into your thinking of the present moment.

Indeed, nothing can enter your present thinking which does not link itself to something in your past experience. The savage Indian in the primeval forest never thought about killing a deer with a rifle merely by pulling a trigger, or of turning a battery of machine guns on his enemies to annihilate them—none of these things were related to his past experience; hence he could not think in such terms.

The Present Interpreted by the Past: Not only can we not think at all except in terms of our past experience, but even if we could, the present would be meaningless to us; for the present is interpreted in the light of the past. The sedate man of affairs who decries athletic sports, and has never taken part in them, cannot understand the wild enthusiasm which prevails between rival teams in a hotly contested event. The fine work of art is to the one who has never experienced the appeal which comes through beauty, only so much of canvas and variegated patches of color. Paul says that Jesus was "unto the Greeks, foolishness." He was foolishness to them because nothing in their experience with their own gods had been enough like the character of Jesus to enable them to interpret Him.

The Future Also Depends on the Past: To the mind incapable of using past experience, the future also would be impossible; for we can look forward into the future only by placing in its experiences the elements of which we have already known. The savage who has never seen the shining yellow metal does not dream of a heaven whose streets are paved with gold, but rather of a "happy hunting ground." If you will analyze your own dreams of the future you will see in them familiar pictures perhaps grouped together in new forms, but coming, in their elements, from your past experience nevertheless. All that would remain to a mind devoid of a past would be the little bridge of time which we call the "present moment," a series of unconnected *now's*. Thought would be impossible, for the mind would have nothing to compare and relate. Personality would not exist; for personality requires continuity of experience, else we should be a new person each succeeding moment, without memory and without plans. Such a mind would be no mind at all.

Rank Determined by Ability to Utilize Past Experience: So important is past experience in determining our present thinking and guiding our future actions, that the place of an individual in the scale of creation is determined largely by the ability to profit by past experience. The scientist tells us of many species of animals now extinct, which lost their lives and suffered their race to die out because when, long ago, the climate began to change and grow much colder, they were unable to use the experience of suffering in the last cold season as an incentive to provide shelter, or move to a warmer climate against the coming of the next and more rigorous one. Man was able to make the adjustment; and, providing himself with clothing and shelter and food, he survived, while myriads of the lower forms perished.

The singed moth again and again dares the flame which tortures it, and at last gives its life, a sacrifice to its folly; the burned child fears the fire, and does not the second time seek the experience. So also can the efficiency of an individual or a nation, as compared with other individuals or nations, be determined. The inefficient are those who repeat the same error or useless act over and over, or else fail to repeat a chance useful act whose repetition might lead to success. They are unable to learn their lesson and be guided by experience. Their past does not sufficiently minister to their present, and through it direct their future.

2. HOW PAST EXPERIENCE IS CONSERVED

Past Experience Conserved in Both Mental and Physical Terms: If past experience plays so important a part in our welfare, how, then, is it to be conserved so that we may secure its benefits? Here, as elsewhere, we find the mind and body working in perfect unison and harmony, each doing its part to further the interests of both. The results of our past experience may be read in both our mental and our physical nature.

On the physical side past experience is recorded in modified structure through the law of habit working on the tissues of the body, and particularly on the delicate tissues of the brain and nervous system. This is easily seen in its outward aspects. The stooped shoulders and bent form of the workman tell a tale of physical toil and exposure; the bloodless lips and pale face of the victim of the city sweat shop tell of foul air, long hours, and insufficient food; the rosy cheek and bounding step of childhood speak of fresh air, good food and happy play.

On the mental side past experience is conserved chiefly by means of *images*, *ideas*, and *concepts*. The nature and function of concepts will be discussed in a later chapter. It will now be our purpose to examine the nature of images and ideas, and to note the part they play in the mind's activities.

The Image and the Idea: To understand the nature of the image, and then of the idea, we may best go back to the percept. You look at a watch which I hold before your eyes and secure a percept of it. Briefly, this is what happens: The light reflected from the yellow object, on striking the retina, results in a nerve current which sets up a certain form of activity in the cells of the visual brain area, and lo! a *percept* of the watch flashes in your mind.

Now I put the watch in my pocket, so that the stimulus is no longer present to your eye. Then I ask you to think of my watch just as it appeared as you were looking at it; or you may yourself choose to think of it without my suggesting it to you. In either case *the cellular activity in the visual area of the cortex is reproduced* approximately as it occurred in connection with the percept, and lo! an *image* of the watch flashes in your mind. An image is thus an approximate copy of a former percept (or several percepts). It is aroused indirectly by means of a nerve current coming by way of some other brain center, instead of directly by the stimulation of a sense organ, as in the case of a percept.

If, instead of seeking a more or less exact mental *picture* of my watch, you only think of its general *meaning* and relations, the fact that it is of gold, that it is for the purpose of keeping time, that it was a present to me, that I wear it in my left pocket, you then have an *idea* of the watch. Our idea of an object is, therefore, the general meaning of relations we ascribe to it. It should be remembered, however, that the terms image and idea are employed rather loosely, and that there is not yet general uniformity among writers in their use.

All Our Past Experience Potentially at Our Command: Images may in a certain sense take the place of percepts, and we can again experience sights, sounds, tastes, and smells which we have known before, without having the stimuli actually present to the senses. In this way all our past experience is potentially available to the present. All the objects we have seen, it is potentially possible again to see in the mind's eye without being obliged to have the objects before us; all the sounds we have heard, all the tastes and smells and temperatures we have experienced, we may again have presented to our minds in the form of mental images without the various stimuli being present to the end-organs of the senses.

Through images and ideas the total number of objects in our experience is infinitely multiplied; for many of the things we have seen, or heard, or smelled, or tasted, we cannot again have present to the senses, and without this power we would never get them again. And besides this fact, it would be inconvenient to have to go and secure afresh each sensation or percept every time we need to use it in our thought. While *habit*, then, conserves our past experience on the physical side, the *image* and the *idea* do the same thing on the mental side.

3. INDIVIDUAL DIFFERENCES IN IMAGERY

Images to Be Viewed by Introspection: The remainder of the description of images will be easier to understand, for each of you can know just what is meant in every case by appealing to your own mind. I beg of you not to think that I am presenting something new and strange, a curiosity connected with our thinking which has been discovered by scholars who have delved more deeply into the matter than we can hope to do. Every day—no, more than that, every hour and every moment—these images are flitting through our minds, forming a large part of our stream of consciousness. Let us see whether we can turn our attention within and discover some of our images in their flight. Let us introspect.

I know of no better way to proceed than that adopted by Francis Galton years ago, when he asked the English men of letters and science to think of their breakfast tables, and then describe the images which appeared. I am about to ask each one of you to do the same thing, but I want to warn you beforehand that the images will not be so vivid as the sensory experiences themselves. They will be much fainter and more vague, and less clear and definite; they will be fleeting, and must be caught on the wing. Often the image may fade entirely out, and the idea only be left.

The Varied Imagery Suggested by One's Dining Table: Let each one now recall the dining table as you last left it, and then answer questions concerning it like the following:

> Can I see clearly in my "mind's eye" the whole table as it stood spread before me? Can I see all parts of it equally clearly? Do I get the snowy white and gloss of the linen? The delicate coloring of the china, so that I can see where the pink shades off into the white? The graceful lines and curves of the dishes? The sheen of the silver? The brown of the toast? The yellow of the cream? The rich red and dark green of the bouquet of roses? The sparkle of the glassware?
>
> Can I again hear the rattle of the dishes? The clink of the spoon against the cup? The moving up of the chairs? The chatter of the voices, each with its own peculiar pitch and quality? The twitter of a bird outside the window? The tinkle of a distant bell? The chirp of a neighborly cricket?
>
> Can I taste clearly the milk? The coffee? The eggs? The bacon? The rolls? The butter? The jelly? The fruit? Can I get the appetizing odor of the coffee? Of the meat? The oranges and bananas? The perfume of the lilac bush outside the door? The perfume from a handkerchief newly treated to a spray of heliotrope?

Can I recall the touch of my fingers on the velvety peach? On the smooth skin of an apple? On the fretted glassware? The feel of the fresh linen? The contact of leather-covered or cane-seated chair? Of the freshly donned garment? Can I get clearly the temperature of the hot coffee in the mouth? Of the hot dish on the hand? Of the ice water? Of the grateful coolness of the breeze wafted in through the open window?

Can I feel again the strain of muscle and joint in passing the heavy dish? Can I feel the movement of the jaws in chewing the beefsteak? Have the throat and lips in talking? Have the chest and diaphragm in laughing? Of the muscles in sitting and rising? In hand and arm in using knife and fork and spoon? Can I get again the sensation of pain which accompanied biting on a tender tooth? From the shooting of a drop of acid from the rind of the orange into the eye? The chance ache in the head? The pleasant feeling connected with the exhilaration of a beautiful morning? The feeling of perfect health? The pleasure connected with partaking of a favorite food?

Power of Imagery Varies in Different People: It is more than probable that some of you cannot get perfectly clear images in all these lines, certainly not with equal facility; for the imagery from any one sense varies greatly from person to person. A celebrated painter was able, after placing his subject in a chair and looking at him attentively for a few minutes, to dismiss the subject and paint a perfect likeness of him from the visual image which recurred to the artist every time he turned his eyes to the chair where the sitter had been placed. On the other hand, a young lady, a student in my psychology class, tells me that she is never able to recall the looks of her mother when she is absent, even if the separation has been only for a few moments. She can get an image of the form, with the color and cut of the dress, but never the features. One person may be able to recall a large part of a concert through his auditory imagery, and another almost none.

In general it may be said that the power, or at least the use, of imagery decreases with age. The writer has made a somewhat extensive study of the imagery of certain high-school students, college students, and specialists in psychology averaging middle age. Almost without exception it was found that clear and vivid images played a smaller part in the thinking of the older group than of the younger. More or less abstract ideas and concepts seemed to have taken the place of the concrete imagery of earlier years.

Imagery Types: Although there is some difference in our ability to use imagery of different sensory types, probably there is less variation here than has been supposed. Earlier pedagogical works spoke of the *visual* type of mind, or the *audile* type, or the *motor* type, as if the possession of one kind of imagery necessarily rendered a person short in other types. Later studies have shown this view incorrect, however. The person who has good images of one type is likely to excel in all types, while one who is lacking in any one of the more important types will probably be found short in all.[4] Most of us probably make more use of visual and auditory than of other kinds of imagery, while olfactory and gustatory images seem to play a minor role.

4. THE FUNCTION OF IMAGES

Binet says that the man who has not every type of imagery almost equally well developed is only the fraction of a man.

While this no doubt puts the matter too strongly, yet images do play an important part in our thinking.

Images Supply Material for Imagination and Memory: Imagery supplies the pictures from which imagination builds its structures. Given a rich supply of images from the various senses, and imagination has the material necessary to construct times and events long since past, or to fill the future with plans or experiences not yet reached. Lacking images, however, imagination is handicapped, and its meager products reveal in their barrenness and their lack of warmth and reality the poverty of material.

Much of our memory also takes the form of images. The face of a friend, the sound of a voice, or the touch of a hand may be recalled, not as a mere fact, but with almost the freshness and fidelity of a percept. That much of our memory goes on in the form of ideas instead of images is true. But memory is often both aided in its accuracy and rendered more vital and significant through the presence of abundant imagery.

Imagery in the Thought Processes: Since logical thinking deals more with relations and meanings than with particular objects, images naturally play a smaller part in reasoning than in memory and imagination. Yet they have their place here as well. Students of geometry or trigonometry often have difficulty in understanding a theorem until they succeed in visualizing the surface or solid involved. Thinking in the field of astronomy, mechanics, and many other sciences is assisted at certain points by the ability to form clear and accurate images.

The Use of Imagery in Literature: Facility in the use of imagery undoubtedly adds much to our enjoyment and appreciation of certain forms of literature. The great writers commonly use all types of images in their description and narration. If we are not able to employ the images they used, many of their most beautiful pictures are likely to be to us but so many words suggesting prosaic ideas.

Shakespeare, describing certain beautiful music, appeals to the sense of smell to make himself understood:

> ... it came o'er my ear like the sweet sound
>
> That breathes upon a bank of violets,
>
> Stealing and giving odor!

Lady Macbeth cries:

> Here's the smell of the blood still:
>
> All the perfumes of Arabia will not sweeten this little hand.

Milton has *Eve* say of her dream of the fatal apple:

> ... The pleasant savory smell
>
> so quickened appetite, that I, me thought,
>
> Could not but taste.

Likewise with the sense of touch:

> ... I take thy hand, this hand
>
> As soft as dove's down, and as white as it.

Imagine a person devoid of delicate tactile imagery, with senseless finger tips and leaden footsteps, undertaking to interpret these exquisite lines:

Thus I set my print less feet
o'er the cowslip's velvet head,
That bends not as I tread.

Shakespeare thus appeals to the muscular imagery:

At last, a little shaking of mine arm
And thrice his head thus waving up and down,
He raised a sigh so piteous and profound
As it did seem to shatter all his bulk
And end his being.

Many passages like the following appeal to the temperature images:

Freeze, freeze, thou bitter sky,
Thou dost not bite so nigh
As benefits forgot!

To one whose auditory imagery is meager, the following lines will lose something of their beauty:

How sweet the moonlight sleeps upon this bank!
Here we will sit and let the sounds of music
Creep in our ears; soft stillness and the night
Become the touches of sweet harmony.

Note how much clear images will add to Browning's words:

Are there not two moments in the adventure of a diver—one when a beggar he prepares to plunge, and one, when a prince he rises with his pearl?

Points Where Images Are of Greatest Service: Beyond question, many images come flooding into our minds which are irrelevant and of no service in our thinking. No one has failed to note many such. Further, we undoubtedly do much of our best thinking with few or no images present. Yet we need images. Where, then, are they most needed? *Images are needed wherever the percepts which they represent would be of service.* Whatever one could better understand or enjoy or appreciate by seeing it, hearing it, or perceiving it through some other sense, he can better understand, enjoy or appreciate through images than by means of ideas only.

5. THE CULTIVATION OF IMAGERY

Images Depend on Sensory Stimuli: The power of imaging can be cultivated the same as any other ability.

In the first place, we may put down as an absolute requisite *such an environment of sensory stimuli as will tempt every sense to be awake and at its best*, that we may be led into a large acquaintance with the objects of our material environment. No one's stock of sensory images is greater than the sum total of his sensory experiences. No one ever has images of sights, or sounds, or tastes, or smells which he has never experienced.

Likewise, he must have had the fullest and freest possible liberty in motor activities. For not only is the motor act itself made possible through the office of imagery, but the motor act clarifies and makes useful the images. The boy who has actually made a table, or a desk, or a box has ever afterward a different and a better image of one of these objects than before; so also when he has owned and ridden a bicycle, his image of this machine will have a different significance from that of the image founded upon the visual perception alone of the wheel he longingly looked at through the store window or in the other boy's dooryard.

The Influence of Frequent Recall: But sensory experiences and motor responses alone are not enough, though they are the basis of good imagery. *There must be frequent recall.* The sunset may have been never so brilliant, and the music never so entrancing; but if they are never thought of and dwelt upon after they were first experienced, little will remain of them after a very short time. It is by repeating them often in experience through imagery that they become fixed, so that they stand ready to do our bidding when we need next to use them.

The Reconstruction of Our Images: To richness of experience and frequency of the recall of our images we must add one more factor; namely, that of their *reconstruction* or working over. Few if any images are exact recalls of former percepts of objects. Indeed, such would be neither possible nor desirable. The images which we recall are recalled for a purpose, or in view of some future activity, and hence must be *selective*, or made up of the elements of several or many former related images.

Thus the boy who wishes to construct a box without a pattern to follow recalls the images of numerous boxes he may have seen, and from them all he has a new image made over from many former percepts and images, and this new image serves him as a working model. In this way he not only gets a copy which he can follow to make his box, but he also secures a new product in the form of an image different from any he ever had before, and is therefore by so much the richer. It is this working over of our stock of old images into new and richer and more suggestive ones that constitutes the essence of constructive imagination.

The more types of imagery into which we can put our thought, the more fully is it ours and the better our images. The spelling lesson needs not only to be taken in through the eye, that we may retain a visual image of the words, but also to be recited orally, so that the ear may furnish an auditory image, and the organs of speech a motor image of the correct forms. It needs also to be written, and thus given into the keeping of the hand, which finally needs most of all to know and retain it.

The reading lesson should be taken in through both the eye and the ear, and then expressed by means of voice and gesture in as full and complete a way as possible, that it may be associated with motor images. The geography lesson needs not only to be read, but to be drawn, or molded, or constructed. The history lesson should be made to appeal to every possible form of imagery. The arithmetic lesson must be not only computed, but measured, weighed, and pressed into actual service.

Thus we might carry the illustration into every line of education and experience, and the same truth holds. *What we desire to comprehend completely and retain well, we must apprehend through all available senses and conserve in every possible type of image and form of expression.*

6. PROBLEMS IN INTROSPECTION AND OBSERVATION

1. Observe a reading class and try to determine whether the pupils picture the scenes and events they read about. How can you tell?

2. Similarly observe a history class. Do the pupils realize the events as actually happening, and the personages as real, living people?

3. Observe in a similar way a class in geography, and draw conclusions. A pupil in computing the cost of plastering a certain room based the figures on the room *filled full of plaster*. How might visual imagery have saved the error?

4. Imagine a three-inch cube. Paint it. Then saw it up into inch cubes, leaving them all standing in the original form. How many inch cubes have paint on three faces? How many on two faces? How many on one face? How many have no paint on them? Answer all these questions by referring to your imagery alone.

5. Try often to recall images in the various sensory lines; determine in what classes of images you are least proficient and try to improve in these lines.

6. How is the singing teacher able, after his class has sung through several scores, to tell that they are flatting?

7. Study your imagery carefully for a few days to see whether you can discover your predominating type of imagery.

CHAPTER IX
IMAGINATION

Everyone desires to have a good imagination, yet not all would agree as to what constitutes a good imagination. If I were to ask a group of you whether you have good imaginations, many of you would probably at once fall to considering whether you are capable of taking wild flights into impossible realms of thought and evolving unrealities out of airy nothings. You would compare yourself with great imaginative writers, such as Stevenson, Poe, De Quincey, and judge your power of imagination by your ability to produce such tales as made them famous.

1. THE PLACE OF IMAGINATION IN MENTAL ECONOMY

But such a measure for the imagination as that just stated is far too narrow. A good imagination, like a good memory, is the one which serves its owner best. If DeQuincey and Poe and Stevenson and Bulwer found the type which led them into such dizzy flights the best for their particular purpose, well and good; but that is not saying that their type is the best for you, or that you may not rank as high in some other field of imaginative power as they in theirs. While you may lack in their particular type of imagination, they may have been short in the type which will one day make you famous.

The artisan, the architect, the merchant, the artist, the farmer, the teacher, the professional man—all need imagination in their vocations not less than the writers need it in theirs, but each needs a specialized kind adapted to the particular work which he has to do.

Practical Nature of Imagination: Imagination is not a process of thought which must deal chiefly with unrealities and impossibilities, and which has for its chief end our amusement when we have nothing better to do than to follow its wanderings. It is, rather, a commonplace, necessary process which illumines the way for our everyday thinking and acting—a process without which we think and act by haphazard chance or blind imitation. It is the process by which the images from our past experiences are marshaled, and made to serve our present. Imagination looks into the future and constructs our patterns and lays our plans. It sets up our ideals and pictures us in the acts of achieving them. It enables us to live our joys and our sorrows, our victories and our defeats before we reach them. It looks into the past and allows us to live with the kings and seers of old, or it goes back to the beginning and we see things in the process of the making. It comes into our present and plays a part in every act from the simplest to the most complex. It is to the mental stream what the light is to the traveler who carries it as he passes through the darkness, while it casts its beams in all directions around him, lighting up what otherwise would be intolerable gloom.

Imagination in the Interpretation of History, Literature, and Art: Let us see some of the most common uses of the imagination. Suppose I describe to you the battle of the Marne. Unless you can take the images which my words suggest and build them into struggling, shouting, bleeding soldiers; into forts and entanglements and breastworks; into roaring cannon and whistling bullet and screaming shell—unless you can take all these separate images and out of them get one great unified complex, then my description will be to you only so many words largely without content, and you will lack the power to comprehend the historical event in any complete way. Unless you can read the poem, and out of the images suggested by the words reconstruct the picture which was in the mind of the author as he wrote "The Village Blacksmith" or "Snowbound," the significance will have dropped out, and the throbbing scenes of life and action become only so many dead words, like the shell of the chrysalis after the butterfly has left its shroud. Without the power of imagination, the history of Washington's winter at Valley Forge becomes a mere formal recital, and you can never get a view of the snow-covered tents, the wind-swept landscape, the tracks in the snow marked by the telltale drops of blood, or the form of the heartbroken commander as he kneels in the silent wood to pray for his army. Without the power to construct this picture as you read, you may commit the words, and be able to recite them, and to pass examination upon them, but the living reality of it will forever escape you.

Your power of imagination determines your ability to interpret literature of all kinds; for the interpretation of literature is nothing, after all, but the reconstruction on our part of the pictures with their meanings which were in the mind of the writer as he penned the words, and the experiencing of the emotions which moved him as he wrote. Small use indeed to read the history of the centuries unless we can see in it living, acting people, and real events occurring in actual environments. Small use to read the world's great books unless their characters are to us real men and women—our brothers and sisters, interpreted to us by the master minds of the ages. Anything less than this, and we are no longer dealing with literature, but with words—like musical sounds which deal with no theme, or like picture frames in which no picture has been set. Nor is the case different in listening to a speaker. His words are to you only so many sensations of sounds of such and such pitches and intensities and quality, unless your mind keeps pace with his and continually builds the pictures which fill his thought as he speaks. Lacking imagination, the sculptures of Michael Angelo and the pictures of Raphael are to you so many pieces of curiously shaped marble and ingeniously colored canvas. What the sculptor and the painter have placed before you must suggest to you images and thoughts from your own experience, to fill out and make alive the marble and the canvas, else to you they are dead.

Imagination and Science: Nor is imagination less necessary in other lines of study. Without this power of building living, moving pictures out of images, there is small use to study science beyond what is immediately present to our senses; for some of the most fundamental laws of science rest upon conceptions which can be grasped only as we have the power of imagination. The student who cannot get a picture of the molecules of matter, infinitely close to each other and yet never touching, all in vibratory motion, yet each within its own orbit, each a complete unit in itself, yet capable of still further division into smaller particles,—the student who cannot see all this in a clear visual image can never at best have more than a most hazy notion of the theory of matter. And this means, finally, that the explanations of light and heat and sound, and much besides, will be to him largely a jumble of words which linger in his memory, perchance, but which never vitally become a possession of his mind.

So with the world of the telescope. You may have at your disposal all the magnificent lenses and the accurate machinery owned by modern observatories; but if you have not within yourself the power to build what these reveal to you, and what the books tell you, into the solar system and still larger systems, you can never study astronomy except in a blind and piecemeal sort of way, and all the planets and satellites and suns will never for you form themselves into a system, no matter what the books may say about it.

Everyday Uses of Imagination: But we may consider a still more practical phase of imagination, or at least one which has more to do with the humdrum daily life of most of us. Suppose you go to your milliner and tell her how you want your spring hat shaped and trimmed. And suppose you have never been able to see this hat *in Toto* in your mind, so as to get an idea of how it will look when completed, but have only a general notion, because you like red velvet, white plumes, and a turned-up rim, that this combination will look well together. Suppose you have never been able to see how you would look in this particular hat with your hair done in this or that way. If you are in this helpless state shall you not have to depend finally on the taste of the milliner, or accept the "model," and so fail to reveal any taste or individuality on your own part?

How many times have you been disappointed in some article of dress, because when you planned it you were unable to see it all at once so as to get the full effect; or else you could not see yourself in it, and so be able to judge whether it suited you! How many homes have in them draperies and rugs and wall paper and furniture which are in constant quarrel because someone could not see before they were assembled that they were never intended to keep company! How many people who plan their own houses, would build them just the same again after seeing them completed? The man who can see a building complete before a brick has been laid or a timber put in place, who can see it not only in its details one by one as he runs them over in his mind, but can see the building in its entirety, is the only one who is safe to plan the structure. And this is the man who is drawing a large salary as an architect, for imaginations of this kind are in demand. Only the one who can see in his "mind's eye," before it is begun, the thing he would create, is capable to plan its construction. And who will say that ability to work with images of these kinds is not of just as high a type as that which results in the construction of plots upon which stories are built!

The Building of Ideals and Plans: Nor is the part of imagination less marked in the formation of our life's ideals and plans. Everyone who is not living blindly and aimlessly must have some ideal, some pattern, by which to square his life and guide his actions. At some time in our life I am sure that each of us has selected the person who filled most nearly our notion of what we should like to become, and measured ourselves by this pattern. But there comes a time when we must idealize even the most perfect individual; when we invest the character with attributes which we have selected from some other person, and thus worship at a shrine which is partly real and partly ideal.

As time goes on, we drop out more and more of the strictly individual element, adding correspondingly more of the ideal, until our pattern is largely a construction of our own imagination, having in it the best we have been able to glean from the many characters we have known. How large a part these ever-changing ideals play in our lives we shall never know, but certainly the part is not an insignificant one. And happy the youth who is able to look into the future and see himself approximating some worthy ideal. He has caught a vision which will never allow him to lag or falter in the pursuit of the flying goal which points the direction of his efforts.

Imagination and Conduct: Another great field for imagination is with reference to conduct and our relations with others. Over and over again the thoughtless person has to say, "I am sorry; I did not think." The "did not think" simply means that he failed to realize through his imagination what would be the consequences of his rash or unkind words. He would not be unkind, but he did not imagine how the other would feel; he did not put himself in the other's place. Likewise with reference to the effects of our conduct on ourselves. What youth, taking his first drink of liquor, would continue if he could see a clear picture of himself in the gutter with bloated face and bloodshot eyes a decade hence? Or what boy, slyly smoking one of his early cigarettes, would proceed if he could see his haggard face and nerveless hand a few years farther along? What spendthrift would throw away his money on vanities could he vividly see himself in penury and want in old age? What prodigal anywhere who, if he could take a good look at himself sin-stained and broken as he returns to his "father's house" after the years of debauchery in the "far country" would not hesitate long before he entered upon his downward career?

Imagination and Thinking: We have already considered the use of imagination in interpreting the thoughts, feelings and handiwork of others. Let us now look a little more closely into the part it plays in our own thinking. Suppose that, instead of reading a poem, we are writing one; instead of listening to a description of a battle, we are describing it; instead of looking at the picture, we are painting it. Then our object is to make others who may read our language, or listen to our words, or view our handiwork, construct the mental images of the situation which furnished the material for our thought.

Our words and other modes of expression are but the description of the flow of images in our minds, and our problem is to make a similar stream flow through the mind of the listener; but strange indeed would it be to make others see a situation which we ourselves cannot see; strange if we could draw a picture without being able to follow its outlines as we draw. Or suppose we are teaching science, and our object is to explain the composition of matter to someone, and make him understand how light, heat, etc., depend on the theory of matter; strange if the listener should get a picture if we ourselves are unable to get it. Or, once more, suppose we are to describe some incident, and our aim is to make its every detail stand out so clearly that no one can miss a single one. Is it not evident that we can never make any of these images more clear to those who listen to us or read our words than they are to ourselves?

2. THE MATERIAL USED BY IMAGINATION

What is the material, the mental content, out of which imagination builds its structures?

Images the Stuff of Imagination: Nothing can enter the imagination the elements of which have not been in our past experience and then been conserved in the form of images. The Indians never dreamed of a heaven whose streets are paved with gold, and in whose center stands a great white throne. Their experience had given them no knowledge of these things; and so, perforce, they must build their heaven out of the images which they had at command, namely, those connected with the chase and the forest. So their heaven was the "happy hunting ground," inhabited by game and enemies over whom the blessed forever triumphed. Likewise the valiant soldiers whose deadly arrows and keen-edged swords and battle-axes won on the bloody field of Hastings, did not picture a far-off day when the opposing lines should kill each other with mighty engines hurling death from behind parapets a dozen miles away. Firearms and the explosive powder were yet unknown, hence there were no images out of which to build such a picture.

I do not mean that your imagination cannot construct an object which has never before been in your experience as a whole, for the work of the imagination is to do precisely this thing. It takes the various images at its disposal and builds them into *wholes* which may never have existed before, and which may exist now only as a creation of the mind. And yet we have put into this new product not a single *element* which was not familiar to us in the form of an image of one kind or another. It is the *form* which is new; the *material* is old. This is exemplified every time an inventor takes the two fundamental parts of a machine, the *lever* and the *inclined plane*, and puts them together in relations new to each other and so evolves a machine whose complexity fairly bewilders us. And with other lines of thinking, as in mechanics, inventive power consists in being able to see the old in new relations, and so constantly build new constructions out of old material. It is this power which gives us the daring and original thinker, the Newton whose falling apple suggested to him the planets falling toward the sun in their orbits; the Darwin who out of the thigh bone of an animal was able to construct in his imagination the whole animal and the environment in which it must have lived, and so add another page to the earth's history.

The Two Factors in Imagination: From the simple facts which we have just been considering, the conclusion is plain that our power of imagination depends on two factors; namely, (1) *the materials available in the form of usable images capable of recall*, and (2) *our constructive ability*, or the power to group these images into new *wholes, the process being guided by some purpose or end*. Without this last provision, the products of our imagination are daydreams with their "castles in Spain," which may be pleasing and proper enough on occasions, but which as an habitual mode of thought are extremely dangerous.

Imagination Limited by Stock of Images: That the mind is limited in its imagination by its stock of images may be seen from a simple illustration: Suppose that you own a building made of brick, but that you find the old one no longer adequate for your needs, and so purpose to build a new one; and suppose, further, that you have no material for your new building except that contained in the old structure. It is evident that you will be limited in constructing your new building by the material which was in the old. You may be able to build the new structure in any one of a multitude of different forms or styles of architecture, so far as the material at hand will lend itself to that style of building, and providing, further, that you are able to make the plans. But you will always be limited finally by the character and amount of material obtainable from the old structure. So with the mind. The old building is your past experience, and the separate bricks are the images out of which you must build your new structure through the imagination. Here, as before, nothing can enter which was not already on hand. Nothing goes into the new structure so far as its constructive material is concerned except images, and there is nowhere to get images but from the results of our past experience.

Limited Also by Our Constructive Ability: But not only is our imaginative output limited by the *amount* of material in the way of images which we have at our command, but also and perhaps not less by our *constructive ability*. Many persons might own the old pile of bricks fully adequate for the new structure, and then fail to get the new because they were unable to construct it. So, many who have had a rich and varied experience in many lines are yet unable to muster their images of these experiences in such a way that new products are obtainable from them. These have the heavy, draft-horse kind of intellect which goes plodding on, very possibly doing good service in its own circumscribed range, but destined after all to service in the narrow field with its low, drooping horizon. They are never able to take a dash at a two-minute clip among equally swift competitors, or even swing at a good round pace along the pleasant highways of an experience lying beyond the confines of the narrow *here* and *now*. These are the minds which cannot discover relations; which cannot *think*. Minds of this type can never be architects of their own fate, or even builders, but must content themselves to be had carriers.

The Need of a Purpose: Nor are we to forget that we cannot intelligently erect our building until we know the *purpose* for which it is to be used. No matter how much building material we may have on hand, nor how skillful an architect we may be, unless our plans are guided by some definite aim, we shall be likely to end with a structure that is fanciful and useless. Likewise with our thought structure. Unless our imagination is guided by some aim or purpose, we are in danger of drifting into mere daydreams which not only are useless in furnishing ideals for the guidance of our lives, but often become positively harmful when grown into a habit. The habit of daydreaming is hard to break, and, continuing, holds our thought in thrall and makes it unwilling to deal with the plain, homely things of everyday life. Who has not had the experience of an hour or a day spent in a fairyland of dreams, and awakened at the end to find himself rather dissatisfied with the prosaic round of duties which confronted him! I do not mean to say that we should *never* dream; but I know of no more pernicious mental habit than that of daydreaming carried to excess, for it ends in our following every will-o'-the-wisp of fancy, and places us at the mercy of every chance suggestion.

3. TYPES OF IMAGINATION

Although imagination enters every field of human experience, and busies itself with every line of human interest, yet all its activities can be classed under two different types. These are (1) *reproductive*, and (2) *creative* imagination.

Reproductive Imagination: Reproductive imagination is the type we use when we seek to reproduce in our minds the pictures described by others, or pictures from our own past experience which lack the completeness and fidelity to make them true memory.

The narration or description of the story book, the history or geography text; the tale of adventure recounted by traveler or hunter; the account of a new machine or other invention; fairy tales and myths—these or any other matter that may be put into words capable of suggesting images to us are the field for reproductive imagination. In this use of the imagination our business is to follow and not lead, to copy and not create.

Creative Imagination: But we must have leaders, originators—else we should but imitate each other and the world would be at a standstill. Indeed, every person, no matter how humble his station or how humdrum his life, should be in some degree capable of initiative and originality. Such ability depends in no small measure on the power to use creative imagination.

Creative imagination takes the images from our own past experience or those gleaned from the work of others and puts them together in new and original forms. The inventor, the writer, the mechanic or the artist who possesses the spirit of creation is not satisfied with *mere* reproduction, but seeks to modify, to improve, to originate. True, many important inventions and discoveries have come by seeming accident, by being stumbled upon. Yet it holds that the person who thus stumbles upon the discovery or invention is usually one whose creative imagination is actively at work *seeking* to create or discover in his field. The world's progress as a whole does not come by accident, but by creative planning. Creative imagination is always found at the van of progress, whether in the life of an individual or a nation.

4. TRAINING THE IMAGINATION

Imagination is highly susceptible of cultivation, and its training should constitute one of the most important aims of education. Every school subject, but especially such subjects as deal with description and narration—history, literature, geography, nature study and science—is rich in opportunities for the use of imagination. Skillful teaching will not only find in these subjects a means of training the imagination, but will so employ imagination in their study as to make them living matter, throbbing with life and action, rather than so many dead words or uninteresting facts.

Gathering of Material for Imagination: Theoretically, then, it is not hard to see what we must do to cultivate our imagination. In the first place, we must take care to secure a large and usable *stock of images* from all fields of perception. It is not enough to have visual images alone or chiefly, for many a time shall we need to build structures involving all the other senses and the motor activities as well. This means that we must have a first-hand contact with just as large an environment as possible—large in the world of Nature with all her varied forms suited to appeal to every avenue of sense; large in our contact with people in all phases of experience, laughing with those who laugh and weeping with those who weep; large in contact with books, the interpreters of the men and events of the past. We must not only let all these kinds of environment drift in upon us as they may chance to do, but we must deliberately *seek* to increase our stock of experience; for, after all, experience lies at the bottom of imagination as of every other mental process. And not only must we thus put ourselves in the way of acquiring new experience, but we must by recall and reconstruction, as we saw in an earlier discussion, keep our imagery fresh and usable. For whatever serves to improve our images, at the same time is bettering the very foundation of imagination.

We Must Not Fail to Build: In the second place, we must not fail *to build*. For it is futile to gather a large supply of images if we let the material lie unused. How many people there are who put in all their time gathering material for their structure, and never take time to do the building! They look and listen and read, and are so fully occupied in absorbing the immediately present that they have no time to see the wider significance of the things with which they deal. They are like the students who are too busy studying to have time to think. They are so taken up with receiving that they never perform the higher act of combining. They are the plodding fact gatherers, many of them doing good service, collecting material which the seer and the philosopher, with their constructive power, build together into the greater wholes which make our systems of thought. They are the ones who fondly think that, by reading books full of wild tales and impossible plots, they are training their imagination. For them, sober history, no matter how heroic or tragic in its quiet movements, is too tame. They have not the patience to read solid and thoughtful literature, and works of science and philosophy are a bore. These are the persons who put in all their time in looking at and admiring other people's houses, and never get time to do any building for themselves.

We Should Carry Our Ideals into Action: The best training for the imagination which I know anything about is that to be obtained by taking our own material and from it building our own structure. It is true that it will help to look through other people's houses enough to discover their style of building: we should read. But just as it is not necessary for us to put in all the time we devote to looking at houses, in inspecting doll houses and Chinese pagodas, so it is not best for us to get all our notions of imaginative structures from the marvelous and the unreal; we get good training for the imagination from reading "Hiawatha," but so can we from reading the history of the primitive Indian tribes. The pictures in "Snowbound" are full of suggestion for the imagination: but so is the history of the Puritans in New England. But even with the best of models before us, it is not enough to follow others' building. We must construct stories for ourselves, must work out plots for our own stories; we must have time to meditate and plan and build, not idly in the daydream, but purposefully, and then make our images real by *carrying them out in activity*, if they are of such a character that this is possible; we must build our ideals and work to them in the common course of our everyday life; we must think for ourselves instead of forever following the thinking of others; we must *initiate* as well as imitate.

5. PROBLEMS FOR OBSERVATION AND INTROSPECTION

1. Explain the cause and the remedy in the case of such errors as the following:

Children who defined mountain as land 1,000 or more feet in height said that the factory smokestack was higher than the mountain because it "went straight up" and the mountain did not.

Children often think of the horizon as fastened to the earth.

Islands are thought of as floating on the water.

2. How would you stimulate the imagination of a child who does not seem to picture or make real the descriptions in reading, geography, etc.? Is it possible that such inability may come from an insufficient basis in observation, and hence in images?

3. Classify the school subjects, including domestic science and manual training, as to their ability to train (1) reproductive and (2) creative imagination.

4. Do you ever skip the descriptive parts of a book and read the narrative? As you read the description of a bit of natural scenery, does it rise before you? As you study the description of a battle, can you see the movements of the troops?

5. Have you ever planned a house as you think you would like it? Can you see it from all sides? Can you see all the rooms in their various finishing and furnishings?

6. What plans and ideals have you formed, and what ones are you at present following? Can you describe the process by which your plans or ideals change? Do you ever try to put yourself in the other person's place?

7. Take some fanciful unreality which your imagination has constructed and see whether you can select from it familiar elements from actual experiences.

8. What use do you make of imagination in the common round of duties in your daily life? What are you doing to improve your imagination?

CHAPTER X
ASSOCIATION

Whence came the thought that occupies you this moment, and what determines the next that is to follow? Introspection reveals no more interesting fact concerning our minds than that our thoughts move in a connected and orderly array and not in a hit-and-miss fashion. Our mental states do not throng the stream of consciousness like so many pieces of wood following each other at random down a rushing current, now this one ahead, now that. On the contrary, our thoughts come, one after the other, as they are beckoned or *caused*. The thought now in the focal point of your consciousness appeared because it sprouted out of the one just preceding it; and the present thought, before it departs, will determine its successor and lead it upon the scene. This is to say that our thought stream possesses not only a continuity, but also a *unity*; it has coherence and system. This coherence and system, which operates in accordance with definite laws, is brought about by what the psychologist calls *association*.

1. THE NATURE OF ASSOCIATION

We may define association, then, as the tendency among our thoughts to form such a system of bonds with each other that the objects of consciousness are vitally connected both (1) as they exist at any given moment, and (2) as they occur in succession in the mental stream.

The Neural Basis of Association: The association of thoughts—ideas, images, memory—or of a situation with its response, rests primarily on a neural basis. Association is the result of habit working in neuron groups. James states its fundamental law as follows: "When two elementary brain-processes have been active together or in immediate succession, one of them, on recurring, tends to propagate its excitement into the other." This is but a technical statement of the simple fact that nerve currents flow most easily over the neuron connections that they have already used.

It is hard to teach an old dog new tricks, because the old tricks employ familiar, much-used neural paths, while new tricks require the connecting up of groups of neurons not in the habit of working together; and the flow of nerve energy is more easily accomplished in the neurons accustomed to working together. One who learns to speak a foreign language late in life never attains the facility and ease that might have been reached at an earlier age. This is because the neural paths for speech are already set for his mother tongue, and, with the lessened plasticity of age, the new paths are hard to establish.

The connections between the various brain areas, or groups of neurons, are, as we have seen in an earlier chapter, accomplished by means of *association fibers*. This function requires millions of neurons, which unite every part of the cortex with every other part, thus making it possible for a neural activity going on in any particular center to extend to any other center whatsoever. In the relatively unripe brain of the child, the association fibers have not yet set up most of their connections.

The age at which memory begins is determined chiefly by the development of a sufficient number of association fibers to bring about recall. The more complex reasoning, which requires many different associative connections, is impossible prior to the existence of adequate neural development. It is this fact that makes it futile to attempt to teach young children the more complicated processes of arithmetic, grammar, or other subjects. They are not yet equipped with the requisite brain machinery to grasp the necessary associations.

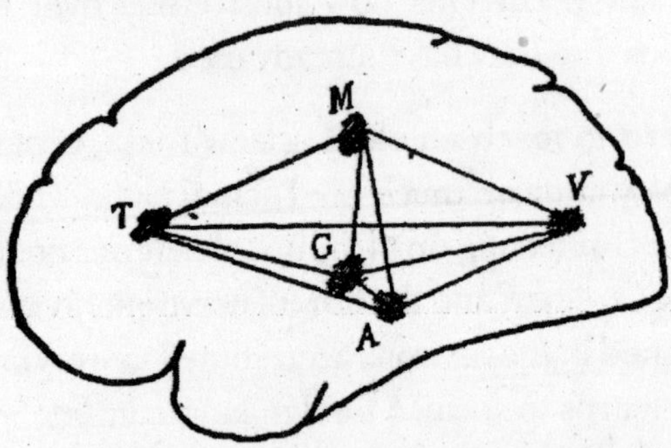

Fig. 18.—Diagrammatic scheme of association, in which V stands for the visual, A for the auditory, G for the gustatory, M for the motor, and T for the thought and feeling centers of the cortex.

Association the Basis of Memory: Without the machinery and processes of association we could have no memory. Let us see in a simple illustration how association works in recall. Suppose you are passing an orchard and see a tree loaded with tempting apples. You hesitate, then climb the fence, pick an apple and eat it, hearing the owner's dog bark as you leave the place. The accompanying diagram will illustrate roughly the centers of the cortex which were involved in the act, and the association fibers which connect them. (See

Fig. 18.) Now let us see how you may afterward remember the circumstance through association. Let us suppose that a week later you are seated at your dining table, and that you begin to eat an apple whose flavor reminds you of the one which you plucked from the tree. From this start how may the entire circumstance be recalled? Remember that the cortical centers connected with the sight of the apple tree, with our thoughts about it, with our movements in getting the apple, and with hearing the dog bark, were all active together with the taste center, and hence tend to be thrown into activity again from its activity. It is easy to see that we may (1) get a visual image of the apple tree and its fruit from a current over the gustatory-visual association fibers; (2) the thoughts, emotions, or deliberations which we had on the former occasion may again recur to us from a current over the gustatory-thought neurons; (3) we may get an image of our movements in climbing the fence and picking the apple from a current over the gustatory-motor fibers; or (4) we may get an auditory image of the barking of the dog from a current over the gustatory-auditory fibers. Indeed, we are *sure* to get some one or more of these unless the paths are blocked in some way, or our attention leads off in some other direction.

Factors Determining Direction of Recall: *Which* of these we get first, which of the images the taste percept calls to take its place as it drops out of consciousness, will depend, other things being equal, on which center was most keenly active in the original situation, and is at the moment most permeable. If, at the time we were eating the stolen fruit, our thoughts were keenly self-accusing for taking the apples without permission, then the current will probably discharge through the path gustatory-thought, and we shall recall these thoughts and their accompanying feelings. But if it chances that the barking of the dog frightened us badly, then more likely the discharge from the taste center will be along the path gustatory-auditory, and we shall get the auditory image of the dog's barking, which in turn may call up a visual image of his savage appearance over the auditory-visual fibers. It is clear, however, that, given any one of the elements of the entire situation back, the rest are potentially possible to us, and any one may serve as a "cue" to call up all the rest. Whether, given the starting point, we get them all, depends solely on whether the paths are sufficiently open between them for the current to discharge between them, granting that the first experience made sufficient impression to be retained.

Since this simple illustration may be made infinitely complex by means of the millions of fibers which connect every center in the cortex with every other center, and since, in passing from one experience to another in the round of our daily activities, these various areas are all involved in an endless chain of activities so intimately related that each one can finally lead to all the others, we have here the machinery both of retention and of recall—the mechanism by which our past may be made to serve the present through being reproduced in the form of memory images or ideas. Through this machinery we are unable to escape our past, whether it be good or bad; for both the good and the bad alike are brought back to us through its operations.

When the repetition of a series of acts has rendered habit secure, the association is relatively certain. If I recite to you A-B-C-D, your thought at once runs on to E, F, G. If I repeat,

"Tell me not in mournful numbers," association leads you to follow with "Life is but an empty dream." Your neuron groups are accustomed to act in this way, so the sequence follows. Memorizing anything from the multiplication table to the most beautiful gems of poetic fervor consists, therefore, in the setting up of the right associative connections in the brain.

Association in Thinking: All thinking proceeds by the discovery or recognition of relations between the terms or objects of our thought. The science of mathematics rests on the relations found to exist between numbers and quantities. The principles and laws of natural science are based on the relations established among the different forms of matter and the energy that operates in this field. So also in the realm of history, art, ethics, or any other field of human experience. Each fact or event must be linked to other facts or events before it possesses significance. Association therefore lies at the foundation of all thinking, whether that of the original thinker who is creating our sciences, planning and executing the events of history, evolving a system of ethics, or whether one is only learning these fields as they already exist by means of study. Other things being equal, he is the best thinker who has his knowledge related part to part so that the whole forms a unified and usable system.

Association and Action: Association plays an equally important part in all our motor responses, the acts by which we carry on our daily lives, do our work and our play, or whatever else may be necessary in meeting and adapting ourselves to our environment. Some sensations are often repeated, and demand practically the same response each time. In such cases the associations soon become fixed, and the response certain and automatic. For example, we sit at the table, and the response of eating follows, with all its complex acts, as a matter of course. We lie down in bed, and the response of sleep comes. We take our place at the piano, and our fingers produce the accustomed music.

It is of course obvious that the influence of association extends to moral action as well. In general, our conduct follows the trend of established associations. We are likely to do in great moral crises about, as we are in the habit of doing in small ones.

2. THE TYPES OF ASSOCIATION

Fundamental Law of Association: Stated on the physiological side, the law of habit as set forth in the definition of association in the preceding section includes all the laws of association. In different phrasing we may say: (1) Neuron groups accustomed to acting together have the tendency to work in unison. (2) The more frequently such groups act together the stronger will be the tendency for one to throw the other into action. Also, (3) the more intense the excitement or tension under which they act together the stronger will be the tendency for activity in one to bring about activity in the other.

The corresponding facts may be expressed in psychological terms as follows: (1) Facts accustomed to being associated together in the mind have a tendency to reappear together. (2) The more frequently these facts appear together the stronger the tendency for the presence of one to insure the presence of the other. (3) The greater the tension, excitement or concentration when these facts appear in conjunction with each other, the more certain the presence of one is to cause the presence of the other.

Psychologists from Aristotle have differentiated several different types of association down. It is to be kept in mind, however, that all association types *go back to the elementary law of habit-connections among the neurons* for their explanation.

Association by Contiguity: The recurrence in our minds of many of the elements from our past experience is due to the fact that at some time, possibly at many times, the recurring facts were contiguous in consciousness with some other element or fact which happens now to be again present. All have had the experience of meeting some person whom we had not seen for several months or years, and having a whole series of supposedly forgotten incidents or events connected with our former associations flood into the mind. Things we did, topics we discussed, trips we took, games we played, now recur at the renewal of our acquaintance. For these are the things that were contiguous in our consciousness with our sense of the personality and appearance of our friend. And who has not in similar fashion had a whiff of perfume or the strains of a song recall to him his childhood days! Contiguity is again the explanation.

At the Mercy of Our Associations: Through the law thus operating we are in a sense at the mercy of our associations, which may be bad as well as good. We may form certain lines of interest to guide our thought, and attention may in some degree direct it, but one's mental make-up is, after all, largely dependent on the character of his associations. Evil thoughts, evil memories, evil imaginations—these all come about through the association of unworthy or impure images along with the good in our stream of thought. We may try to forget the base deed and banish it forever from our thinking, but lo! In an unguarded moment the nerve current shoots into the old path, and the impure thought flashes into the mind, unsought and unwelcome. Every young man who thinks he must indulge in a little sowing of wild oats before he settles down to a correct life, and so deals in unworthy thoughts and deeds, is putting a mortgage on his future; for he will find the inexorable machinery of his nervous system grinding the hated images of such things back into his mind as surely as the mill returns to the sack of the miller what he feeds into the hopper. He may refuse to harbor these thoughts, but he can no more hinder their seeking admission to his mind than he can prevent the tramp from knocking at his door. He may drive such images from his mind the moment they are discovered, and indeed is guilty if he does not; but not taking offense at this rebuff, the unwelcome thought again seeks admission.

The only protection against the return of the undesirable associations is to choose lines of thought as little related to them as possible. But even then, do the best we may, an occasional "connection" will be set up, we know not how, and the unwelcome image stands staring us in the face, as the corpse of Eugene Aram's victim confronted him at every turn, though he thought it safely buried. A minister of my acquaintance tells me that in the holiest moments of his most exalted thought, images rise in his mind which he loathes, and from which he recoils in horror. Not only does he drive them away at once, but he seeks to lock and bar the door against them by firmly resolving that he will never think of them again. But alas! that is beyond his control. The tares have been sown among the wheat, and will persist along with it until the end. In his boyhood these images were given into the keeping of his brain cells, and they are only being faithful to their trust.

Association by Similarity and Contrast: All are familiar with the fact that like tends to suggest like. One friend reminds us of another friend when he manifests similar traits of character, shows the same tricks of manner, or has the same peculiarities of speech or gesture. The telling of a ghost or burglar story in a company will at once suggest a similar story to every person of the group, and before we know it the conversation has settled down to ghosts or burglars. One boastful boy is enough to start the gang to recounting their real or imaginary exploits. Good and beautiful thoughts tend to call up other good and beautiful thoughts, while evil thoughts are likely to produce after their own kind; like produces like.

Another form of relationship is, however, quite as common as similar in our thinking. In certain directions we naturally think in *opposites*. Black suggests white, good suggests bad, fat suggests lean, wealth suggests poverty, happiness suggests sorrow, and so on.

The tendency of our thought thus to group in similar and opposites is clear when we go back to the fundamental law of association. The fact is that we more frequently assemble our thoughts in these ways than in haphazard relations. We habitually group similar together, or compare opposites in our thinking; hence these are the terms between which associative bonds are formed.

Partial, or Selective, Association: The past is never wholly reinstated in present consciousness. Many elements, because they had formed fewer associations, or because they find some obstacle to recall, are permanently dropped out and forgotten. In other words, association is always *selective*, favoring now this item of experience, now that, above the rest.

It is well that this is so; for to be unable to escape from the great mass of minutia and unimportant detail in one's past would be intolerable, and would so cumber the mind with useless rubbish as to destroy its usefulness. We have surely all had some experience with the type of persons whose associations are so complete and impartial that all their conversation teems with unessential and irrelevant details. They cannot recount the simplest incident in its essential points but, slaves to literalness, make themselves insufferable bores by entering upon every lane and by-path of circumstance that leads nowhere and matters not the least in their story. Dickens, Thackeray, George Eliot, Shakespeare, and many other writers have seized upon such characters and made use of them for their comic effect. James, in illustrating this mental type, has quoted the following from Miss Austen's "Emma":

"'But where could *you* hear it?' cried Miss Bates. 'Where could you possibly hear it, Mr. Knightley? For it is not five minutes since I received Mrs. Cole's note—no, it cannot be more than five—or at least ten—for I had got my bonnet and spencer on, just ready to come out—I was only gone down to speak to Patty again about the pork—Jane was standing in the passage—were not you, Jane?—for my mother was so afraid that we had not any salting-pan large enough. So I said I would go down and see, and Jane said: "Shall I go down instead? for I think you have a little cold, and Patty has been washing the kitchen." "Oh, my dear," said I—well, and just then came the note.'"

The Remedy: The remedy for such wearisome and fruitless methods of association is, as a matter of theory, simple and easy. It is to emphasize, intensify, and dwell upon the *significant and essential* in our thinking. The person who listens to a story, who studies a lesson, or who is a participant in any event must apply a *sense of value*, recognizing and fixing the important and relegating the trivial and unimportant to their proper level. Not to train one's self to think in this discriminating way is much like learning to play a piano by striking each key with equal force!

3. TRAINING IN ASSOCIATION

Since association is at bottom nothing but habit at work in the mental processes, it follows that it, like other forms of habit, can be encouraged or suppressed by training. Certainly, no part of one's education is of greater importance than the character of his associations. For upon these will largely depend not alone the *content* of his mental stream, the stuff of his thinking, but also its *organization*, or the use made of the thought material at hand. In fact, the whole science of education rests on the laws and principles involved in setting up right systems of associative connections in the individual.

The Pleasure-Pain Motive in Association: A general law seems to obtain throughout the animal world that associative responses accompanied by pleasure tend to persist and grow stronger, while those accompanied by pain tend to weaken and fall away. The little child of two years may not understand the gravity of the offense in tearing the leaves out of books, but if its hands are sharply spotted whenever they tear a book, the association between the sight of books and tearing them will soon cease. In fact, all punishment should have for its object the use of pain in the breaking of associative bonds between certain situations and wrong responses to them.

On the other hand, the dog that is being trained to perform his tricks is rewarded with a tidbit or a pat when the right response has been made. In this way the bond for this particular act is strengthened through the use of pleasure. All matter studied and learned under the stimulus of good feeling, enthusiasm, or a pleasurable sense of victory and achievement not only tends to set up more permanent and valuable associations than if learned under opposite conditions, but it also exerts a stronger appeal to our interest and appreciation.

The influence of mental attitude on the matter we study raises a question as to the wisdom of assigning the committing of poetry, or Bible verses, or the reading of so many pages of a literary masterpiece as a punishment for some offense. How many of us have carried away associations of dislike and bitterness toward some gem of verse or prose or Scripture because of having our learning of it linked up with the thought of an imposed task set as penance for wrong-doing! One person tells me that to this day she hates the sight of Tennyson because this was the volume from which she was assigned many pages to commit in atonement for her youthful delinquencies.

Interest as a Basis for Association: Associations established under the stimulus of strong interest are relatively broad and permanent, while those formed with interest flagging are more narrow and of doubtful permanence. This statement is, of course, but a particular application of the law of attention. Interest brings the whole self into action. Under it's urging the mind is active and alert. The new facts learned are completely registered, and are assimilated to other facts to which they are related. Many associative connections are formed, hence the new matter is more certain of recall, and possess more significance and meaning.

Association and Methods of Learning: The number and quality of our associations depends in no small degree on our methods of learning. We may be satisfied merely to impress what we learn on our memory, committing it uncritically as so many facts to be stored away as a part of our education. We may go a step beyond this and grasp the simplest and most obvious meanings, but not seek for the deeper and more fundamental relations. We may learn separate sections or divisions of a subject, accepting each as a more or less complete unit, without connecting these sections and divisions into a logical whole.

But all such methods are a mistake. They do not provide for the associative bonds between the various facts or groups of facts in our knowledge, without which our facts are in danger of becoming but so much lumber in the mind. Meanings, relations, definitely recognized associations, should attach to all that we learn. Better far a smaller amount of *usable* knowledge than any quantity of unorganized and undigested information, even if the latter sometimes allows us to pass examinations and receive honor grades. In short, real mastery demands that we *think*, that is *relate* and *associate*, instead of merely *absorbing* as we learn.

4. PROBLEMS IN OBSERVATION AND INTROSPECTION

1. Test the uncontrolled associations of a group of pupils by pronouncing to the class some word, as *blue*, and having the members write down 20 words in succession as rapidly as

they can, taking in each instance the first word that occurs to them. The difference in the scope, or range, of associations, can easily be studied by applying this test to, say, a fourth grade and an eighth grade and then comparing results.

2. Have you ever been puzzled by the appearance in your mind of some fact or incident not thought of before for years? Were you able to trace out the associative connection that caused the fact to appear? Why are we sometimes unable to recall, when we need them, facts that we perfectly well know?

3. You have observed that it is possible to be able to spell certain words when they occur in a spelling lesson, but to miss them when employing them in composition. It is possible to learn a conjugation or a declension in tabular form, and then not be able to use the correct forms of words in speech or writing. Relate these facts to the laws of association, and recommend a method of instruction that will remove the discrepancy.

4. To test the quickness of association in a class of children, copy the following words clearly in a vertical column on a chart; have your class all ready at a given signal; then display the chart before them for sixty seconds, asking them to write down on paper the exact *opposite* of as many words as possible in one minute. Be sure that all know just what they are expected to do.

> Bad, inside, slow, short, little, soft, black, dark, sad, true, dislike, poor, well, sorry, thick, full, peace, few, below, enemy.
>
> Count the number of correct opposites got by each pupil.

5. Can you think of garrulous persons among your acquaintance the explanation of whose tiresomeness is that

their association is of the *complete* instead of the *selective* type? Watch for such illustrations in conversation and in literature (e.g., Juliet's nurse).

6. Observe children in the schoolroom for good and poor training in association. Have you ever had anything that you otherwise presumably would enjoy rendered distasteful because of unpleasant associations? Pass your own methods of learning in review, and also inquire into the methods used by children in study, to determine whether they are resulting in the best possible use of association.

CHAPTER XI
MEMORY

Every hour of our lives we call upon memory to supply us with some fact or detail from out our past. Let memory wholly fail us, and we find ourselves helpless and out of joint in a world we fail to understand. A poor memory handicaps one in the pursuit of education, hampers him in business or professional success, and puts him at a disadvantage in every relation of life. On the other hand, a good memory is an asset on which the owner realizes anew each succeeding day.

1. THE NATURE OF MEMORY

Now that you come to think of it, you can recall perfectly well that Columbus discovered America in 1492; that your house is painted white; that it rained a week ago today. But where were these once-known facts, now remembered so easily, while they were out of your mind? Where did they stay while you were not thinking of them? The common answer is, "Stored away in my memory." Yet no one believes that the memory is a warehouse of facts, which we pack away there when we for a time have no use for him or her, as we store away our old furniture.

What is Retained: The truth is that the simple question I asked you is by no means an easy one, and I will answer it myself by asking you an easier one: As we sit with the sunlight streaming into our room, where is the darkness which filled it last night? And where will all this light be at midnight tonight? Answer these questions, and the ones I asked about your remembered facts will be answered. While it is true that, regardless of the conditions in our little room, darkness still exists wherever there is no light, and light still exists wherever there is no darkness, yet for this particular room *there is no darkness when the sun shines in*, and *there is no light when the room is filled with darkness*. So in the case of a remembered fact. Although the fact that Columbus discovered America some four hundred years ago, that your house is of a white color, that it rained a week ago today, exists as a fact regardless of whether your minds think of these things at all, yet the truth remains as before: for the particular mind which remembers these things, *the facts did not exist while they were out of the mind*.

It is not the remembered fact which is retained, BUT THE POWER TO REPRODUCE THE FACT WHEN WE REQUIRE IT.

The Physical Basis of Memory: The power to reproduce a once-known fact depends ultimately on the brain. This is not hard to understand if we go back a little and consider that brain activity was concerned in every perception we have ever had, and in every fact we have ever known. Indeed, it was through a certain neural activity of the cortex that you were able originally to know that Columbus discovered America, that your house is white, and that it rained on a day in the past. Without this cortical activity, these facts would have existed just as truly, but *you* would never have known them. Without this neural activity in the brain there is no consciousness, and to it we must look for the recurrence in consciousness of remembered facts, as well as for those, which appear for the first time.

How We Remember: Now, if we are to have a once-known fact repeated in consciousness, or in other words *remembered*, what we must do on the physiological side is to provide for a repetition of the neural activity which was at first responsible for the fact's appearing in consciousness. The mental accompaniment of the repeated activity *is the memory*. Thus, as *memory is the approximate repetition of once-experienced mental states or facts, together with the recognition of their belonging to our past, so it is accomplished by an approximate repetition of the once-performed neural process in the cortex, which originally accompanied these states or facts.*

The part played by the brain in memory makes it easy to understand why we find it so impossible to memorize or to recall when the brain is fatigued from long hours of work or lack of sleep. It also explains the derangement in memory that often comes from an injury to the brain, or from the toxins of alcohol, drugs or disease.

Dependence of Memory on Brain Quality: Differences in memory ability, while depending in part on the training memory receives, rest ultimately on the memory-quality of the brain. James tells us that four distinct types of brains may be distinguished, and he describes them as follows:

Brains that are:

(1) Like *marble* to receive and like *marble* to retain.

(2) Like *wax* to receive and like *wax* to retain.

(3) Like *marble* to receive and like *wax* to retain.

(4) Like *wax* to receive and like *marble* to retain.

The first type gives us those who memorize slowly and with much heroic effort, but who keep well what they have committed. The second type represents the ones who learn in a flash, who can cram up a lesson in a few minutes, but who forgets as easily and as quickly as they learn. The third type characterizes the unfortunates who must labor hard and long for what they memorize, only to see it quickly slipping from their grasp. The fourth type is a rare boon to its possessor, enabling him easily to stock his memory with valuable material, which is readily available to him upon demand.

The particular type of brain we possess is given us through heredity, and we can do little or nothing to change the type. Whatever our type of brain, however, we can do much to improve our memory by obeying the laws upon which all good memory depends.

2. THE FOUR FACTORS INVOLVED IN MEMORY

Nothing is more obvious than that memory cannot return to us what has never been given into its keeping, what has not been retained, or what for any reason cannot be recalled. Further, if the facts given back by memory are not recognized as belonging to our past, memory would be incomplete. Memory, therefore, involves the following four factors: (1) *registration*, (2) *retention*, (3) *recall*, (4) *recognition*.

Registration: By registration we mean the learning or committing of the matter to be remembered. On the brain side this involves producing in the appropriate neurons the activities which, when repeated again later, cause the fact to be recalled. It is this process that constitutes what we call "impressing the facts upon the brain."

Nothing is more fatal to good memory than partial or faulty registration. A thing but half learned is sure to be forgotten. We often stop in the mastery of a lesson just short of the full impression needed for permanent retention and sure recall. We sometimes say to our teachers, "I cannot remember," when, as a matter of fact, we have never learned the thing we seek to recall.

Retention: Retention, as we have already seen, resides primarily in the brain. It is accomplished through the law of habit working in the neurons of the cortex. Here, as elsewhere, habit makes an activity once performed more easy of performance each succeeding time. Through this law a neural activity once performed tends to be repeated; or, in other words, a fact once known in consciousness tends to be remembered. That so large a part of our past is lost in oblivion, and out of the reach of our memory, is probably much more largely due to a failure to *recall* than to *retain*. We say that we have forgotten a fact or a name which we cannot recall, try as hard as we may; yet surely all have had the experience of a long-striven-for fact suddenly appearing in our memory when we had given it up and no longer had use for it. It was retained all the time, else it never could have come back at all.

An aged man of my acquaintance lay on his deathbed. In his childhood he had first learned to speak German; but, moving with his family when he was eight or nine years of age to an English-speaking community, he had lost his ability to speak German, and had been unable for a third of a century to carry on a conversation in his mother tongue. Yet during the last days of his sickness he lost almost wholly the power to use the English language, and spoke fluently in German. During all these years his brain paths had retained the power to reproduce the forgotten words, even though for so long a time the words could not be recalled. James quotes a still more striking case of an aged woman who was seized with a fever and, during her delirious ravings, was heard talking in Latin, Hebrew and Greek. She herself could neither read nor write, and the priests said she was possessed of a devil. But a physician unraveled the mystery. When the girl was nine years of age, a pastor, who was a noted scholar, had taken her into his home as a servant, and she had remained there until his death. During this time she had daily heard him read aloud from his books in these languages. Her brain had indelibly retained the record made upon it, although for years she could not have recalled a sentence, if, indeed, she had ever been able to do so.

Recall: Recall depends entirely on association. There is no way to arrive at a certain fact or name that is eluding us except by means of some other facts, names, or what-not so related to the missing term as to be able to bring it into the fold. Memory arrives at any desired fact only over a bridge of associations. It therefore follows that the more associations set up between the fact to be remembered and related facts already in the mind, the more certain the recall. Historical dates and events should when learned be associated with important central dates and events to which they naturally attach. Geographical names, places or other information should be connected with related material already in the mind. Scientific knowledge should form a coherent and related whole. In short, everything that is given over to the memory for its keeping should be linked as closely as possible to material of the same sort. This is all to say that we should not expect our memory to retain and reproduce isolated, unrelated facts, but should give it the advantage of as many logical and well grounded associations as possible.

Recognition: A fact reproduced by memory but not recognized, as belonging to our past experience would impress us as a new fact. This would mean that memory would fail to link the present to the past. Often we are puzzled to know whether we have before met a certain person, or on a former occasion told a certain story, or previously experienced a certain present state of mind which seems half familiar. Such baffling mental states are usually but instances of partial and incomplete recognition. Recognition no longer applies to much of our knowledge; for example, we say we remember that four times six is twenty-four, but probably none of us can recall when and where we learned this fact—we cannot *recognize* it as belonging to our past experience. So with ten thousand other things, which we *know* rather than remember in the strict sense.

3. THE STUFF OF MEMORY

What are the forms in which memory presents the past to us? What are the elements with which it deals? What is the stuff of which it consists?

Images as the Material of Memory: In the light of our discussion upon mental imagery, and with the aid of a little introspection, the answer is easy. I ask you to remember your home, and at once a visual image of the familiar house, with its well-known rooms and their characteristic furnishings, comes to your mind. I ask you to remember the last concert you attended, or the chorus of birds you heard recently in the woods; and there comes a flood of images, partly visual, but largely auditory, from the melodies you heard. Or I ask you to remember the feast of which you partook yesterday, and gustatory and olfactory images are prominent among the others which appear. And so I might keep on until I had covered the whole range of your memory; and, whether I ask you for the simple trivial experiences of your past, for the tragic or crucial experiences, or for the most abstruse and abstract facts which you know and can recall, the case is the same: much of what memory presents to you comes in the form of *images* or of *ideas* of your past.

Images Vary as to Type: We do not all remember what we call the same fact in like images or ideas. When you remembered that Columbus discovered America in 1492, some of you had an image of Columbus the mariner standing on the deck of his ship, as the old picture shows him; and accompanying this image was an idea of "long ago ness." Others, in recalling the same fact, had an image of the coast on which he landed, and perchance felt the rocking of the boat and heard it scraping on the sand as it neared the shore. And still others saw on the printed page the words stating that Columbus discovered America in 1492. And so in an infinite variety of images or ideas we may remember what we call the same fact, though of course the fact is not really the same fact to any two of us, nor to any one of us when it comes to us on different occasions in different images.

Other Memory Material: But sensory images are not the only material with which memory has to deal. We may also recall the bare fact that it rained a week ago today without having images of the rain. We may recall that Columbus discovered America in 1492 without visual or other images of the event. As a matter of fact we do constantly recall many facts of abstract nature, such as mathematical or scientific formula with no imagery other than that of the words or symbols, if indeed these were present. Memory may therefore use as its stuff not only images, but also a wide range of facts, ideas and meanings of all sorts.

4. LAWS UNDERLYING MEMORY

The development of a good memory depends in no small degree on the closeness with which we follow certain well-demonstrated laws.

The Law of Association: The law of association, as we have already seen, is fundamental. Upon it the whole structure of memory depends. Stating this law in neural terms we may say: Brain areas which are *active together at the same time tend to establish associative paths*, so that when one of them is again active the other is also brought into activity. Expressing the same truth in mental terms: If two facts or experiences *occur together in consciousness*, and one of them is later recalled, it tends to cause the other to appear also.

The Law of Repetition: The law of repetition is but a restatement of the law of habit, and may be formulated as follows: The *more frequently* a certain cortical activity occurs, the more easily is its repetition brought about. Stating this law in mental terms we may say: The more often a fact is recalled in consciousness the easier and more certain the recall becomes. It is upon the law of repetition that reviews and drills to fix things in the memory are based.

The Law of Decency: We may state the law of decency in physiological terms as follows: The *more recently* brain centers have been employed in a certain activity, the more easily are they thrown into the same activity. This, on the mental side, means: The more recently any facts have been present in consciousness the more easily are they recalled. It is in obedience to this law that we want to rehearse a difficult lesson just before the recitation hour, or cram immediately before an examination. The working of this law also explains the tendency of all memories to fade out as the years pass by.

The Law of Vividness: The law of vividness is of primary importance in memorizing. On the physical side it may be expressed as follows: The *higher the tension* or the more intense the activity of neural centers the more easily the activity is repeated. The counterpart of this law in mental terms is: *The higher the degree of attention* or concentration when the fact is registered the more certain it is of recall. Better far one impression of a high degree of vividness than several repetitions with the attention wandering or the brain too fatigued to respond. Not drill alone, but drill with concentration, is necessary to sure memory,—in proof of which witness the futile results on the part of the small boy who "studies his spelling lesson over fifteen times," the while he is at the same time counting his marbles.

5. RULES FOR USING THE MEMORY

Much careful and fruitful experimentation in the field of memory has taken place in recent years. The scientists are now able to give us certain simple rules which we can employ in using our memories, even if we lack the time or opportunity to follow all their technical discussions.

Wholes Versus Parts: Probably most people in setting to work to commit to memory a poem, oration, or other such material, have a tendency to learn it first by stanzas or sections and then put the parts together to form the whole. Many tests, however, have shown this to be a less effective method than to go over the whole poem or oration time after time, finally giving special attention to any particularly difficult places. The only exception to this rule would seem to be in the case of very long productions, which may be broken up into sections of reasonable length. The method of committing by wholes instead of parts not only economizes time and effort in the learning, but also gives a better sense of unity and meaning to the matter memorized.

Rate of Forgetting: The rate of forgetting is found to be very much more rapid immediately following the learning than after a longer time has elapsed. This is to say that of what one is going to forget of matter committed to memory approximately one-half will fall away within the first twenty-four hours and three-fourths within the first three days. Since it is always economy to fix afresh matter that is fading out before it has been wholly forgotten, it will manifestly pay to review important memory material within the first day or two after it has once been memorized.

Divided Practice: If to commit a certain piece of material we must go over it, say, ten different times, the results are found to be much better when the entire number of repetitions are not had in immediate succession, but with reasonable intervals between. This is due, no doubt, to the well-known fact that associations tend to take form and grow more secure even after we have ceased to think specifically of the matter in hand. The intervals allow time for the associations to form their connections. It is in this sense that James says we "learn to swim during the winter and to skate during the summer."

Forcing the Memory to Act: In committing matter by reading it, the memory should be forced into activity just as fast as it is able to carry part of the material. If, after reading a poem over once, parts of it can be repeated without reference to the text, the memory should be compelled to reproduce these parts. So with all other material. Re-reading should be applied only at such points as the memory has not yet grasped.

Not a Memory, But Memories: Professor James has emphasized the fact, which has often been demonstrated by experimental tests, that we do not possess a memory, but a collection of memories. Our memory may be very good in one line and poor in another. Nor can we "train our memory" in the sense of practicing it in one line and having the improvement extend equally to other lines. Committing poetry may have little or no effect in strengthening the memory for historical or scientific data. In general, the memory must be trained in the specific lines in which it is to excel. General training will not serve except as it may lead to better modes of learning what is to be memorized.

6. WHAT CONSTITUTES A GOOD MEMORY

Let us next inquire what are the qualities which enter into what we call a good memory. The merchant or politician will say, "Ability to remember well people's faces and names"; the teacher of history, "The abiiity to recall readily dates and events"; the teacher of mathematics, "The power to recall mathematical formula"; the hotel waiter, "The ability to keep in mind half-a-dozen orders at a time"; the manager of a corporation, "The ability to recall all the necessary details connected with the running of the concern." While these answers are very divergent, yet they may all be true for the particular person testifying; for out of them all there emerges this common truth, that *the best memory is the one which best serves its possessor*. That is, one's memory not only must be ready and exact, but must produce the right kind of material; it must bring to us what we need in our thinking. A very easy corollary at once grows out of this fact; namely, that in order to have the memory return to us the right kind of matter, we must store it with the right kind of images and ideas, for the memory cannot give back to us anything which we have not first given into its keeping.

A Good Memory Selects Its Material: The best memory is not necessarily the one which impartially repeats the largest number of facts of past experience. Everyone has many experiences which he never needs to have reproduced in memory; useful enough they may have been at the time, but wholly useless and irrelevant later. They have served their purpose, and should henceforth slumber in oblivion. They would be but so much rubbish and lumber if they could be recalled. Everyone has surely met that particular type of bore whose memory is so faithful to details that no incident in the story he tells, no matter however trivial, is ever omitted in the recounting. His associations work in such a tireless round of minute succession, without ever being able to take a jump or a short cut, that he is powerless to separate the wheat from the chaff; so he dumps the whole indiscriminate mass into our long-suffering ears.

Dr. Carpenter tells of a member of Parliament who could repeat long legal documents and acts of Parliament after one reading. When he was congratulated on his remarkable gift, he replied that, instead of being an advantage to him, it was often a source of great inconvenience, because when he wished to recollect anything in a document he had read, he could do it only by repeating the whole from the beginning up to the point which he wished to recall. Maudsley says that the kind of memory which enables a person "to read a photographic copy of former impressions with his mind's eye is not, indeed, commonly associated with high intellectual power," and gives as a reason that such a mind is hindered by the very wealth of material furnished by the memory from discerning the relations between separate facts upon which judgment and reasoning depend. It is likewise a common source of surprise among teachers that many of the pupils who could outstrip their classmates in learning and memory do not turn out to be able men. But this, says Whately, "is as reasonable as to wonder that a cistern if filled should not be a perpetual fountain." It is possible for one to be so lost in a tangle of trees that he cannot see the woods.

A Good Memory Requires Good Thinking: It is not, then, mere re-presentation of facts that constitutes a good memory. The pupil who can reproduce a history lesson by the page has not necessarily as good a memory as the one who remembers fewer facts, but sees the relations between those remembered, and hence is *able to choose what he will remember.* Memory must be *discriminative.* It must fasten on that which is important and keep that for us. Therefore we can agree that "*the art of remembering is the art of thinking.*" Discrimination must select the important out of our mental stream, and these images must be associated with as many others as possible which are already well fixed in memory, and hence are sure of recall when needed. In this way the old will always serve as a cue to call up the new.

Memory Must Be Specialized: And not only must memory, if it is to be a good memory, omit the generally worthless, or trivial, or irrelevant, and supply the generally useful, significant, and relevant, but it must in some degree be a *specialized memory*. It must minister to the particular needs and requirements of its owner. Small consolation to you if you are a Latin teacher, and are able to call up the binomial theorem or the date of the fall of Constantinople when you are in dire need of a conjugation or a declension, which eludes you. It is much better for the merchant and politician to have a good memory for names and faces than to be able to repeat the succession of English monarchs from Alfred the Great to Edward VII and not be able to tell John Smith from Tom Brown. It is much more desirable for the lawyer to be able to remember the necessary details of his case than to be able to recall all the various athletic records of the year; and so on.

In order to be a good memory for *us*, our memory must be faithful in dealing with the material, which constitutes the needs of our vocations. Our memory may, and should, bring to us many things outside of our immediate vocations, else our lives will be narrow; but its chief concern and most accurate work must be along the path of our everyday requirements at its hands. And this works out well in connection with the physiological laws, which were stated a little while since, providing that our vocations are along the line of our interests. For the things with which we work daily, and in which we are interested, will be often thought of together, and hence will become well associated. They will be frequently recalled, and hence more easily remembered; they will be vividly experienced as the inevitable result of interest, and this goes far to insure recall.

7. MEMORY DEVICES

Many devices have been invented for training or using the memory, and conscienceless fakers upon uninformed people have imposed not a few worthless "systems". All memorizing finally must go back to the fundamental laws of brain activity and the rules growing out of these laws. There is no "royal road" to a good memory.

The Effects of Cramming: Not a few students depend on cramming for much of their learning. If this method of study would yield as valuable permanent results, it would be by far the most sensible and economical method to use; for under the stress of necessity we often are able to accomplish results much faster than when no pressure is resting upon us. The difficulty is, however, that the results are not permanent; the facts learned do not have time to seek out and link themselves to well-established associates; learned in an hour, their retention is as ephemeral as the application which gave them to us.

Facts cramming may profitably learn which are needed but temporarily and which cannot become a part of our body of permanent knowledge. The lawyer needs many details for the case he is trying, which not only are valueless to him as soon as the case is decided, but would positively be in his way. He may profitably cram such facts. But those facts, which are to become a permanent part of his mental equipment, such as the fundamental principles of law, he cannot cram. These he must have in a logical chain, which will not leave their recall dependent upon a chance cue. Crammed facts may serve us during a recitation or an examination, but they never really become a part of us. Nothing can take the place of the logical placing of facts if they are to be remembered with facility, and be usable in thinking when recalled.

Remembering Isolated Facts: But after all this is taken into consideration there still remain a large number of facts which refuse to fit into any connected or logical system. Or, if they do belong with some system, their connection is not very close, and we have more need for the few individual facts than for the system as a whole. Hence we must have some means of remembering such facts other than by connecting them with their logical associations. Such facts as may be typified by the multiplication table, certain dates, events, names, numbers, errands, and engagements of various kinds—all these need to be remembered accurately and quickly when the occasion for them arises. We must be able to recall them with facility, so that the occasion will not have passed by before we can secure them and we have failed to do our part because of the lapse.

With facts of this type the means of securing a good memory are the same as in the case of logical memory, except that we must of necessity forego the linking to naturally related associates. We can, however, take advantage of the three laws, which have been given. If these methods are used faithfully, then we have done what we can in the way of insuring the recall of facts of this type, unless we associate them with some artificial cue, such as tying a thread around our finger to remember an errand, or learning the multiplication table by singing it. We are not to be too ready to excuse ourselves, however, if we have forgotten to mail the letter or deliver the message; for our attention may have been very lax when we recorded the direction in the first place, and we may never have taken the trouble to think of the matter between the time it was given into our keeping and the time we were to perform the errand.

Mnemonic Devices: Many ingenious devices have been invented to assist the memory. No doubt each one of you has some way of your own of remembering certain things committed to you, or some much-needed fact, which has a tendency to elude you. You may not tie the traditional string around your finger or place your watch in the wrong pocket; but if not, you have invented some method, which suits your convenience better. While many books have been written, and many lectures given exploiting mnemonic systems, they are, however, all founded upon the same general principle: namely, that of *association of ideas* in the mind. They all make use of the same basis for memory that any of us use every time we remember anything, from the commonest event, which occurred last hour to the most abstruse bit of philosophy, which we may have in our minds. They all tie the fact to be remembered to some other fact which is sure of recall, and then trust the old fact to bring the new along with it when it again comes into the mind.

Artificial devices may be permissible in remembering the class of facts which have no logical associates in which we can relate them; but even then I cannot help feeling that if we should use the same care and ingenuity in carefully recording the seemingly unrelated facts that we do in working out the device and making the association in it, we should discover hidden relations for most of the facts we wish to remember, and we should be able to insure their recall as certainly and in a better way than through the device. Then, also, we should not be in danger of handing over to the device various facts for which we should discover relations, thus placing them in the logical body of our usable knowledge where they belong.

8. PROBLEMS IN OBSERVATION AND INTROSPECTION

1. Carefully consider your own powers of memory and see whether you can decide which of the four types of brain you have. Apply similar tests to your classmates or a group of school children that you have a chance to observe. Be sure to take into account the effects of past training or habits of memory.

2. Watch in your own memorizing and also that of school children for failures in recall caused by lack of proper associations. Why is it particularly hard to commit what one does not understand?

3. Observe a class in a recitation or an examination and seek to discover whether any defects of memory revealed are to be explained by lack of (1) repetition, (2) decency, (3) vividness in learning.

4. Make a study of your own class and also of a group of children in school to discover their methods of memorizing. Have in mind the rules for memorizing given in section 5 of this chapter.

5. Observe by introspection your method of recall of historical events you have studied, and note whether *images* form an important part of your memory material; or does your recall consist chiefly of bare *facts*? In how far does this depend on your method of *learning* the facts in the first place?

6. Carefully consider your experience from cramming your lessons. Does the material learned in this way stay with you? Do you *understand* it and find yourself able to *use* it as well as stuff learned during a longer interval and with more time for associations to form?

CHAPTER XII
THINKING

No word is more constantly on our lips than the word *think*. A hundred times a day we tell what we think about this thing or that. Any exceptional power of thought classes us among the efficient of our generation. It is in their ability to think that men stand preeminently above the animals.

1. DIFFERENT TYPES OF THINKING

The term *think*, or *thinking*, is employed in so many different senses that it will be well first of all to come to an understanding as to its various uses. Four different types of thinking which we shall note are:[5] (1) *chance*, or idle, thinking; (2) thinking in the form of *uncritical belief*; (3) *assimilative* thinking; and (4) *deliberative* thinking.

Chance or Idle Thinking: Our thinking is of the chance or idle kind when we think to no conscious end. No particular problem is up for solution, and the stream of thought drifts along in idleness. In such thinking, immediate interest, some idle fancy, the impulse of the moment, or the suggestions from our environment determine the train of associations and give direction to our thought. In a sense, we surrender our mental bark to the winds of circumstance to drive it whithersoever they will without let or hindrance from us. Since no results are sought from our thinking, none are obtained. The best of us spend more time in these idle trains of thought than we would like to admit, while inferior and untrained minds seldom rise above this barren thought level. Not infrequently even when we are studying a lesson, which demands our best thought power, we find that an idle chain of associations has supplanted the more rigid type of thinking and appropriated the field.

Uncritical Belief: We often say that we think a certain thing is true or false when we have, as a matter of fact, done little or no thinking about it. We only *believe*, or uncritically accept, the common point of view as to the truth or untruth of the matter concerned. The ancients believed that the earth was flat, and the savages that eclipses were caused by animals eating up the moon. Not a few people today believe that potatoes and other vegetables should be planted at a certain phase of the moon, that sickness is a visitation of Providence, and that various "charms" are potent to bring good fortune or ward off disaster. Probably not one in a thousand of those who accept such beliefs could give, or have ever tried to give, any rational reason for their point of view.

But we must not be too harsh toward such crude illustrations of uncritical thinking. It is entirely possible that not all of us who pride ourselves on our trained powers of thought could give good reasons discovered by our own thinking why we think our political party, our church, or our social organization is better than some other one. How few of us, after all, really *discover* our creed, *join* a church, or *choose* a political party! We adopt the points of view of our nation or our group much as we adopt their customs and dress — not because thinking convinces we that they are best, but because they are less trouble.

Assimilative Thinking: It is this type of thinking that occupies us when we seek to appropriate new facts or ideas and understand them; that is, relate them to knowledge already on hand. We think after this fashion in much of our study in schools and textbooks. The problem for our thought is not so much one of invention or discovery as of grasp and assimilation. Our thinking is to apprehend meanings and relations, and so unify and give coherence to our knowledge.

In the absence of this type of thinking one may commit to memory many facts that he does not understand, gather much information that contains little meaning to him, and even achieve very creditable scholastic grades that stand for a small amount of education or development. For all information, to become vital and usable must be thought into relation to our present active, functioning body of knowledge; therefore assimilative thinking is fundamental to true mastery and learning.

Deliberative Thinking: Deliberative thinking constitutes the highest type of thought process. In order to do deliberative thinking there is necessary, first of all, what Dewey calls a "split-road" situation. A traveler going along a well-beaten highway, says Dr. Dewey, does not deliberate; he simply keeps on going. But let the highway split into two roads at a fork, only one of which leads to the desired destination, and now a problem confronts him; he must take one road or the other, but *which*? The intelligent traveler will at once go to *seeking for evidence* as to which road he should choose. He will balance this fact against that fact, and this probability against that probability, in an effort to arrive at a solution of his problem.

Before we can engage in deliberative thinking we must be confronted by some problem, some such "*split-road*" situation in our mental stream—we must have something to think about. It is this fact that makes one writer say that the great purpose of one's education is not to solve all his problems for him. It is rather to help him (1) to *discover* problems, or "*split-road*" situations, (2) to assist him in gathering the facts necessary for their solution, and (3) to train him in the weighing of his facts or evidence, that is, in deliberative thinking. Only as we learn to recognize the true problems that confront us in our own lives and in society about us can we become thinkers in the best sense. Our own plans and projects, the questions of right and wrong that are constantly arising, the social, political and religious problems awaiting solution, all afford the opportunity and the necessity for deliberative thinking. And unhappy is the pupil whose school work does not set the problems and employ the methods, which will insure training in this as well as in the assimilative type of thinking. Every school subject, besides supplying certain information to be "learned," should present its problems requiring true deliberative thinking within the range of development and ability of the pupil, and no subject—literature, history, science, language—is without many such problems.

2. THE FUNCTION OF THINKING

All true thinking is for the purpose of discovering relations between the things we think about. Imagine a world in which nothing is related to anything else; in which every object perceived, remembered, or imagined, stands absolutely by itself, independent and self-sufficient! What a chaos it would be! We might perceive, remember, and imagine all the various objects we please, but without the power to think them together, they would all be totally unrelated, and hence have no meaning.

Meaning Depends on Relations: To have a rational meaning for us, things must always be defined in terms of other things, or in terms of their uses. *Fuel* is that which feeds *fire*. *Food* is what is eaten for *nourishment*. A *locomotive* is a machine for *drawing a train*. *Books* are to *read*, *pianos* to *play*, *balls* to *throw*, *schools* to *instruct*, *friends* to *enjoy*, and so on through the whole list of objects, which we know or can define. Everything depends for it's meaning on its relation to other things; and the more of these relations we can discover, the more fully do we see the meaning. Thus balls may have other uses than to throw, schools other functions than to instruct, and friends mean much more to us than mere enjoyment. And just in the degree in which we have realized these different relations, have we defined the object, or, in other words, have we seen its meaning.

The Function of Thinking is to Discover Relations: Now it is by *thinking* that these relations are discovered. This is the function of thinking. Thinking takes the various separate items of our experience and discovers to us the relations existing among them, and builds them together into a unified, related, and usable body of knowledge, threading each little bit on the string of relationship, which runs through the whole. It was, no doubt, this thought which Tennyson had in mind when he wrote:

Flower in the crannied wall,
I pluck you out of the crannies,
I hold you here, root and all, in my hand,
Little flower—but if I could understand
What you are, root and all, and all in all,
I should know what God and man is.

Starting in with even so simple a thing as a little flower, if he could discover all the relations which every part bears to every other part and to all other things besides, he would finally reach the meaning of God and man. For each separate thing, be it large or small, forms a link in an unbroken chain of relationships which binds the universe into an ordered whole.

Near and Remote Relations: The relations discovered through our thinking may be very close and simple ones, as when a child sees the relation between his bottle and his dinner; or they may be very remote ones, as when Newton saw the relation between the falling of an apple and the motion of the planets in their orbits. But whether simple or remote, the seeing of the relationships is in both cases alike thinking; for thinking is nothing, in its last analysis, but the discovering of the relationships which exist between the various objects in our mental stream.

Thinking passes through all grades of complexity, from the first faint dawning's in the mind of the babe when it sees the relation between the mother and it's feeding, on to the mighty grasp of the sage who is able to "think God's thoughts after Him." But it all comes to the same end finally—the bringing to light of new meanings through the discovery of new relations. And whatever does this is thinking.

Child and Adult Thinking: What constitutes the difference in the thinking of the child and that of the sage? Let us see whether we can discover this difference. In the first place the relations seen by the child are *immediate* relations: they exist between simple percepts or images; the remote and the general are beyond his reach. He has not had sufficient experience to enable him to discover remote relations. He cannot think things which are absent from him, or which he has never known. The child could by no possibility have seen in the falling apple what Newton saw; for the child knew nothing of the planets in their orbits, and hence could not see relations in which these formed one of the terms. The sage, on the other hand, is not limited to his immediate percepts or their images. He can see remote relations. He can go beyond individuals, and think in classes. The falling apple is not a mere falling apple to him, but one of a *class of falling bodies*. Besides a rich experience full of valuable facts, the trained thinker has acquired also the habit of looking out for relations; he has learned that this is the method *par excellence* of increasing his store of knowledge and of rendering effective the knowledge he has. He has learned how to think.

The chief business of the child is the collection of the materials of thought, seeing only the more necessary and obvious relations as he proceeds; his chief business when older grown is to seek out the network of relations which unites this mass of material, and through this process to systematize and give new meanings to the whole.

3. THE MECHANISM OF THINKING

It is evident from the foregoing discussion that we may include under the term thinking all sorts of mental processes by which relations are apprehended between different objects of thought. Thus young children think as soon as they begin to understand something of the meaning of the objects of their environment. Even animals think by means of simple and direct associations. Thinking may therefore go on in terms of the simplest and most immediate, or the most complex and distant relationships.

Sensations and Percepts as Elements in Thinking: Relations seen between sensations would mean something, but not much; relations seen between *objects* immediately present to the senses would mean much more; but our thinking must go far beyond the present, and likewise far beyond individual objects. It must be able to annihilate both time and space, and to deal with millions of individuals together in one group or class. Only in this way can our thinking go beyond that of the lower animals; for a wise rat, even, may come to see the relation between a trap and danger, or a horse the relation between pulling with his teeth at the piece of string on the gate latch, and securing his liberty.

But it takes the farther-reaching mind of man to *invent* the trap and the latch. Perception alone does not go far enough. It is limited to immediately present objects and their most obvious relations. The perceptual image is likewise subject to similar limitations. While it enables us to dispense with the immediate presence of the object, yet it deals with separate individuals; and the world is too full of individual objects for us to deal with them separately. It is in *conception*, *judgment*, and *reasoning* that true thinking takes place. Our next purpose will therefore be to study these somewhat more closely, and see how they combine in our thinking.

4. THE CONCEPT

Fortunately for our thinking, the great external world, with its millions upon millions of individual objects, is so ordered that these objects can be grouped into comparatively few great classes; and for many purposes we can deal with the class as a whole instead of with the separate individuals of the class. Thus there are an infinite number of individual objects in the world, which are composed of *matter*. Yet all these myriads of individuals may be classed under the two great heads of *inanimate* and *animate*. Taking one of these again: all animate forms may be classed as either *plants* or *animals*. And these classes may again be subdivided indefinitely. Animals include mammals, birds, reptiles, insects, mollusks, and many other classes besides, each class of which may be still further separated into its *orders*, *families*, *genera*, *species*, and *individuals*. This arrangement economizes our thinking by allowing us to think in large terms.

The Concepts Serve to Group and Classify: But the somewhat complicated form of classification just described did not come to man ready-made. Someone had to *see* the relationship existing among the myriads of animals of a certain class, and group these together under the general term *mammals*. Likewise with birds, reptiles, insects, and all the rest. In order to accomplish this, many individuals of each class had to be observed, the qualities common to all members of the class discriminated from those not common, and the common qualities retained as the measure by which to test the admission of other individuals into this class. The process of classification is made possible by what the psychologist calls the *concept.* The concept enables us to think *birds* as well as bluebirds, robins, and wrens; it enables us to think *men* as well as Tom, Dick, and Harry. In other words, *the concept lies at the bottom of all thinking, which rises above the seeing of the simplest relations between immediately present objects.*

Growth of a Concept: We can perhaps best understand the nature of the concept if we watch its growth in the thinking of a child. Let us see how the child forms the concept *dog*, under which he is able finally to class the several hundred or the several thousand different dogs with which his thinking requires him to deal. The child's first acquaintance with a dog is, let us suppose, with a pet poodle, white in color, and named *Gyp*. At this stage in the child's experience, *dog* and *Gyp* are entirely synonymous, including Gyp's color, size, and all other qualities, which the child has discovered. But now let him see another pet poodle, which is like Gyp except that it is black in color. Here comes the first cleavage between *Gyp* and *dog* as synonyms: *dog* no longer means white, but may mean *black*. Next let the child sees a brown spaniel. Not only will white and black now no longer answer to *dog*, but the roly-poly poodle form also has been lost; for the spaniel is more slender. Let the child go on from this until he has seen many different dogs of all varieties: poodles, bulldogs, setters, shepherds, cockers, and a host of others. What has happened to his *dog*, which at the beginning meant the one particular little individual with which he played?

Dog is no longer white or black or brown or gray: *color* is not an essential quality, so it has dropped out; *size* is no longer essential except within very broad limits; *shagginess* or *smoothness* of coat is a very inconstant quality, so this is dropped; *form* varies so much from the fat pug to the slender hound that it is discarded, except within broad limits; *good nature*, *playfulness*, *friendliness*, and a dozen other qualities are likewise found not to belong in common to *all* dogs, and so have had to go; and all that is left to his *dog* is *four-footedness*, and a certain general *form*, and a few other dog qualities of habit of life and disposition. As the term *dog* has been gaining in *extent*, that is, as more individuals have been observed and classed under it, it has correspondingly been losing in *content*, or it has been losing in the specific qualities, which belong to it. Yet it must not be thought that the process is altogether one of elimination; for new qualities which are present in all the individuals of a class, but at first overlooked, are continually being discovered as experience grows, and built into the developing concept.

Definition of Concept: A concept, then, is *our general idea or notion of a class of individual objects*. Its function is to enable us to classify our knowledge, and thus deal with classes or universals in our thinking. Often the basis of a concept consists of an *image*, as when you get a hazy visual image of a mass of people when I suggest *mankind* to you. Yet the core, or the vital, functioning part of a concept is its *meaning*. Whether this meaning attaches to an image or a word or stands relatively or completely independent of either, does not so much matter; but our meanings must be right, else all our thinking is wrong.

Language and the Concept: We think in words. None has failed to watch the flow of his thought as it is carried along by words like so many little boats moving along the mental stream, each with its freight of meaning. And no one has escaped the temporary balking of his thought by failure to find a suitable word to convey the intended meaning. What the grammarian calls the *common nouns* of our language are the words by which we name our concepts and are able to speak of them to others. We define a common noun as "the name of a class," and we define a concept as the meaning or idea we have of a class. It is easy to see that when we have named these class *ideas* we have our list of common nouns. The study of the language of a people may therefore reveal much of their type of thought.

The Necessity for Growing Concepts: The development of our concepts constitutes a large part of our education. For it is evident that, since thinking rests so fundamentally on concepts, progress in our mental life must depend on a constant growth in the number and character of our concepts. Not only must we keep on adding new concepts, but also the old must not remain static. When our concepts stop growing, our minds have ceased to grow—we no longer learn. This arrest of development is often seen in persons who have settled into a life of narrow routine, where the demands are few and of a simple nature. Unless they rise above their routine, they early become "old fogies." Their concepts petrify from lack of use and the constant reconstruction which growth necessitates.

On the other hand, the person who has upon him the constant demand to meet new situations or do better in old ones will keep on enriching his old concepts and forming new ones, or else, unable to do this, he will fail in his position. And the person who keeps on steadily enriching his concepts has discovered the secret of perpetual youth so far as his mental life is concerned. For him there is no old age; his thought will be always fresh, his experience always accumulating, and his knowledge growing more valuable and usable.

5. JUDGMENT

But in the building up of percepts and concepts, as well as in making use of them after they are formed, another process of thinking enters; namely, the process of *judging*.

Nature of Judgment: Judging enters more or less into all our thinking, from the simplest to the most complex. The babe lies staring at his bottle, and finally it dawns on his sluggish mind that this is the object from which he gets his dinner. He has performed a judgment. That is, he has alternately directed his attention to the object before him and to his image of former nursing, discovered the relation existing between the two, and affirmed to him, "This is what gives me my dinner." "Bottle" and "what-gives-me-my-dinner" are essentially identical to the child. *Judgment is, then, the affirmation of the essential identity of meaning of two objects of thought.* Even if the proposition in which we state our judgment has in it a negative, the definition will still hold, for the mental process is the same in either case. It is as much a judgment if we say, "The day is not-cold," as if we say, "The day is cold."

Judgment Used in Percepts and Concepts: How judgment enters into the forming of our percepts may be seen from the illustration just given. The act by which the child perceived his bottle had in it a large element of judging. He had to compare two objects of thought—the one from past experience in the form of images, and the other from the present object, in the form of sensations from the bottle—and then affirm their essential identity. Of course it is not meant that what I have described *consciously* takes place in the mind of the child;

but some such process lies at the bottom of every perception, whether of the child or anyone else.

Likewise it may be seen that the forming of concepts depends on judgment. Every time that we meet a new object, which has to be assigned its place in our classification, judgment is required. Suppose the child, with his immature concept *dog*, sees for the first time a greyhound. He must compare this new specimen with his concept *dog*, and decide that this is or is not a dog. If he discovers the identity of meaning in the essentials of the two objects of thought, his judgment will be affirmative, and his concept will be modified in whatever extent *greyhound* will affect it.

Judgment Leads to General Truths: But judgment goes much farther than to assist in building percepts and concepts. It takes our concepts after they are formed and discovers and affirms relations between them, thus enabling us finally to relate classes as well as individuals. It carries our thinking over into the realm of the universal, where we are not hampered by particulars. Let us see how this is done. Suppose we have the concept *man* and the concept *animal*, and that we think of these two concepts in their relation to each other. The mind analyzes each into its elements, compares them, and finds the essential identity of meaning in a sufficient number to warrant the judgment, *man is an animal.* This judgment has given a new bit of knowledge, in that it has discovered to us a new relation between two great classes, and hence given both, in so far, a new meaning and a wider definition. And as this new relation does not pertain to any particular man or any particular animal, but includes all individuals in each class, it has carried us over into universals, so that we have a *general* truth and will not have to test each individual man henceforth to see whether he fits into this relation.

Judgments also, as we will see later, constitute the material for our reasoning. Hence upon their validity will depend the validity of our reasoning?

The Validity of Judgments: Now, since every judgment is made up of an affirmation of relation existing between two terms, it is evident that the validity of the judgment will depend on the thoroughness of our knowledge of the terms compared. If we know but few of the attributes of either term of the judgment, the judgment is clearly unsafe. Imperfect concepts lie at the basis of many of our wrong judgments. A young man complained because his friend had been expelled from college for alleged misbehavior. He said, "Mr. A—— was the best boy in the institution." It is very evident that someone had made a mistake in judgment. Surely no college would want to expel the best boy in the institution. Either my complainant or the authorities of the college had failed to understand one of the terms in the judgment. Either "Mr. A——" or "the best boy in the institution" had been wrongly interpreted by someone. Likewise, one person will say, "Jones is a good man," while another will say, "Jones is a rascal." Such a discrepancy in judgment must come from a lack of acquaintance with Jones or a lack of knowledge of what constitutes a good man or a rascal.

No doubt most of us are prone to make judgments with too little knowledge of the terms we are comparing, and it is usually those who have the least reason for confidence in their judgments who are the most certain that they cannot be mistaken. The remedy for faulty judgments is, of course, in making ourselves more certain of the terms involved, and this in turn sends us back for a review of our concepts or the experience upon which the terms depend. It is evident that no two persons can have just the same concepts, for all have not had the same experience out of which their concepts came. The concepts may be named the same, and may be nearly enough alike so that we can usually understand each other; but, after all, I have mine and you have yours, and if we could each see the other's in their true light, no doubt we should save many misunderstandings and quarrels.

6. REASONING

All the mental processes, which we have so far described, find their culmination and highest utility in *reasoning*. Not that reasoning comes last in the list of mental activities, and cannot take place until all the others have been completed, for reasoning is in some degree present almost from the dawn of consciousness. The difference between the reasoning of the child and that of the adult is largely one of degree—of reach. Reasoning goes farther than any of the other processes of cognition, for it takes the relations expressed in judgments and out of these relations evolves still other and more ultimate relations.

Nature of Reasoning: It is hard to define reasoning so as to describe the precise process which occurs; for it is so intermingled with perception, conception, and judgment, that one can hardly separate them even for purposes of analysis, much less to separate them functionally. We may, however, define reasoning provisionally as *thinking by means of a series of judgments with the purpose of arriving at some definite end or conclusion*. What does this mean? Professor Angell has stated the matter so clearly that I will quote his illustration of the case:

"Suppose that we are about to make a long journey which necessitates the choice from among a number of possible routes. This is a case of the genuinely problematic kind. It requires reflection, a weighing of the *pros* and *cons*, and giving of the final decision in favor of one or other of several alternatives. In such a case the procedure of most of us is after this order. We think of one route as being picturesque and wholly novel, but also as being expensive. We think of another as less interesting, but also as less expensive. A third is, we discover, the most expedient, but also the most costly of the three. We find ourselves confronted, then, with the necessity of choosing with regard to the relative merits of cheapness, beauty, and speed. We proceed to consider these points in the light of all our interests, and the decision more or less makes itself. We find, for instance, that we must, under the circumstances, select the cheapest route."

How Judgments Function in Reasoning: Such a line of thinking is very common to everyone, and one that we carry out in one form or another a thousand times every day we live. When we come to look closely at the steps involved in arriving at a conclusion, we detect a series of judgments—often not very logically arranged, to be sure, but yet so related that the result is safely reached in the end. We compare our concept of, say, the first route and our concept of picturesque ness, decide they agree, and affirm the judgment, "This route is picturesque." Likewise we arrive at the judgment, "This route is also expensive, it is interesting, etc." Then we take the other routes and form our judgments concerning them. These judgments are all related to each other in some way, some of them being more intimately related than others. Which judgments remain as the significant ones, the ones that are used to solve the problem finally, depends on which concepts are the most vital for us with reference to the ultimate end in view. If time is the chief element, then the form of our reasoning would be something like this: "Two of the routes require more than three days: hence I must take the third route." If economy were the important end, the solution would be as follows: "Two routes cost more than $1,000; I cannot afford to pay more than $800; I therefore must patronize the third route."

In both cases it is evident that the conclusion is reached through a comparison of two or more judgments. This is the essential difference between judgment and reasoning. Whereas judgment discovers relations between concepts, *reasoning discovers relations between judgments, and from this evolves a new judgment, which is, the conclusion sought.* The example given well illustrates the ordinary method by which we reason to conclusions.

Deduction and the Syllogism: Logic may take the conclusion, with the two judgments on which it is based, and form the three into what is called a *syllogism*, of which the following is a classical type:

All men are mortal;

Socrates is a man,

Therefore

Socrates is mortal.

The first judgment is in the form of a proposition, which is called the *major premise*, because it is general in its nature, including all men. The second is the *minor premise*, since it deals with a particular man. The third is the *conclusion*, in which a new relation is discovered between Socrates and mortality.

This form of reasoning is *deductive*, that is, it proceeds from the general to the particular. Much of our reasoning is an abbreviated form of the syllogism, and will readily expand into it. For instance, we say, "It will rain tonight, for there is lightning in the west." Expanded into the syllogism form it would be, "Lightning in the west is a sure sign of rain; there is lightning in the west this evening; therefore, it will rain tonight." While we do not commonly think in complete syllogisms, it is often convenient to cast our reasoning in this form to test its validity. For example, a fallacy lurks in the generalization, "Lightning in the west is a sure sign of rain." Hence the conclusion is of doubtful validity.

Induction: Deduction is a valuable form of reasoning, but a moment's reflection will show that something must precede the syllogism in our reasoning. The *major premise must be accounted for*. How are we able to say that all men are mortal, and that lightning in the west is a sure sign of rain? How was this general truth arrived at? There is only one way, namely, through the observation of a large number of particular instances, or through *induction*.

Induction is the method of proceeding from the particular to the general. Many men are observed, and it is found that all who have been observed have died under a certain age. It is true that not all men have been observed to die, since many are now living, and many more will no doubt come and live in the world whom *we* cannot observe, since mortality will have overtaken us before their advent. To this it may be answered that the men now living have not yet lived up to the limit of their time, and, besides, they have within them the causes working whose inevitable effect has always been and always will be death; likewise with the men yet unborn, they will possess the same organism as we, whose very nature necessitates mortality. In the case of the premonitions of rain, the generalization is not so safe, for there have been exceptions. Lightning in the west at night is not always followed by rain, nor can we find inherent causes as in the other case, which necessitates rain as an effect.

The Necessity for Broad Induction: Thus it is seen that our generalizations, or major premises, are of all degrees of validity. In the case of some, as the mortality of man, millions of cases have been observed and no exceptions found, but on the contrary, causes discovered whose operation renders the result inevitable. In others, as, for instance, in the generalization once made, "All cloven-footed animals chew their cud," not only had the examination of individual cases not been carried so far as in the former case when the generalization was made, but there were found no inherent causes residing in cloven-footed animals which make it necessary for them to chew their cud. That is, cloven feet and cud chewing do not of necessity go together, and the case of the pig disproves the generalization.

In practically no instance, however, is it possible for us to examine every case upon which a generalization is based; after examining a sufficient number of cases, and particularly if there are supporting causes, we are warranted in making the "inductive leap," or in proceeding at once to state our generalization as a working hypothesis. Of course it is easy to see that if we have a wrong generalization, if our major premise is invalid, all that follows in our chain of reasoning will be worthless. This fact should render us careful in making generalizations on too narrow a basis of induction. We may have observed that certain red-haired people of our acquaintance are quick-tempered, but we are not justified from this in making the general statement that all red-haired people are quick-tempered. Not only have we not examined a sufficient number of cases to warrant such a conclusion, but also we have found in the red hair not even a cause of quick temper, but only an occasional concomitant.

The Interrelation of Induction and Deduction: Induction and deduction must go hand in hand in building up our world of knowledge. Induction gives us the particular facts out of which our system of knowledge is built, furnishes us with the data out of which general truths are formed; deduction allows us to start with the generalization furnished us by induction, and from this vantage ground to organize and systematize our knowledge and, through the discovery of its relations, to unify it and make it usable. Deduction starts with a general truth and asks the question, "What new relations are made necessary among particular facts by this truth?" Induction starts with particulars, and asks the question, "To what general truth do these separate facts lead?" Each method of reasoning needs the other. Deduction must have induction to furnish the facts for its premises; induction must have deduction to organize these separate facts into a unified body of knowledge. "He only sees well who sees the whole in the parts, and the parts in the whole."

7. PROBLEMS IN OBSERVATION AND INTROSPECTION

1. Watch your own thinking for examples of each of the four types described. Observe a class of children in a recitation or at study and try to decide which type each child is employing. What proportion of the time supposedly given to study is given over to *chance* or idle thinking? To *assimilative* thinking? To *deliberative* thinking?

2. Observe children at work in school with the purpose of determining whether they are being taught to *think*, or only to memorize certain facts. Do you find that definitions whose meaning is not clear are often required of children? Which should come first, the definition or the meaning and application of it?

3. It is of course evident from the relation of induction and deduction that the child's natural mode of learning a subject is by induction. Observe the teaching of children to determine whether inductive methods are commonly used. Outline an inductive lesson in arithmetic, physiology, geography, civics, etc.

4. What concepts have you now which you are aware are very meager? What is your concept of *mountain?* How many have you seen? Have you any concepts, which you are working very hard to enrich?

5. Recall some judgment, which you have made and which proved to be false, and see whether you can now discover what was wrong with it. Do you find the trouble to be an inadequate concept? What constitutes "good judgment"? "Poor judgment"? Did you ever make a mistake in an example in, say, percentage, by saying "This is the base," when it proved not to be? What was the cause of the error?

6. Can you recall any instance in which you made too hasty a generalization when you had observed but few cases upon which to base your premise? What of your reasoning which followed?

7. See whether you can show that validity of reasoning rests ultimately on correct perceptions. What are you doing at present to increase your power of thinking?

8. How ought this chapter to help one in making a better teacher? A better student?

CHAPTER XIII
INSTINCT

Nothing is more wonderful than nature's method of endowing each individual at the beginning with all the impulses, tendencies and capacities that are to control and determine the outcome of the life. The acorn has the perfect oak tree in its heart; the complete butterfly exists in the grub; and man at his highest powers is present in the babe at birth. Education *adds* nothing to what heredity supplies, but only develops what is present from the first.

We are a part of a great-unbroken procession of life, which began at the beginning and will go on till the end. Each generation receives, through heredity, the products of the long experience through which the race has passed. The generation receiving the gift today lives its own brief life, makes its own little contribution to the sum total and then passes on as millions have done before. Through heredity, the achievements, the passions, the fears, and the tragedies of generations long since moldered to dust stir our blood and tone our nerves for the conflict of today.

1. THE NATURE OF INSTINCT

Every child born into the world has resting upon him an unseen hand reaching out from the past, pushing him out to meet his environment, and guiding him in the start upon his journey. This impelling and guiding power from the past we call *instinct.* In the words of Mosso: "Instinct is the voice of past generations reverberating like a distant echo in the cells of the nervous system. We feel the breath, the advice, the experience of all men, from those who lived on acorns and struggled like wild beasts, dying naked in the forests, down to the virtue and toil of our father, the fear and love of our mother."

The Babe's Dependence on Instinct.—The child is born ignorant and helpless. It has no memory, no reason, no imagination. It has never performed a conscious act, and does not know how to begin. It must get started, but how? It has no experience to direct it, and is unable to understand or imitate others of its kind. It is at this point that instinct comes to the rescue. The race has not given the child a mind ready made—that must develop; but it has given him a ready-made nervous system, ready to respond with the proper movements when it receives the touch of its environment through the senses.

And this nervous system has been so trained during a limitless past that its responses are the ones, which are necessary for the welfare of its owner. It can do a hundred things without having to wait to learn them. Burdette says of the newborn child, "Nobody told him what to do. Nobody taught him. He knew. Placed suddenly on the guest list of this old caravansary, he knew his way at once to two places in it—his bedroom and the dining-room." A thousand generations of babies had done the same thing in the same way, and each had made it a little easier for this particular baby to do his part without learning how.

Definition of Instinct: *Instincts are the tendency to act in certain definite ways, without previous education and without a conscious end in view.* They are a tendency to *act*; for some movement, or motor adjustment, is the response to an instinct. They do not require previous *education*, for none is possible with many instinctive acts: the duck does not have to be taught to swim or the baby to suck. They have no conscious *end* in view, though the result may be highly desirable.

Says James: "The cat runs after the mouse, runs or shows fight before the dog, avoids falling from walls and trees, shuns fire and water, etc., not because he has any notion either of life or death, or of self, or of preservation. He has probably attained to no one of these conceptions in such a way as to react definitely upon it. He acts in each case separately, and simply because he cannot help it; being so framed that when that particular running thing called a mouse appears in his field of vision he *must* pursue; that when that particular barking and obstreperous thing called a dog appears he *must* retire, if at a distance, and scratch if close by; that he *must* withdraw his feet from water and his face from flame, etc. His nervous system is to a great extent a pre-organized bundle of such reactions. They are as fatal as sneezing, and exactly correlated to their special excitants as it to its own."

You ask, Why does the lark rise on the flash of a sunbeam from his meadow to the morning sky, leaving a trail of melody to mark his flight? Why does the beaver build his dam, and the oriole hang her nest? Why are myriads of animal forms on the earth today doing what they were countless generations ago? Why does the lover seek the maid, and the mother cherish her young? *Because the voice of the past speaks to the present, and the present has no choice but to obey.*

Instincts Are Racial Habits: Instincts are the habits of the race which it bequeaths to the individual; the individual takes these for his start, and then modifies them through education, and thus adapts himself to his environment. Through his instincts, the individual is enabled to short-cut racial experience, and begin at once on life activities which the race has been ages in acquiring. Instinct preserves to us what the race has achieved in experience, and so starts us out where the race left off.

Unmodified Instinct is Blind: Many of the lower animal forms act on instinct blindly, unable to use past experience to guide their acts, incapable of education. Some of them carry out seemingly marvelous activities, yet their acts are as automatic as those of a machine and as devoid of foresight. A species of mud wasp carefully selects clay of just the right consistency, finds a somewhat sheltered nook under the eaves, and builds its nest, leaving one open door. Then it seeks a certain kind of spider, and having stung it so as to benumb without killing, carries it into the new-made nest, lays its eggs on the body of the spider so that the young wasps may have food immediately upon hatching out, then goes out and plasters the door over carefully to exclude all intruders. Wonderful intelligence? Not intelligence at all. Its acts were dictated not by plans for the future, but by pressure from the past. Let the supply of clay fail, or the race of spiders become extinct, and the wasp is helpless and its species will perish. Likewise the *race* of bees and ants have done wonderful things, but *individual* bees and ants are very stupid and helpless when confronted by any novel conditions to which their race has not been accustomed.

Man starts in as blindly as the lower animals; but, thanks to his higher mental powers, this blindness soon gives way to foresight, and he is able to formulate purposeful ends and adapt his activities to their accomplishment. Possessing a larger number of instincts than the lower animals have, man finds possible a greater number of responses to a more complex environment than do they. This advantage, coupled with his ability to reconstruct his experience in such a way that he secures constantly increasing control over his environment, easily makes man the superior of all the animals, and enables him to exploit them for his own further advancement.

2. LAW OF THE APPEARANCE AND DISAPPEARANCE OF INSTINCTS

No child is born with all its instincts ripe and ready for action. Yet each individual contains within his own inner nature the law, which determines the order and time of their development.

Instincts Appear in Succession as Required: It is not well that we should be started on too many different lines of activity at once, hence our instincts do not all appear at the same time. Only as fast as we need additional activities do they ripen. Our very earliest activities are concerned chiefly with feeding; hence we first have the instincts, which prompt us to take our food and to cry for it when we are hungry. Also we find useful such abbreviated instincts, called *reflexes*, as sneezing, snuffling, gagging, vomiting, starting, etc.; hence we have the instincts enabling us to do these things. Soon comes the time for teething, and, to help the matter along, the instinct of biting enters, and the rubber ring is in demand. The time approaches when we are to feed ourselves, so the instinct arises to carry everything to the mouth. Now we have grown strong and must assume an erect attitude, hence the instinct to sit up and then to stand. Locomotion comes next, and with it the instinct to creep and walk. Also a language must be learned, and we must take part in the busy life about us and do as other people do; so the instinct to imitate arises that we may learn things quickly and easily.

Wc need a spur to keep us up to our best effort, so the instinct of emulation emerges. We must defend ourselves, so the instinct of pugnacity is born. We need to be cautious, hence the instinct of fear. We need to be investigative, hence the instinct of curiosity. Much self-directed activity is necessary for our development, hence the play instinct. It is best that we should come to know and serve others, so the instincts of sociability and sympathy arise. We need to select a mate and care for offspring, hence the instinct of love for the other sex, and the parental instinct. This is far from a complete list of our instincts, and I have not tried to follow the order of their development, but I have given enough to show the origin of many of our life's most important activities.

Many Instincts Are Transitory: Not only do instincts ripen by degrees, entering our experience one by one as they are needed, but they drop out when their work is done. Some, like the instinct of self-preservation, are needed our lifetime through, hence they remain to the end. Others, like the play instinct, serve their purpose and disappear or are modified into new forms in a few years, or a few months. The life of the instinct is always as transitory as is the necessity for the activity to which it gives rise. No instinct remains wholly unaltered in man, for it is constantly being made over in the light of each new experience. The instinct of self-preservation is modified by knowledge and experience, so that the defense of the man against threatened danger would be very different from that of the child; yet the instinct to protect oneself in *some* way remains. On the other hand, the instinct to romp and play is less permanent. It may last into adult life, but few middle-aged or old people care to race about, as do children. Their activities are occupied in other lines, and they require less physical exertion.

Contrast with these two examples such instincts as sucking, creeping, and crying, which are much more fleeting than the play instinct, even. With dentition comes another mode of eating, and sucking is no more serviceable. Walking is a better mode of locomotion than creeping, so the instinct to creep soon dies. Speech is found a better way than crying to attract attention to distress, so this instinct drops out. Many of our instincts not only would fail to be serviceable in our later lives, but would be positively in the way. Each serves its day, and then passes over into so modified a form as not to be recognized, or else drops out of sight altogether.

Seemingly Useless Instincts: Indeed it is difficult to see that some instincts serve a useful purpose at any time. The pugnacity and greediness of childhood, its foolish fears, the bashfulness of youth—these seem to be either useless or detrimental to development. In order to understand the workings of instinct, however, we must remember that it looks in two directions; into the future for its application, and into the past for its explanation. We should not be surprised if the experiences of a long past have left behind some tendencies which are not very useful under the vastly different conditions of today.

Nor should we be too sure that an activity whose precise function in relation to development we cannot discover has no use at all. Each instinct must be considered not alone in the light of what it means to its possessor today, but of what it means to all his future development. The tail of a polliwog seems a very useless appendage so far as the adult frog is concerned, yet if the polliwog's tail is cut off a perfect frog never develops.

Instincts to Be Utilized When They Appear: A man may set the stream to turning his mill wheels today or wait for twenty years—the power is there ready for him when he wants it. Instincts must be utilized when they present themselves; else they disappear—never, in most cases, to return. Birds kept caged past the flying time never learn to fly well. The hunter must train his setter when the time is ripe, or the dog can never be depended upon. Ducks kept away from the water until full grown have almost as little inclination for it as chickens.

The child whom the pressure of circumstances or unwise authority of parents keeps from mingling with playmates and participating in their plays and games when the social instinct is strong upon him, will in later life find himself a hopeless recluse to whom social duties are a bore. The boy who does not hunt and fish and race and climb at the proper time for these things, will find his taste for them fade away, and he will become wedded to a sedentary life. The youth and maiden must be permitted to "dress up" when the impulse comes to them, or they are likely ever after to be careless in their attire.

Instincts as Starting Points: Most of our habits have their rise in instincts, and all desirable instincts should be seized upon and transformed into habits before they fade away. Says James in his remarkable chapter on Instinct: "In all pedagogy the great thing is to strike while the iron is hot, and to seize the wave of the pupils' interest in each successive subject before its ebb has come, so that knowledge may be got and a habit of skill acquired—a headway of interest, in short, secured, on which afterwards the individual may float. There is a happy moment for fixing skill in drawing, for making boys collectors in natural history, and presently dissectors and botanists; then for initiating them into the harmonies of mechanics and the wonders of physical and chemical law. Later, introspective psychology and the metaphysical and religious mysteries take their turn; and, last of all, the drama of human affairs and worldly wisdom in the widest sense of the term. In each of us a saturation point is soon reached in all these things; the impetus of our purely intellectual zeal expires, and unless the topic is associated with some urgent personal need that keeps our wits constantly whetted about it, we settle into an equilibrium, and live on what we learned when our interest was fresh and instinctive, without adding to the store."

> There is a tide in the affairs of men
> which, taken at the flood, leads on to fortune;
> Omitted, all the voyage of their life
> is bound in shallows and in miseries.

The More Important Human Instincts: It will be impossible in this brief statement to give a complete catalogue of the human instincts, much less to discuss each in detail. We must content ourselves therefore with naming the more important instincts, and finally discussing a few of them: *Sucking, biting, chewing, clasping objects with the fingers, carrying to the mouth, crying, smiling, sitting up, standing, locomotion, vocalization, imitation, emulation, pugnacity, resentment, anger, sympathy, hunting and fighting, fear, acquisitiveness, play, curiosity, sociability, modesty, secretiveness, shame, love, and jealousy* may be said to head the list of our instincts. It will be impossible in our brief space to discuss this entire list. Only a few of the more important will be noticed.

3. THE INSTINCT OF IMITATION

No individual enters the world with a large enough stock of instincts to start him doing all the things necessary for his welfare. Instinct prompts him to eat when he is hungry, but does not tell him to use a knife and fork and spoon; it prompts him to use vocal speech, but does not say whether he shall use English, French, or German; it prompts him to be social in his nature, but does not specify that he shall say please and thank you, and take off his hat to ladies. The race did not find the specific *modes* in which these and many other things are to be done of sufficient importance to crystallize them in instincts; hence the individual must learn them, as he needs them. The simplest way of accomplishing this is for each generation to copy the ways of doing things, which are followed, by the older generation among whom they are born. This is done largely through *imitation*.

Nature of Imitation: *Imitation is the instinct to respond to a suggestion from another by repeating his act.* The instinct of imitation is active in the year-old child, it requires another year or two to reach its height, then it gradually grows less marked, but continues in some degree throughout life. The young child is practically helpless in the matter of imitation. Instinct demands that he shall imitate, and he has no choice but to obey. His environment furnishes the models, which he must imitate, whether they are good or bad. Before he is old enough for intelligent choice, he has imitated a multitude of acts about him; and habit has seized upon these acts and is weaving them into conduct and character. Older grown we may choose what we will imitate, but in our earlier years we are at the mercy of the models which are placed before us.

If our mother tongue is the first we hear spoken, that will be our language; but if we first hear Chinese, we will learn that with almost equals facility. If whatever speech we hear is well spoken, correct, and beautiful, so will our language be; if it is vulgar, or incorrect, or slangy, our speech will be of this kind. If the first manners, which serve us as models, are coarse and boorish, ours will resemble them; if they are cultivated and refined, ours will be like them. If our models of conduct and morals are questionable, our conduct and morals will be of like type. Our manner of walking, of dressing, of thinking, of saying our prayers, even, originates in imitation. By imitation we adopt ready-made our social standards, our political faith, and our religious creeds. Our views of life and the values we set on its attainments are largely a matter of imitation.

Individuality in Imitation: Yet, given the same model, no two of us will imitate precisely alike. Your acts will be yours, and mine will be mine. This is because no two of us have just the same heredity, and hence cannot have precisely similar instincts. There reside in our different personalities different powers of invention and originality, and these determine by how much the product of imitation will vary from the model. Some remain imitators all their lives, while others use imitation as a means to the invention of better types than the original models. The person, who is an imitator only, lacks individuality and initiative; the nation, which is an imitator, only is stagnant and unprogressive. While imitation must be blind in both cases at first, it should be increasingly intelligent as the individual or the nation progresses.

Conscious and Unconscious Imitation: The much-quoted dictum that "all consciousness is motor" has a direct application to imitation. It only means that *we have a tendency to act on whatever idea occupies the mind.* Think of yawning or clearing the throat, and the tendency is strong to do these things. We naturally respond to smile with smile and to frown with frown. And even the impressions coming to us from our material environment have their influence on our acts. Our response to these ideas may be a conscious one, as when a boy purposely stutters in order to mimic an unfortunate companion; or it may be unconscious, as when the boy unknowingly falls into the habit of stammering from hearing this kind of speech. The child may consciously seek to keep himself neat and clean so as to harmonize with a pleasant and well-kept home, or he may unconsciously become slovenly and cross-tempered from living in an ill kept home where constant bickering is the rule.

Often we deliberately imitate what seems to us desirable in other people, but probably far the greater proportion of the suggestions to which we respond are received and acted upon unconsciously. In conscious imitation we can select what models we shall imitate, and therefore protect ourselves in so far as our judgment of good and bad models is valid. In unconscious imitation, however, we are constantly responding to a stream of suggestions pouring in upon us hour after hour and day after day, with no protection but the leadings of our interests as they direct our attention now to this phase of our environment, and now to that.

Influence of Environment: No small part of the influences which mold our lives comes from our material environment. Good clothes, artistic homes, beautiful pictures and decoration, attractive parks and lawns, well-kept streets, well-bound books—all these have a direct moral and educative value; on the other hand, squalor, disorder, and ugliness are an incentive to ignorance and crime.

Hawthorne tells in "The Great Stone Face" of the boy Ernest, listening to the tradition of a coming Wise Man who one day is to rule over the Valley. The story sinks deep into the boy's heart, and he thinks and dreams of the great and good man; and as he thinks and dreams, he spends his boyhood days gazing across the valley at a distant mountain side whose rocks and cliffs nature had formed into the outlines of a human face remarkable for the nobleness and benignity of its expression. He comes to love this Face and looks upon it as the prototype of the coming Wise Man, until lo! as he dwells upon it and dreams about it, the beautiful character which its expression typifies grows into his own life, and he himself becomes the long-looked-for Wise Man.

The Influence of Personality: More powerful than the influence of material environment, however, is that of other personalities upon us—the touch of life upon life. A living personality contains a power which grips hold of us, electrifies us, inspires us, and compels us to new endeavor, or else degrades and debases us. None has failed to feel at some time this life-touch, and to bless or curse the day when its influence came upon him. Either consciously or unconsciously such a personality becomes our ideal and model; we idolize it, idealize it, and imitate it, until it becomes a part of us. Not only do we find these great personalities living in the flesh, but we find them also in books, from whose pages they speak to us, and to whose influence we respond.

And not in the *great* personalities alone does the power to influence reside. From *every life*, which touches ours, a stream of influence great or small is entering our life and helping to mold it. Nor are we to forget that this influence is reciprocal, and that we are reacting upon others up to the measure of the powers that are in us.

4. THE INSTINCT OF PLAY

Small use to be a child unless one can play. Says Karl Groos: "Perhaps the very existence of youth is due in part to the necessity for play; the animal does not play because he is young, but he is young because he must play." Play is a constant factor in all grades of animal life. The swarming insects, the playful kitten, the frisking lambs, the racing colt, the darting swallows, the maddening aggregation of blackbirds—these are but illustrations of the common impulse of all the animal world to play. Wherever freedom and happiness reside, there play is found; wherever play is lacking, there the curse has fallen and sadness and oppression reign. Play is the natural rule in the paradise of youth; it is childhood's chief occupation. To toil without play, places man on a level with the beasts of burden.

The Necessity for Play: But why is play so necessary? Why is this impulse so deep-rooted in our natures? Why not compel our young to expend their boundless energy on productive labor? Why all this waste? Why have our child labor laws? Why not shut recesses from our schools, and so save time for work? Is it true that all work and no play make Jack a dull boy? Too true. For proof we need but gaze at the dull and lifeless faces of the prematurely old children as they pour out of the factories where child labor is employed. We need but follow the children, who have had a play less childhood, into a narrow and barren manhood. We need but to trace back the history of the dull and brutish men of today, and find that they were the play less children of yesterday. Play is as necessary to the child as food, as vital as sunshine, as indispensable as air.

The keynote of play is *freedom*, freedom of physical activity, and mental initiative. In play the child makes his own plans, his imagination has free rein, originality is in demand, and constructive ability is placed under tribute. Here are developed a thousand tendencies, which would never find expression in the narrow treadmill of labor alone. The child needs to learn to work; but along with his work must be the opportunity for free and unrestricted activity, which can come only through play. The boy needs a chance to be a barbarian, a hero, an Indian. He needs to ride his broomstick on a dangerous raid, and to charge with lath sword the redoubts of a stubborn enemy. He needs to be a leader as well as a follower. In short, without in the least being aware of it, he needs to develop himself through his own activity—he needs freedom to play.

If the child be a girl, there is no difference except in the character of the activities employed.

Play in Development and Education: And it is precisely out of these play activities that the later and more serious activities of life emerge. Play is the gateway by which we best enter the various fields of the world's work, whether our particular sphere be that of pupil or teacher in the schoolroom, of man in the busy marts of trade or in the professions, or of farmer or mechanic. Play brings the *whole self* into the activity; it trains to habits of independence and individual initiative, to strenuous and sustained effort, to endurance of hardship and fatigue, to social participation and the acceptance of victory and defeat. And these are the qualities needed by the man of success in his vocation.

These facts make the play instinct one of the most important in education. Froebel was the first to recognize the importance of play, and the kindergarten was an attempt to utilize its activities in the school. The introduction of this new factor into education has been attended, as might be expected, by many mistakes. Some have thought to recast the entire process of education into the form of games and plays, and thus to lead the child to possess the "Promised Land" through aimlessly chasing butterflies in the pleasant fields of knowledge. It is needless to say that they have not succeeded. Others have mistaken the shadow for the substance, and introduced games and plays into the schoolroom which lack the very first element of play; namely, *freedom of initiative and action* on the part of the child. Educational theorists and teachers have invented games and occupations and taught them to the children, who go through with them much as they would with any other task, enjoying the activity but missing the development which would come through a larger measure of self-direction.

Work and Play Are Complements: Work cannot take the place of play, neither can play be substituted for work. Nor are the two antagonistic, but each is the complement of the other; for the activities of work grow immediately out of those of play, and each lends zest to the other. Those who have never learned to work and those who have never learned to play are equally lacking in their development. Further, it is not the name or character of an activity which determines whether it is play for the participant, but *his attitude toward the activity*. If the activity is performed for its own sake and not for some ulterior end, if it grows out of the interest of the child and involves the free and independent use of his powers of body and mind, if it is *his*, and not someone's else—then the activity possesses the chief characteristics of play. Lacking these, it cannot be play, whatever else it may be.

Play, like other instincts, besides serving the present, looks in two directions, into the past and into the future. From the past come the shadowy interests which, taking form from the touch of our environment, determine the character of the play activities. From the future come the premonitions of the activities that are to be. The boy adjusting himself to the requirements of the game, seeking control over his companions or giving in to them, is practicing in miniature the larger game which he will play in business or profession a little later. The girl in her playhouse, surrounded by a nondescript family of dolls and pets, is unconsciously looking forward to a more perfect life when the responsibilities shall be a little more real. So let us not grudge our children the play day of youth.

5. OTHER USEFUL INSTINCTS

Many other instincts ripen during the stage of youth and play their part in the development of the individual.

Curiosity: It is inherent in every normal person to want to investigate and *know*. The child looks out with wonder and fascination on a world he does not understand, and at once begins to ask questions and try experiments. Every new object is approached in a spirit of inquiry. Interest is omnivorous, feeding upon every phase of environment. Nothing is too simple or too complex to demand attention and exploration, so that it vitally touches the child's activities and experience.

The momentum given the individual by curiosity toward learning and mastering his world is incalculable. Imagine the impossible task of teaching children what they had no desire or inclination to know! Think of trying to lead them to investigate matters concerning which they felt only a supreme indifference! Indeed one of the greatest problems of education is to keep curiosity alive and fresh so that its compelling influence may promote effort and action. One of the greatest secrets of eternal youth is also found in retaining the spontaneous curiosity of youth after the youthful years are past.

Manipulation: This is the rather unsatisfactory name for the universal tendency to *handle*, *do* or *make* something. The young child builds with its blocks, constructs fences and pens and caves and houses, and a score of other objects. The older child, supplied with implements and tools, enters upon more ambitious projects and revels in the joy of creation as he makes boats and boxes, soldiers and swords, kites, playhouses and what-not. Even as adults we are moved by a desire to express ourselves through making or creating that which will represent our ingenuity and skill. The tendency of children to destroy is not from wantonness, but rather from a desire to manipulate.

Education has but recently begun to make serious use of this important impulse. The success of all laboratory methods of teaching, and of such subjects as manual training and domestic science, is abundant proof of the adage that we learn by doing. We would rather construct or manipulate an object than merely learn its verbal description. Our deepest impulses lead to creation rather than simple mental appropriation of facts and descriptions.

The Collecting Instinct: The words *my* and *mine* enter the child's vocabulary at a very early age. The sense of property ownership and the impulse to make collections of various kinds go hand in hand. Probably there are few of us who have not at one time or another made collections of autographs, postage stamps, coins, bugs, or some other thing of as little intrinsic value. And most of us, if we have left youth behind, are busy even now in seeking to collect fortunes, works of art, rare volumes or other objects on which we have set our hearts.

The collecting instinct and the impulse to ownership can be made important agents in the school. The child who, in nature study, geography or agriculture, is making a collection of the leaves, plants, soils, fruits, or insects used in the lessons has an incentive to observation and investigation impossible from book instruction alone. One who, in manual training or domestic science, is allowed to own the article made will give more effort and skill to its construction than if the work be done as a mere school task.

The Dramatic Instinct: Every person is, at one stage of his development, something of an actor. All children like to "dress up" and impersonate someone else—in proof of which, witness the many play scenes in which the character of nurse, doctor, pirate, teacher, merchant or explorer is taken by children who, under the stimulus of their spontaneous imagery and as yet untrammeled by self-consciousness, freely enter into the character they portray. The dramatic impulse never wholly dies out. When we no longer aspire to do the acting ourselves we have others do it for us in the theaters or the movies.

Education finds in the dramatic instinct a valuable aid. Progressive teachers are using it freely, especially in the teaching of literature and history. Its application to these fields may be greatly increased, and also extended more generally to include religion, morals, and art.

The Impulse to Form Gangs and Clubs: Few boys and girls grow up without belonging at some time to a secret gang, club or society. Usually this impulse grows out of two different instincts, the *social* and the *adventurous*. It is fundamental in our natures to wish to be with our kind—not only our human kind, but also those of the same age, interests and ambitions. The love of secrecy and adventure is also deep seated in us. So we are clannish; and we love to do the unusual, to break away from the commonplace and routine of our lives. There is often a thrill of satisfaction—even if it were later followed by remorse—in doing the forbidden or the unconventional.

The problem here as in the case of many other instincts is one of guidance rather than of repression. Out of the gang impulse we may develop our athletic teams, our debating and dramatic clubs, our tramping clubs, and a score of other recreational, benevolent, or social organizations. Not repression, but proper expression should be our ideal.

6. FEAR

Probably in no instinct more than in that of fear can we find the reflections of all the past ages of life in the world with its manifold changes, its dangers, its tragedies, its sufferings, and its deaths.

Fear Heredity: The fears of childhood "are remembered at every step," and so are the fears through which the race has passed. Says Chamberlain: "Every ugly thing told to the child, every shock, every fright given him, will remain like splinters in the flesh, to torture him all his life long. The bravest old soldier, the most daring young reprobate, is incapable of forgetting them all—the masks, the bogies, ogres, hobgoblins, witches, and wizards, the things that bite and scratch, that nip and tear, that pinch and crunch, the thousand and one imaginary monsters of the mother, the nurse, or the servant, have had their effect; and hundreds of generations have worked to denaturalize the brains of children. Perhaps no animal, not even those most susceptible to fright, has behind it the fear heredity of the child."

President Hall calls attention to the fact that night is now the safest time of the twenty-four hours; serpents are no longer our most deadly enemies; strangers are not to be feared; neither are big eyes or teeth; there is no adequate reason why the wind, or thunder, or lightning should make children frantic as they do. But "the past of man forever seems to linger in his present"; and the child, in being afraid of these things, is only summing up the fear experiences of the race and suffering all too many of them in his short childhood.

Fear of the Dark: Most children are afraid in the dark. Who does not remember the terror of a dark room through which he had to pass, or, worse still, in which he had to go to bed alone, and there lie in cold perspiration induced by a mortal agony of fright! The unused doors which would not lock, and through which he expected to see the goblin come forth to get him! The dark shadows back under the bed where he was afraid to look for the hidden monster, which he was sure, was hiding there and yet dare not face! The lonely lane through which the cows were to be driven late at night, while every fence corner bristled with shapeless monsters lying in wait for boys!

And that hated dark closet where he was shut up "until he could learn to be good!" And the useless trapdoor in the ceiling. How often have we lain in the dim light at night and seen the lid lift just a peep for ogre eyes to peer out, and, when the terror was growing beyond endurance, close down, only to lift once and again, until from sheer weariness and exhaustion we fell into a troubled sleep and dreamed of the hideous monster which inhabited the unused garret! Tell me that the old trapdoor never bent its hinges in response to either man or monster for twenty years? I know it is true, and yet I am not convinced. My childish fears have left a stronger impression than proof of mere facts can ever overrule.

Fear of Being Left Alone: And the fear of being left alone. How big and dreadful the house seemed with the folks all gone! How we suddenly made close friends with the dog or the cat, even, in order that this bit of life might be near us! Or, failing in this, we have gone out to the barn among the chickens and the pigs and the cows, and deserted the empty house with its torture of loneliness. What was there so terrible in being alone? I do not know. I know only that to many children it is a torture more exquisite than the adult organism is fitted to experience.

But why multiply the recollections? They bring a tremor to the strongest of us today. Who of us would choose to live through those childish fears again? Dream fears, fears of animals, fears of furry things, fears of ghosts and of death, dread of fatal diseases, fears of fire and of water, of strange persons, of storms, fears of things unknown and even unimagined, but all the more fearful! Would you all like to relive your childhood for its pleasures if you had to take along with them its sufferings? Would the race choose to live its evolution over again? I do not know. But, for my own part, I should very much hesitate to turn the hands of time backward in either case. Would that the adults at life's noonday, in remembering the childish fears of life's morning, might feel a sympathy for the children of today, who are not yet escaped from the bonds of the fear instinct. Would that all might seek to quiet every foolish childish fear, instead of laughing at it or enhancing it!

7. OTHER UNDESIRABLE INSTINCTS

We are all provided by nature with some instincts, which, while they may serve a good purpose in our development, need to be suppressed or at least modified when they have done their work.

Selfishness: All children, and perhaps all adults, are selfish. The little child will appropriate all the candy, and give none to his playmate. He will grow angry and fight rather than allow brother or sister to use a favorite plaything. He will demand the mother's attention and care even when told that she is tired or ill, and not able to minister to him. But all of this is true to nature and, though it needs to be changed to generosity and unselfishness, is, after all, a vital factor in our natures. For it is better in the long run that each one *should* look out for himself, rather than to be so careless of his own interests and needs as to require help from others. The problem in education is so to balance selfishness and greed with unselfishness and generosity that each serves as a check and a balance to the other. Not elimination but equilibrium is to be our watchword.

Pugnacity, or the Fighting Impulse: Almost every normal child is a natural fighter, just as every adult should possess the spirit of conquest. The long history of conflict through which our race has come has left its mark in our love of combat. The pugnacity of children, especially of boys, is not so much to be deprecated and suppressed as guided into right lines and rendered subject to right ideals. The boy who picks a quarrel has been done a kindness when given a drubbing that will check this tendency. On the other hand, one who risks battle in defense of a weaker comrade does no ignoble thing. Children need very early to be taught the baseness of fighting for the sake of conflict, and the glory of going down to defeat fighting in a righteous cause. The world could well stand more of this spirit among adults!

Let us then hear the conclusion of the whole matter. The undesirable instincts do not need encouragement. It is better to let them fade away from disuse, or in some cases even by attaching punishment to their expression. They are echoes from a distant past, and not serviceable in this better present. *The desirable instincts we are to seize upon and utilize as starting points for the development of useful interests, good habits, and the higher emotional life. We should take them as they come, for their appearance is a sure sign that the organism is ready for and needs the activity they foreshadow; and, furthermore, if they are not used when they present themselves, they disappear, never to return.*

8. PROBLEMS IN OBSERVATION AND INTROSPECTION

1. What instincts have you noticed developing in children? What ones have you observed to fade away? Can you fix the age in both cases? Apply these questions to your own development as you remember it or can get it by tradition from your elders.

2. What use of imitation may be made in teaching (1) literature, (2) composition, (3) music, (4) good manners, (5) morals?

3. Should children be *taught* to play? Make a list of the games you think all children should know and be able to play. It has been said that it is as important for a people to be able to use their leisure time wisely as to use their work time profitably. Why should this be true?

4. Observe the instruction of children to discover the extent to which use is made of the *constructive* instinct. The *collecting* instinct. The *dramatic* instinct. Describe a plan by which each of these instincts can be successfully used in some branch of study.

5. What examples can you recount from your own experience of conscious imitation? Of unconscious imitation? Of the influence of environment? What is the application of the preceding question to the esthetic quality of our school buildings?

6. Have you ever observed that children under a dozen years of age usually cannot be depended upon for "team work" in their games? How do you explain this fact?

CHAPTER XIV
FEELING AND ITS FUNCTIONS

In the psychical world as well as the physical we must meet and overcome inertia. Our lives must be compelled by motive forces strong enough to overcome this natural inertia, and enable us besides to make headway against many obstacles. *The motive power that drives us consists chiefly of our feelings and emotions.* Knowledge, cognition, supplies the rudder that guides our ship, but feeling and emotion supply the power.

To convince one's head is, therefore, not enough; his feelings must be stirred if you would be sure of moving him to action. Often have we *known* that a certain line of action was right, but failed to follow it because feeling led in a different direction? When decision has been hanging in the balance we have piled on one side obligation, duty, sense of right, and a dozen other reasons for action, only to have them all outweighed by the one single: *It is disagreeable.* Judgment, reason, and experience may unite to tell us that a contemplated course is unwise, and imagination may reveal to us its disastrous consequences, and yet its pleasures so appeal to us that we yield. Our feelings often prove a stronger motive than knowledge and will combined; they are a factor constantly to be reckoned with among our motives.

1. THE NATURE OF FEELING

It will be our purpose in the next few chapters to study the *affective* content of consciousness—the feelings and emotions. The present chapter will be devoted to the feelings and the one that follows to the emotions.

The Different Feeling Qualities: At least six (some writers say even more) distinct and qualitatively different feeling states are easily distinguished. These are: *pleasure*, *pain*; *desire*, *repugnance*; *interest*, *apathy*. Pleasure and pain, and desire and repugnance, are directly opposite or antagonistic feelings. Interest and apathy are not opposites in a similar way, since apathy is but the absence of interest, and not its antagonist. In place of the terms pleasure and pain, the *pleasant* and the *unpleasant*, or the *agreeable* and the *disagreeable*, are often used. *Aversion* is frequently employed as a synonym for repugnance.

It is somewhat hard to believe on first thought that feeling comprises but the classes given. For have we not often felt the pain from a toothache, from not being able to take a long-planned trip, from the loss of a dear friend? Surely these are very different classes of feelings! Likewise we have been happy from the very joy of living, from being praised for some well doing, or from the presence of friend or lover. And here again we seem to have widely different classes of feelings.

We must remember, however, that feeling is always based on something *known*. It never appears alone in consciousness as *mere* pleasures or pains. The mind must have something about which to feel. The "what" must precede the "how."? What we commonly call a feeling *is a complex state of consciousness in which feeling predominates*, but which has, nevertheless, *a basis of sensation, or memory, or some other cognitive process*. And what so greatly vary in the different cases of the illustrations just given are precisely this knowledge element, and not the feeling element. A feeling of unpleasantness is a feeling of unpleasantness whether it comes from an aching tooth or from the loss of a friend. It may differ in degree, and the entire mental states of which the feeling is a part may differ vastly, but the simple feeling itself is of the same quality.

Feeling Always Present in Mental Content: No phase of our mental life is without the feeling element. We look at the rainbow with its beautiful and harmonious blending of colors, and a feeling of pleasure accompanies the sensation; then we turn and gaze at the glaring sun, and a disagreeable feeling is the result. A strong feeling of pleasantness accompanies the experience of the voluptuous warmth of a cozy bed on a cold morning, but the plunge between the icy sheets on the preceding evening was accompanied by the opposite feeling. The touch of a hand may occasion a thrill of ecstatic pleasure, or it may be accompanied by a feeling equally disagreeable. And so on through the whole range of sensation; we not only *know* the various objects about us through sensation and perception, but we also *feel* while we know. Cognition, or the knowing processes, gives us our "whats"; and feeling, or the affective processes, gives us our "hows." What is yonder object? A bouquet. How does it affect you? Pleasurably.

If, instead of the simpler sensory processes, which we have just considered, we take the more complex processes, such as memory, imagination, and thinking, the case is no different.

Who has not reveled in the pleasure accompanying the memories of past joys? On the other hand, who is free from all unpleasant memories—from regrets, from pangs of remorse? Who has not dreamed away an hour in pleasant anticipation of some desired object, or spent a miserable hour in dreading some calamity which imagination pictured to him? Feeling also accompanies our thought processes. Everyone has experienced the feeling of the pleasure of intellectual victory over some difficult problem, which had baffled the reason, or over some doubtful case in which our judgment proved correct. And likewise none has escaped the feeling of unpleasantness, which accompanies intellectual defeat. Whatever the contents of our mental stream, "we find in them, everywhere present, a certain color of passing estimate, an immediate sense that they are worth something to us at any given moment, or that they then have an interest to us."

The Seeming Neutral Feeling Zone: It is probable that there is so little feeling connected with many of the humdrum and habitual experiences of our everyday lives, that we are but slightly, if at all, aware of a feeling state in connection with them. Yet a state of consciousness with absolutely no feeling side to it is as unthinkable as the obverse side of a coin without the reverse. Some sort of feeling tone or mood is always present. The width of the affective neutral zone—that is, of a feeling state so little marked as not to be discriminated as either pleasure or pain, desire or aversion—varies with different persons, and with the same person at different times. It is conditioned largely by the amount of attention given in the direction of feeling, and also on the fineness of the power of feeling discrimination. It is safe to say that the zero range is usually so small as to be negligible.

2. MOOD AND DISPOSITION

The sum total of all the feeling accompanying the various sensory and thought processes at any given time results in what we may call our *feeling tone, or mood.*

How Mood is Produced: During most of our waking hours, and, indeed, during our sleeping hours as well, a multitude of sensory currents are pouring into the cortical centers. At the present moment we can hear the rumble of a wagon, the chirp of a cricket, the chatter of distant voices, and a hundred other sounds besides. At the same time the eye is appealed to by an infinite variety of stimuli in light, color, and objects; the skin responds to many contacts and temperatures; and every other type of end organ of the body is acting as a "sender" to telegraph a message in to the brain. Add to these the powerful currents, which are constantly being sent to the cortex from the visceral organs—those of respiration, of circulation, of digestion and assimilation. And then finally add the central processes, which accompany the flight of images through our minds—our meditations, memories, and imaginations, our cogitations and volitions.

Thus we see what a complex our feelings must be, and how impossible to have any moment in which some feeling is not present as a part of our mental stream. It is this complex, now made up chiefly on the basis of the sensory currents coming in from the end-organs or the visceral organs, and now on the basis of those in the cortex connected with our thought life, which constitutes the entire feeling tone, or *mood.*

Mood Colors All Our Thinking: Mood depends on the character of the aggregate of nerve currents entering the cortex, and changes as the character of the current varies. If the currents run on much the same from hour to hour, then our mood is correspondingly constant; if the currents are variable, our mood also will be variable. Not only is mood dependent on our sensations and thoughts for its quality, but also it in turn colors our entire mental life. It serves as a background or setting whose hue is reflected over all our thinking. Let the mood be somber and dark, and the entire world looks gloomy; on the other hand, let the mood be bright and cheerful, and the world puts on a smile.

It is told of one of the early circuit riders among the New England ministry, that he made the following entries in his diary, thus well illustrating the point: "Wed. Eve. Arrived at the home of Bro. Brown late this evening, hungry and tired after a long day in the saddle. Had a bountiful supper of cold pork and beans, warm bread, bacon and eggs, coffee, and rich pastry. I go to rest feeling that my witness is clear; the future is bright; I feel called to a great and glorious work in this place. Bro. Brown's family is godly people." The next entry was as follows: "Thur. Morn. Awakened late this morning after a troubled night. I am very much depressed in soul; the way looks dark; far from feeling called to work among this people, I am beginning to doubt the safety of my own soul. I am afraid the desires of Bro. Brown and his family are set too much on carnal things." A dyspeptic is usually a pessimist, and an optimist always keeps a bright mood.

Mood Influences Our Judgments and Decisions: The prattle of children may be grateful music to our ears when we are in one mood, and excruciatingly discordant noise when we are in another. What appeals to us as a good practical joke one day, may seem a piece of unwarranted impertinence on another. A proposition which looks entirely plausible under the sanguine mood induced by a persuasive orator may appear wholly untenable a few hours later. Decisions, which seemed warranted when we were in an angry mood, often appear unwise or unjust when we have become calmer. Motives, which easily impel us to action when the world looks bright, fail to move us when the mood is somber. The feelings of impending peril and calamity, which are an inevitable accompaniment of the "blues," are speedily dissipated when the sun breaks through the clouds and we are ourselves again.

Mood Influences Effort: A bright and hopeful mood quickens every power and enhances every effort, while a hopeless mood limits power and cripples effort. The football team, which goes into the game, discouraged never plays to the limit. The student who attacks his lesson under the conviction of defeat can hardly hope to succeed, while the one who enters upon his work confident of his power to master it has the battle already half won. The world's best work is done not by those who live in the shadow of discouragement and doubt, but by those in whose breast hope springs eternal. The optimist is a benefactor of the race if for no other reason than the sheer contagion of his hopeful spirit; the pessimist contributes neither to the world's welfare nor its happiness. Youth's proverbial enthusiasm and dauntless energy rest upon the supreme hopefulness, which characterizes the mood of the young. For these reasons, if for no other, the mood of the schoolroom should be one of happiness and good cheer.

Disposition a Resultant of Moods.—The sum total of our moods gives us our *disposition.* Whether these are pleasant or unpleasant, cheerful or gloomy will depend on the predominating character of the moods which enter into them. As well expect to gather grapes of thorns or figs of thistles, as to secure a desirable disposition out of undesirable moods. A sunny disposition never comes from gloomy moods, or a hopeful one out of the "blues." And it is our disposition, more than the power of our reason, which, after all, determines our desirability as friends and companions.

The person of surly disposition can hardly make a desirable companion, no matter what his intellectual qualities may be. We may live very happily with one who cannot follow the reasoning of a Newton, but it is hard to live with a person chronically subject to "black moods." Nor can we put the responsibility for our disposition off on our ancestors. It is not an inheritance, but a growth. Slowly, day-by-day, and mood-by-mood, we build up our disposition until finally it comes to characterize us.

Temperament: Some are, however, more predisposed to certain types of mood than are others. The organization of our nervous system, which we get through heredity undoubtedly, has much to do with the feeling tone into which we most easily fall. We call this predisposition *temperament.* On the effects of temperament, our ancestors must divide the responsibility with us. I say *divide* the responsibility, for even if we find ourselves predisposed toward a certain undesirable type of moods, there is no reason why we should give up to them. Even in spite of hereditary predispositions, we can still largely determine for ourselves what our moods are to be.

If we have a tendency toward cheerful, quiet, and optimistic moods, the psychologist names our temperament the *sanguine*; if we are tense, easily excited and irritable, with a tendency toward sullen or angry moods, the *choleric*; if we are given to frequent fits of the "blues," if we usually look on the dark side of things and have a tendency toward moods of discouragement and the "dumps," the *melancholic*; if hard to rouse, and given to indolent and indifferent moods, the *phlegmatic*. Whatever be our temperament, it is one of the most important factors in our character.

3. PERMANENT FEELING ATTITUDES, OR SENTIMENTS

Besides the more or less transitory feeling states which we have called moods, there exists also a class of feeling attitudes, which contain more of the complex intellectual element, are withal of rather a higher nature, and much more permanent than our moods. We may call these our *sentiments*, or *attitudes*. Our sentiments comprise the somewhat constant level of feeling combined with cognition, which we name *sympathy*, *friendship*, *love*, *patriotism*, *religious faith*, *selfishness*, *pride*, *vanity*, *etc.* Like our dispositions, our sentiments are a growth of months and years. Unlike our dispositions, however, our sentiments are relatively independent of the physiological undertone, and depend more largely upon long-continued experience and intellectual elements as a basis. A sluggish liver might throw us into an irritable mood and, if the condition were long continued, might result in a surly disposition; but it would hardly permanently destroy one's patriotism and make him turn traitor to his country. One's feeling attitude on such matters is too deep seated to be modified by changing whims.

How Sentiments Develop: Sentiments have their beginning in concrete experiences in which feeling is a predominant element, and grow through the multiplication of these experiences much as the concept is developed through many percepts. There is a residual element left behind each separate experience in both cases. In the case of the concept the residual element is intellectual, and in the case of the sentiment it is a complex in which the feeling element is predominant.

How this comes about is easily seen by means of an illustration or two. The mother feeds her child when he is hungry, and an agreeable feeling is produced; she puts him into the bath and snuggles him in her arms, and the experiences are pleasant. The child comes to look upon the mother as one whose especial function is to make things pleasant for him, so he comes to be happy in her presence, and long for her in her absence. He finally grows to love his mother not alone for the countless times she has given him pleasure, but for what she herself is. The feelings connected at first wholly with pleasant experiences coming through the ministrations of the mother, strengthened no doubt by instinctive tendencies toward affection, and later enhanced by a fuller realization of what a mother's care and sacrifice mean, grow at last into a deep, forceful, abiding sentiment of love for the mother.

The Effect of Experience: Likewise with the sentiment of patriotism. In so far as our patriotism is a true patriotism and not a noisy clamor, it had its rise in feelings of gratitude and love when we contemplated the deeds of heroism and sacrifice for the flag, and the blessings, which come to us from our relations as citizens to our country. If we have had concrete cases brought to our experience, as, for example, our property saved from destruction at the hands of a mob or our lives saved from a hostile foreign foe, the patriotic sentiment will be all the stronger.

So we may carry the illustration into all the sentiments. Our religious sentiments of adoration, love, and faith have their origin in our belief in the care, love, and support from a higher Being typified to us as children by the care, love, and support of our parents. Pride arises from the appreciation or over-appreciation of oneself, his attainments, or his belongings. Selfishness has its genesis in the many instances in which pleasure results from ministering to self. In all these cases it is seen that our sentiments develop out of our experiences: they are the permanent but ever-growing results which we have to show for experiences which are somewhat long continued, and in which a certain feeling quality is a strong accompaniment of the cognitive part of the experience.

The Influence of Sentiment: Our sentiments, like our dispositions, are not only a natural growth from the experiences upon which they are fed, but they in turn have large influence in determining the direction of our further development. Our sentiments furnish the soil, which is either favorable or hostile to the growth of new experiences. One in whom the sentiment of true patriotism is deep-rooted will find it much harder to respond to a suggestion to betray his country's honor on battlefield, in legislative hall, or in private life, than one lacking in this sentiment. The boy who has a strong sentiment of love for his mother will find this a restraining influence in the face of temptation to commit deeds, which would wound her feelings. A deep and abiding faith in God is fatal to the growth of pessimism, distrust, and a self-centered life. One's sentiments are a safe gauge of his character. Let us know a man's attitude or sentiments on religion, morality, friendship, honesty, and the other great questions of life, and little remains to be known. If he is right on these, he may well be trusted in other things; if he is wrong on these, there is little to build upon.

Literature has drawn its best inspiration and choicest themes from the field of our sentiments. The sentiment of friendship has given us our David and Jonathan, our Damon and Pythias, and our Tennyson and Hallam. The sentiment of love has inspired countless masterpieces; without its aid most of our fiction would lose its plot, and most of our poetry its charm. Religious sentiment inspired Milton to write the world's greatest epic, "Paradise Lost." The sentiment of patriotism has furnished an inexhaustible theme for the writer and the orator. Likewise if we go into the field of music and art, we find that the best efforts of the masters are clustered around some human sentiment which has appealed to them, and which they have immortalized by expressing it on canvas or in marble, that it may appeal to others and cause the sentiment to grow in us.

Sentiments as Motives: The sentiments furnish the deepest, the most constant, and the most powerful motives which control our lives. Such sentiments as patriotism, liberty, and religion have called a thousand armies to struggle and die on ten thousand battlefields, and have given martyrs courage to suffer in the fires of persecution. Sentiments of friendship and love have prompted countless deeds of self-sacrifice and loving devotion. Sentiments of envy, pride, and jealousy have changed the boundary lines of nations, and have prompted the committing of ten thousand unnamable crimes. Slowly day by day from the cradle to the grave we are weaving into our lives the threads of sentiment, which at last become so many cables to bind us to good or evil.

4. PROBLEMS IN OBSERVATION AND INTROSPECTION

1. Are you subject to the "blues," or other forms of depressed feeling? Are your moods very changeable, or rather constant? What kind of a disposition do you think you have? How did you come by it; that is, in how far is it due to hereditary temperament, and in how far to your daily moods?

2. Can you recall an instance in which some undesirable mood was caused by your physical condition? By some disturbing mental condition? What is your characteristic mood in the morning after sleeping in an ill-ventilated room? After sitting for half a day in an ill-ventilated schoolroom? After eating indigestible food before going to bed?

3. Observe a number of children or your classmates closely and see whether you can determine the characteristic mood of each. Observe several different schools and see whether you can note a characteristic mood for each room. Try to determine the causes producing the differences noted. (Physical conditions in the room, personality of the teacher, methods of governing, teaching, etc.)

4. When can you do your best work, when you are happy, or unhappy? Cheerful, or "blue"? Confident and hopeful, or discouraged? In a spirit of harmony and cooperation with your teacher, or antagonistic? Now relate your conclusions to the type of atmosphere that should prevail in the schoolroom or the home. Formulate a statement as to why the "spirit" of the school is all-important. (Effect on effort, growth, disposition, sentiments, character, etc.)

5. Can you measure more or less accurately the extent to which your feelings serve as *motives* in your life? Are feelings alone a safe guide to action? Make a list of the important sentiments that should be cultivated in youth. Now show how the work of the school may be used to strengthen worthy sentiments.

CHAPTER XV
THE EMOTIONS

Feeling and emotion are not to be looked upon as two different *kinds* of mental processes. In fact, emotion is but *a feeling state of a high degree of intensity and complexity*. Emotion transcends the simpler feeling states whenever the exciting cause is sufficient to throw us out of our regular routine of affective experience. The distinction between emotion and feeling is a purely arbitrary one, since the difference is only one of complexity and degree, and many feelings may rise to the intensity of emotions. A feeling of sadness on hearing of a number of fatalities in a railway accident may suddenly become an emotion of grief if we learn that a member of our family is among those killed. A feeling of gladness may develop into an emotion of joy, or a feeling of resentment be kindled into an emotion of rage.

1. THE PRODUCING AND EXPRESSING OF EMOTION

Nowhere more than in connection with our emotions is the close inter-relations of mind and body seen. All are familiar with the fact that the emotion of anger tends to find expression in the blow, love in the caress, fear in flight, and so on. But just how our organism acts in *producing* an emotion is less generally understood. Professor James and Professor Lange have shown us that emotion not only tends to produce some characteristic form of response, but that *the emotion is itself caused by certain deep-seated physiological reactions*. Let us seek to understand this statement a little more fully.

Physiological Explanation of Emotion: We must remember first of all that *all* changes in mental states are accompanied by corresponding physiological changes. Hard, concentrated thinking quickens the heart beat; keen attention is accompanied by muscular tension; certain sights or sounds increase the rate of breathing; offensive odors produce nausea, and so on. So complete and perfect is the response of our physical organism to mental changes that one psychologist declares it possible, had we sufficiently delicate apparatus, to measure the reactions caused throughout the body of a sleeping child by the shadow from a passing cloud falling upon the closed eyelids.

The order of the entire event resulting in an emotion is as follows: (1) something is *known*; some object enters consciousness coming either from immediate perception or through memory or imagination. This fact, or thing known, must be of such nature that it will, (2) set up deep-seated and characteristic *organic response*; (3) the feeling *accompanying and caused by these physiological reactions constitutes the emotion*. For example, we may be passing along the street in a perfectly calm and equable state of mind, when we come upon a teamster who is brutally beating an exhausted horse because it is unable to draw an overloaded wagon up a slippery incline. The facts grasped as we take in the situation constitute the *first* element in an emotional response developing in our consciousness. But instantly our muscles begin to grow tense, the heart beat and breath quicken, the face takes on a different expression, the hands clench—the entire organism is reacting to the disturbing situation; the *second* factor in the rising emotion, the physiological response, thus appears. Along with our apprehension of the cruelty and the organic disturbances, which result, we feel waves of indignation and anger surging through us. This is the *third* factor in the emotional event, or the emotion itself. In some such way as this are all of our emotions aroused.

Origin of Characteristic Emotional Reactions: Why do certain facts or objects of consciousness always cause certain characteristic organic responses?

In order to solve this problem we shall have first to go beyond the individual and appeal to the history of the race. What the race has found serviceable, the individual repeats. But even then it is hard to see why the particular type of physical response such as shrinking, pallor, and trembling, which naturally follow stimuli threatening harm, should be the best. It is easy to see, however, that the feeling, which prompts to flight or serves to deter from harm's way might be useful. It is plain that there is an advantage in the tense muscle, the set teeth, the held breath, and the quickened pulse which accompany the emotion of anger, and also in the feeling of anger itself, which prompts to the conflict. But even if we are not able in every case to determine at this day why all the instinctive responses and their correlate of feeling were the best for the life of the race, we may be sure that such was the case; for Nature is inexorable in her dictates that only that shall persist which has proved serviceable in the largest number of cases.

An interesting question arises at this point as to why we feel emotion accompanying some of our motor responses, and not others. Perceptions are crowding in upon us hour after hour; memory, thought, and imagination are in constant play; and a continuous motor discharge results each moment in physical expressions great or small. Yet, in spite of these facts, feeling which is strong enough to rise to an emotion is only an occasional thing. If emotion accompanies any form of physical expression, why not all? Let us see whether we can discover any reason. One day I saw a boy leading a dog along the street. All at once the dog slipped the string over its head and ran away. The boy stood looking after the dog for a moment, and then burst into a fit of rage. What all had happened? The moment before the dog broke away everything was running smoothly in the experience of the boy. There was no obstruction to his thought or his plans. Then in an instant the situation changes. The smooth flow of experience is checked and baffled. The discharge of nerve currents which meant thought, plans, action, is blocked. A crisis has arisen which requires readjustment. The nerve currents must flow in new directions, giving new thought, new plans, new activities—the dog must be recaptured. It is in connection with this damming up of nerve currents from following their wonted channels that the emotion emerges. Or, putting it into mental terms, the emotion occurs when the ordinary current of our thought is violently disturbed—when we meet with some crisis which necessitates a readjustment of our thought relations and plans, either temporarily or permanently.

The Duration of an Emotion: If the required readjustment is but temporary, then the emotion is short-lived, while if the readjustment is necessarily of longer duration, the emotion also will live longer. The fear which follows the thunder is relatively brief; for the shock is gone in a moment, and our thought is but temporarily disturbed. If the impending danger is one that persists, however, as of some secret assassin threatening our life, the fear also will persist. The grief of a child over the loss of someone dear to him is comparatively short, because the current of the child's life has not been so closely bound up in a complexity of experiences with the lost object as in the case of an older person, and hence the readjustment is easier. The grief of an adult over the loss of a very dear friend lasts long, for the object grieved over has so become a part of the bereaved one's experience that the loss requires a very complete readjustment of the whole life. In either case, however, as this readjustment is accomplished the emotion gradually fades away.

Emotions Accompanying Crises in Experience: If our description of the feelings has been correct, it will be seen that the simpler and milder feelings are for the common run of our everyday experience; they are the common values of our thought and acts from hour to hour. The emotions, or more intense feeling states, are, however, the occasional high tide of feeling, which occurs in crises or emergencies. We are angry on some particular provocation, we fear some extraordinary factor in our environment, we are joyful over some unusual good fortune.

2. THE CONTROL OF EMOTIONS

Dependence on Expression: Since all emotions rest upon some form of physical or physiological expression primarily, and upon some thought back of this secondarily, it follows that the first step in controlling an emotion is to secure *the removal of the state of consciousness* which serves as its basis. This may be done, for instance, with a child, either by banishing the terrifying dog from his presence, or by convincing him that the dog is harmless. The motor response will then cease, and the emotion pass away. If the thought is persistent, however, through the continuance of its stimulus, then what remains is to seek to control the physical expression, and in that way suppress the emotion. If, instead of the knit brow, the tense muscles, the quickened heart beat, and all the deeper organic changes which go along with these, we can keep a smile on the face, the muscles relaxed, the heart beat steady, and a normal condition in all the other organs, we shall have no cause to fear an explosion of anger. If we are afraid of mice and feel an almost irresistible tendency to mount a chair every time we see a mouse, we can do wonders in suppressing the fear by resolutely refusing to give expression to these tendencies. Inhibition of the expression inevitably means the death of the emotion.

This fact has its bad side as well as its good in the feeling life, for it means that good emotions as well as bad will fade out if we fail to allow them expression. We are all perfectly familiar with the fact in our own experience that an interest which does not find means of expression soon passes away. Sympathy unexpressed ere long passes over into indifference. Even love cannot live without expression. Religious emotion which does not go out in deeds of service cannot persist. The natural end and aim of our emotions is to serve as motives to activity; and missing this opportunity, they have not only failed in their office, but will themselves die of inaction.

Relief through Expression: Emotional states not only have their rise in organic reactions, but they also tend to result in acts. When we are angry, or in love, or in fear, we have the impulse *to do something about it.* And, while it is true that suppressing the physical expressions on which it is founded may inhibit emotion, so may some forms of expression relieve a state of emotional tension. None have failed to experience the relief, which comes to the overcharged nervous system from a good cry. There is no sorrow so bitter as a dry sorrow, when one cannot weep. An explosion of some kind relieves a state of anger or annoyance, whether in a blow or its equivalent in speech. We often feel better when we have told a man "what we think of him."

At first glance this all seems opposed to what we have been laying down as the explanation of emotion. Yet it is not so if we look well into the case. We have already seen that emotion occurs when there is a blocking of the usual pathways of discharge for the nerve currents, which must then seek new outlets, and thus result in the setting up of new motor responses. In the case of grief, for example, there is a disturbance in the whole organism; the heart beat is deranged, the blood pressure diminished, and the nerve tone lowered. What is needed is for the currents, which are finding an outlet in directions resulting in these particular responses to find a pathway of discharge, which will not produce such deep-seated results. This may be found in crying. The energy thus expended is diverted from producing internal disturbances. Likewise, the explosion in anger may serve to restore the equilibrium of disturbed nerve currents.

Relief Does Not Follow if Image is Held Before the Mind: All this is true, however, only when the expression does not serve to keep the idea before the mind which was originally responsible for the emotion. A person may work himself into a passion of anger by beginning to talk about an insult and, as he grows increasingly violent, bringing the situation more and more sharply into his consciousness. The effect of terrifying images is easily to be observed in the case of one's starting to run when he is afraid after night. There is probably no doubt that the running would relieve his fear providing he could do it and not picture the threatening something as pursuing him. But, with his imagination conjuring up dire images of frightful catastrophes at every step, all control is lost and fresh waves of terror surge over the shrinking soul.

Growing Tendency toward Emotional Control: Among civilized peoples there is a constantly growing tendency toward emotional control. Primitive races express grief, joy, fear, or anger much more freely than do civilized races. This does not mean that primitive man feels more deeply than civilized man; for, as we have already seen, the crying, laughing, or blustering is but a small part of the whole physical expression, and one's entire organism may be stirred to its depths without any of these outward manifestations. Man has found it advisable as he has advanced in civilization not to reveal all he feels to those around him. The face, which is the most expressive part of the body, has come to be under such perfect control that it is hard to read through it the emotional state, although the face of civilized man is capable of expressing far more than is that of the savage. The same difference is observable between the child and the adult. The child reveals each passing shade of emotion through his expression, while the adult may feel much that he does not show.

3. CULTIVATION OF THE EMOTIONS

There is no other mental factor, which has more to do with the enjoyment we get out of life than our feelings and emotions.

The Emotions and Enjoyment: Few of us would care to live at all, if all feeling were eliminated from human experience. True, feeling often makes us suffer; but in so far as life's joys triumph over its woes, do our feelings minister to our enjoyment. Without sympathy, love, and appreciation, life would be barren indeed. Moreover, it is only through our own emotional experience that we are able to interpret the feeling side of the lives about us. Failing in this, we miss one of the most significant phases of social experience, and are left with our own sympathies undeveloped and our life by so much impoverished.

The interpretation of the subtler emotions of those about us is in no small degree an art. The human face and form present a constantly changing panorama of the soul's feeling states to those who can read their signs. The ability to read the finer feelings, which reveal themselves in expression too delicate to be read by the eye of the gross or unsympathetic observer, lies at the basis of all fine interpretation of personality. Feelings are often too deep for outward expression, and we are slow to reveal our deepest selves to those who cannot appreciate and understand them.

How Emotions Develop: Emotions are to be cultivated as the intellect or the muscles are to be cultivated; namely, through proper exercise. Our thought is to dwell on those things to which proper emotions attach, and to shun lines, which would suggest emotions of an undesirable type.

Emotions, which are to be developed must, as has already been said, find expression; we must act in response to their leadings, else they become but idle vaporings. If love prompts us to say a kind word to a suffering fellow mortal, the word must be spoken or the feeling itself fades away. On the other hand, the emotions, which we wish to suppress, are to be refused expression. The unkind and cutting word is to be left unsaid when we are angry, and the fear of things, which are harmless, left, unexpressed and thereby doomed to die.

The Emotional Factor in Our Environment: Much material for the cultivation of our emotions lies in the everyday life all about us if we can but interpret it. Few indeed of those whom we meet daily but are hungering for appreciation and sympathy. Lovable traits exist in every character, and will reveal themselves to the one who looks for them. Miscarriages of justice abound on all sides, and demand our indignation and wrath and the effort to right the wrong. Evil always exists to be hated and suppressed, and dangers to be feared and avoided. Human life and the movement of human affairs constantly appeal to the feeling side of our nature if we understand at all what life and action mean.

A certain blindness exists in many people, however, which makes our own little joys, or sorrows, or fears the most remarkable ones in the world, and keeps us from realizing that others may feel as deeply as we. Of course this self-centered attitude of mind is fatal to any true cultivation of the emotions. It leads to an emotional life which lacks not only breadth and depth, but also perspective.

Literature and the Cultivation of the Emotions: In order to increase our facility in the interpretation of the emotions through teaching us what to look for in life and experience, we may go to literature. Here we find life interpreted for us in the ideal by masters of interpretation; and, looking through their eyes, we see new depths and breadths of feeling which we had never before discovered. Indeed, literature deals far more in the aggregate with the feeling side than with any other aspect of human life. And it is just this, which makes literature a universal language, for the language of our emotions is more easily interpreted than that of our reason. The smile, the cry, the laugh, the frown, the caress, is understood all around the world among all peoples. They are universal.

There is always this danger to be avoided, however. We may become so taken up with the overwrought descriptions of the emotions as found in literature or on the stage that the common humdrum of everyday life around us seems flat and stale. The interpretation of the writer or the actor is far beyond what we are able to make for ourselves, so we take their interpretation rather than trouble ourselves to look in our own environment for the material, which might appeal to our emotions. It is not rare to find those who easily weep over the woes of an imaginary person in a book or on the stage unable to feel sympathy for the real suffering which exists all around them. The story is told of a lady at the theater who wept over the suffering of the hero in the play; and at the moment she was shedding the unnecessary tears, her own coachman, whom she had compelled to wait for her in the street, was frozen to death. Our seemingly prosaic environment is full of suggestions to the emotional life, and books and plays should only help to develop in us the power rightly to respond to these suggestions.

Harm in Emotional Overexcitement: Danger may exist also in still another line; namely, that of emotional overexcitement. There is a great nervous strain in high emotional tension. Nothing is more exhausting than a severe fit of anger; it leaves its victim weak and limp. A severe case of fright often incapacitates one for mental or physical labor for hours, or it may even result in permanent injury. The whole nervous tone is distinctly lowered by sorrow, and even excessive joy may be harmful.

In our actual, everyday life, there is little danger from emotional overexcitement unless it is in the case of fear in children, as was shown in the discussion on instincts, and in that of grief over the loss of objects that are dear to us. Most of our childish fears we could just as well avoid if our elders were wiser in the matter of guarding us against those that are unnecessary. The griefs we cannot hope to escape, although we can do much to control them. Long-continued emotional excitement, unless it is followed by corresponding activity, gives us those who weep over the wrongs of humanity, but never do anything to right them; who are sorry to the point of death over human suffering, but cannot be induced to lend their aid to its alleviation. We could very well spare a thousand of those in the world who merely feel, for one who acts, James tells us.

We should watch, then, that our good feelings do not simply evaporate as feelings, but that they find some place to apply themselves to accomplish good; that we do not, like Hamlet, rave over wrongs which need to be righted, but never bring ourselves to the point where we take a hand in their righting. If our emotional life is to be rich and deep in its feeling and effective in its results on our acts and character, it must find its outlet in deeds.

4. EMOTIONS AS MOTIVES

Emotion is always dynamic, and our feelings constitute our strongest motives to action and achievement.

How Our Emotions Compel Us: Love has often done in the reformation of a fallen life what strength of will was not able to accomplish; it has caused dynasties to fall, and has changed the map of nations. Hatred is a motive hardly less strong. Fear will make savage beasts out of men who fall under its sway, causing them to trample helpless women and children under feet, whom in their saner moments they would protect with their lives. Anger puts out all the light of reason, and prompts peaceful and well-meaning men to commit murderous acts.

Thus feeling, from the faintest and simplest feeling of interest, the various ranges of pleasures and pain, the sentiments which underlie all our lives, and so on to the mighty emotions which grip our lives with an overpowering strength, constitutes a large part of the motive power which is constantly urging us on to do and dare. Hence it is important from this standpoint, also, that we should have the right type of feelings and emotions well developed, and the undesirable ones eliminated.

Emotional Habits: Emotion and feeling are partly matters of habit. That is, we can form emotional as well as other habits, and they are as hard to break. Anger allowed to run uncontrolled leads into habits of angry outbursts, while the one who habitually controls his temper finds it submitting to the habit of remaining within bounds. One may cultivate the habit of showing his fear on all occasions, or of discouraging its expression. He may form the habit of jealousy or of confidence. It is possible even to form the habit of falling in love, or of so suppressing the tender emotions that love finds little opportunity for expression.

And here, as elsewhere, habits are formed through performing the acts upon which the habit rests. If there are emotional habits we are desirous of forming, what we have to do is to indulge the emotional expression of the type we desire, and the habit will follow. If we wish to form the habit of living in a chronic state of the blues, then all we have to do is to be blue and act blue sufficiently, and this form of emotional expression will become a part of us. If we desire to form the habit of living in a happy, cheerful state, we can accomplish this by encouraging the corresponding expression.

5. PROBLEMS IN OBSERVATION AND INTROSPECTION

1. What are the characteristic bodily expressions by which you can recognize a state of anger? Fear? Jealousy? Hatred? Love? Grief? Do you know persons who are inclined to be too expressive emotionally? Who show too little emotional expression? How would you classify yourself in this respect?

2. Are you naturally responsive to the emotional tone of others; that is, are you sympathetic? Are you easily affected by reading emotional books? By emotional plays or other appeals? What is the danger from overexciting the emotions without giving them a proper outlet in some practical activity?

3. Have you observed a tendency among adults not to take seriously the emotions of a child; for example, to look upon childish grief as trivial, or fear as something to be laughed at? Is the child's emotional life as real as that of the adult? (See Ch. IX, Betts, "Fathers and Mothers.")

4. Have you known children to repress their emotions for fear of being laughed at? Have you known parents or others to remark about childish love affairs to the children themselves in a light or joking way? Ought this ever to be done?

5. Note certain children who give way to fits of anger; what is the remedy? Note other children who cry readily; what would you suggest as a cure? (Why should ridicule not be used?)

6. Have you observed any teacher using the lesson in literature or history to cultivate the finer emotions? What emotions have you seen appealed to by a lesson in nature study? What emotions have you observed on the playground that needed restraint? Do you think that on the whole the emotional life of the child receives enough consideration in the school? In the home?

CHAPTER XVI
INTEREST

The feeling that we call interest is so important a motive in our lives and so colors our acts and gives direction to our endeavors that we will do well to devote a chapter to its discussion.

1. THE NATURE OF INTEREST

We saw in an earlier chapter that personal habits have their rise in race habits or instincts. Let us now see how interest helps the individual to select from his instinctive acts those, which are useful to build into personal habits. Instinct impartially starts the child in the performance of many different activities, but does not dictate what particular acts shall be retained to serve as the basis for habits. Interest comes in at this point and says, "This act is of more value than that act; continue this act and drop that." Instinct prompts the babe to countless movements of body and limb. Interest picks out those that are most vitally connected with the welfare of the organism, and the child comes to prefer these rather than the others. Thus it is that out of the random movements of arms and legs and head and body we finally develop the coordinated activities, which are infinitely more useful than the random ones were. And these activities, originating in instincts, and selected by interest, are soon crystallized into habits.

Interest a Selective Agent: The same truth holds for mental activities as for physical. A thousand channels lie open for your stream of thought at this moment, but your interest has beckoned it into the one particular channel which, for the time, at least, appears to be of the greatest subjective value; and it is now following that channel unless your will has compelled it to leave that for another. Your thinking as naturally follows your interest as the needle does the magnet, hence your thought activities are conditioned largely by your interests. This is equivalent to saying that your mental habits rest back finally upon your interests.

Everyone knows what it is to be interested; but interest, like other elementary states of consciousness, cannot be rigidly defined. (1) Subjectively considered, interest may be looked upon as *a feeling attitude, which assigns our activities their place in a subjective scale of values*, and hence selects among them. (2) Objectively considered, an interest is *the object, which calls forth the feeling*. (3) Functionally considered, interest is *the dynamic phase of consciousness*.

Interest Supplies a Subjective Scale of Values: If you are interested in driving a horse rather than in riding a bicycle, it is because the former has a greater subjective value to you than the latter. If you are interested in reading these words instead of thinking about the next social function or the last picnic party, it is because at this moment the thought suggested appeals to you as of more value than the other lines of thought. From this it follows that your standards of values are revealed in the character of your interests. The young man who is interested in the race track, in gaming, and in low resorts confesses by the fact that these things occupy a high place among the things which appeal to him as subjectively valuable. The mother whose interests are chiefly in clubs and other social organizations places these higher in her scale of values than her home. The reader who can become interested only in light, trashy literature must admit that matter of this type ranks higher in his subjective scale of values than the works of the masters. Teachers and students whose strongest interest is in grade marks value these more highly than true attainment. For, whatever may be our claims or assertions, interest is finally an infallible barometer of the values we assign to our activities.

In the case of some of our feelings it is not always possible to ascribe an objective side to them. An unanalyzable complex of causes may produce a feeling of ennui, of impending evil, or of bounding vivacity. But interest, while it is related primarily to the activities of the self, is carried over from the activity to the object, which occasions the activity. That is, interest has both an objective and a subjective side. On the subjective side a certain activity connected with self-expression is worth so much; on the objective side a certain object is worth so much as related to this self-expression. Thus we say, I have an interest in books or in business; my daily activities, my self-expression, are governed with reference to these objects. They are my interests.

Interest Dynamic: Many of our milder feelings terminate within ourselves, never attaining sufficient force as motives to impel us to action. Not so with interest. Its very nature is dynamic. Whatever it seizes upon becomes *ipso facto* an object for some activity, for some form of expression of the self. Are we interested in a new book, we must read it; in a new invention, we must see it, handle it, test it; in some vocation or avocation, we must pursue it. Interest is impulsive. It gives its possessor no opportunity for lethargic rest and quiet, but constantly urges him to action. Grown ardent, interest becomes enthusiasm, "without which," says Emerson, "nothing great was ever accomplished." Are we an Edison, with a strong interest centered in mechanical invention, it will drive us day and night in a ceaseless activity which scarcely gives us time for food and sleep. Are we a Lincoln, with an undying interest in the Union, this motive will make possible superhuman efforts for the accomplishment of our end. Are we man or woman anywhere, in any walk of life, so we are dominated by mighty interests grown into enthusiasm for some object, we shall find great purposes growing within us, and our life will be one of activity and achievement. On the contrary, a life, which has developed no great interest, lacks motive power. Of necessity such a life must be devoid of purpose and hence barren of results, counting little while it is being lived, and little missed by the world when it is gone.

Habit Antagonistic to Interest: While, as we have seen, interest is necessary to the formation of habits, yet habits once formed are antagonistic to interest. That is, acts, which are so habitually performed that they "do themselves", are accompanied by a minimum of interest. They come to be done without attentive consciousness, hence interest cannot attach to their performance. Many of the activities, which make up the daily round of our lives, are of this kind. As long as habit is being modified in some degree, as long as we are improving in our ways of doing things, interest will still cling to the process; but let us once settle into an unmodified rut, and interest quickly fades away. We then have the conditions present, which make of us either a machine or a drudge.

2. DIRECT AND INDIRECT INTEREST

We may have an interest either (1) in the doing of an act, or (2) in the end sought through the doing. In the first instance we call the interest *immediate* or *direct*; in the second instance, *mediate* or *indirect*.

Interest in the End versus Interest in the Activity: If we do not find an interest in the doing of our work, or if it has become positively disagreeable so that we loathe its performance, then there must be some ultimate end for which the task is being performed, and in which there is a strong interest, else the whole process will be the varies drudgery. If the end is sufficiently interesting it may serve to throw a halo of interest over the whole process connected with it. The following instance illustrates this fact:

His father told a twelve-year-old boy that if he would make the body of an automobile at his bench in the manual training school, the father would purchase the running gear for it and give the machine to the boy. In order to secure the coveted prize, the boy had to master the arithmetic necessary for making the calculations, and the drawing necessary for making the plans to scale before the teacher in manual training would allow him to take up the work of construction. The boy had always lacked interest in both arithmetic and drawing, and consequently was dull in them. Under the new incentive, however, he took hold of them with such avidity that he soon surpassed all the remainder of the class, and was able to make his calculations and drawings within a term. He secured his automobile a few months later, and still retained his interest in arithmetic and drawing.

Indirect Interest as a Motive: Interest of the indirect type, which does not attach to the process, but comes from some more or less distant end, most of us find much less potent than interest, which is immediate. This is especially true unless the end be one of intense desire and not too distant. The assurance to a boy that he must get his lessons well because he will need to be an educated man ten years hence when he goes into business for himself does not compensate for the lack of interest in the lessons of today.

Yet it is necessary in the economy of life that both children and adults should learn to work under the incitement of indirect interests. Much of the work we do is for an end, which is more desirable than the work itself. It will always be necessary to sacrifice present pleasure for future good. Ability to work cheerfully for a somewhat distant end saves much of our work from becoming drudgery. If interest is removed from both the process and the end, no inducement is left to work except compulsion; and this, if continued, results in the lowest type of effort. It puts a man on a level with the beast of burden, which constantly shirks its work.

Indirect Interest Alone Insufficient: Interest coming from an end instead of inhering in the process may finally lead to an interest in the work itself; but if it does not, the worker is in danger of being left a drudge at last. To be more than a slave to his work one must ultimately find the work worth doing for its own sake. The man who performs his work solely because he has a wife and babies at home will never be an artist in his trade or profession; the student who masters a subject only because he must know it for an examination is not developing the traits of a scholar. The question of interest in the process makes the difference between the one who works because he loves to work and the one who toils because he must—it makes the difference between the artist and the drudge. The drudge does only what he must when he works, the artist all he can. The drudge longs for the end of labor, the artist for it to begin. The drudge studies how he may escape his labor, the artist how he may better his and ennoble it.

To labor when there is joy in the work is elevating, to labor under the lash of compulsion is degrading. It matters not so much what a man's occupation as how it is performed. A coachman driving his team down the crowded street better than anyone else could do it, and glorying in that fact, may be a true artist in his occupation, and be ennobled through his work. A statesman molding the affairs of a nation as no one else could do it, or a scholar leading the thought of his generation is subject to the same law; in order to give the best grade of service of which he is capable, man must find a joy in the performance of the work as well as in the end sought through its performance. No matter how high the position or how refined the work, the worker becomes a slave to his labor unless interest in its performance saves him.

3. TRANSITORINESS OF CERTAIN INTERESTS

Since our interests are always connected with our activities it follows that many interests will have their birth, grow to full strength, and then fade away as the corresponding instincts, which are responsible for, the activities pass through these same stages. This only means that interest in play develops at the time when the play activities are seeking expression; that interest in the opposite sex becomes strong when instinctive tendencies are directing the attention to the choice of a mate; and that interest in abstract studies comes when the development of the brain enables us to carry on logical trains of thought. All of us can recall many interests, which were once strong, and are now weak or else have altogether passed away. Hide-and-seek, Pussy-wants-a-corner, excursions to the little fishing pond, securing the colored chromo at school, the care of pets, reading blood-and-thunder stories or sentimental ones—interest in these things belongs to our past, or has left but a faint shadow. Other interests have come, and these in turn will also disappear and other new ones yet appear as long as we keep on acquiring new experience.

Interests Must Be Utilized When They Appear: This means that we must take advantage of interests when they appear if we wish to utilize and develop them. How many people there are who at one time felt an interest impelling them to cultivate their taste for music, art, or literature and said they would do this at some convenient season, and finally found themselves without a taste for these things! How many of us have felt an interest in some benevolent work, but at last discovered that our inclination had died before we found time to help the cause! How many of us, young as we are, do not at this moment lament the passing of some interest from our lives, or are now watching the dying of some interest which we had fondly supposed was as stable as Gibraltar? The drawings of every interest, which appeals to us are a voice crying, "Now are the appointed time!" What impulse urges us today to become or to do, we must begin at once to be or perform, if we would attain to the coveted end.

The Value of a Strong Interest: Nor are we to look upon these transitory interests as useless. They come to us not only as a race heritage, but they impel us to activities which are immediately useful, or else prepare us for the later battles of life. But even aside from this important fact it is worth everything just to be interested. For it is only through the impulsion of interest that we first learn to put forth effort in any true sense of the word, and interest furnishes the final foundation upon which volition rests. Without interest the greatest powers may slumber in us unawakened, and abilities capable of the highest attainment rest satisfied with commonplace mediocrity. No one will ever know how many Gladstones and Leibnitzes the world has lost simply because their interests were never appealed to in such a way as to start them on the road to achievement. It matters less what the interest be, so it be not bad, than that there shall be some great interest to compel endeavor, test the strength of endurance, and lead to habits of achievement.

4. SELECTION AMONG OUR INTERESTS

I said early in the discussion that interest is selective among our activities, picking out those, which appear to be of the most value to us. In the same manner there must be a selection among our interests themselves.

The Mistake of Following Too Many Interests: It is possible for us to become interested in so many lines of activity that we do none of them well. This leads to a life so full of hurry and stress that we forget life in our busy living. Says James with respect to the necessity of making a choice among our interests:

> "With most objects of desire, physical nature restricts our choice to but one of many represented goods, and even so it is here. I am often confronted by the necessity of standing by one of my empirical selves and relinquishing the rest. Not

that I would not, if I could, be both handsome and fat, and well dressed, and a great athlete, and make a million a year; be a wit, a bon vivant, and a lady-killer, as well as a philosopher; a philanthropist, statesman, warrior, and African explorer, as well as a 'tone poet' and saint. But the thing is simply impossible. The millionaire's work would run counter to the saint's; the bon vivant and the philosopher and the lady-killer could not well keep house in the same tenement of clay. Such different characters may conceivably at the outset of life be alike possible to man. But to make any one of them actual, the rest must more or less be suppressed. The seeker of his truest, strongest, deepest self must review the list carefully, and pick out the one on which to stake his salvation."

Interests May Be Too Narrow: On the other hand, it is just as possible for our interests to be too narrow as too broad. The one who has cultivated no interests outside of his daily round of humdrum activities does not get enough out of life. It is possible to become so engrossed with making a living that we forget to live—to become so habituated to some narrow treadmill of labor with the limited field of thought suggested by its environment, that we miss the richest experiences of life. Many there are who live a barren, trivial, and self-centered life because they fail to see the significant and the beautiful which lie just beyond where their interests reach! Many there are so taken up with their own petty troubles that they have no heart or sympathy for fellow humanity! Many there are so absorbed with their own little achievements that they fail to catch step with the progress of the age!

Specialization Should Not Come Too Early: It is not well to specialize too early in our interests. We miss too many rich fields, which lie ready for the harvesting, and whose gleaning would enrich our lives. The student who is so buried in books that he has no time for athletic recreations or social diversions is making a mistake equally with the one who is so enthusiastic an athlete and social devotee that he neglects his studies. Likewise, the youth who is so taken up with the study of one particular line that he applies himself to this at the expense of all other lines is inviting a distorted growth. Youth is the time for pushing the skyline back on all sides; it is the time for cultivating diverse and varied lines of interests if we would grow into a rich experience in our later lives. The physical must be developed, but not at the expense of the mental, and vice versa. The social must not be neglected, but it must not be indulged to such an extent that other interests suffer. Interest in amusements and recreations should be cultivated, but these should never run counter to the moral and religious.

Specialization is necessary, but specialization in our interests should rest upon a broad field of fundamental interests, in order that the selection of the special line may be an intelligent one, and that our specialty shall not prove a rut in which we become so deeply buried that we are lost to the best in life.

A Proper Balance to Be Sought: It behooves us, then, to find a proper balance in cultivating our interests, making them neither too broad nor too narrow. We should deliberately seek to discover those which are strong enough to point the way to a life vocation, but this should not be done until we have had an opportunity to become acquainted with various lines of interests. Otherwise our decision in this important matter may be based merely on a whim.

We should also decide what interests we should cultivate for our own personal development and happiness, and for the service we are to render in a sphere outside our immediate vocation. We should consider avocations as well as vocations. Whatever interests are selected should be carried to efficiency. Better a reasonable number of carefully selected interests well developed and resulting in efficiency than a multitude of interests which lead us into so many fields that we can at best get but a smattering of each, and that by neglecting the things which should mean the most to us. Our interests should lead us to live what Wagner calls a "simple life," but not a narrow one.

5. INTEREST FUNDAMENTAL IN EDUCATION

Some educators have feared that in finding our occupations interesting, we shall lose all power of effort and self-direction; that the will, not being called sufficiently into requisition, must suffer from non-use; that we shall come to do the interesting and agreeable things well enough, but fail before the disagreeable.

Interest Not Antagonistic to Effort: The best development of the will does not come through our being forced to do acts in which there is absolutely no interest. Work done under compulsion never secures the full self in its performance. It is done mechanically and usually under such a spirit of rebellion on the part of the doer, that the advantage of such training may well be doubted. Nor are we safe in assuming that tasks done without interest as the motive are always performed under the direction of the will. It is far more likely that they are done under some external compulsion, and that the will has, after all, but very little to do with it. A boy may get an uninteresting lesson at school without much pressure from his will, providing he is sufficiently afraid of the master. In order that the will may receive training through compelling the performance of certain acts, it must have a reasonably free field, with external pressure removed. The compelling force must come from within,. and not from without.

On the other hand, there is not the least danger that we shall ever find a place in life where all the disagreeable is removed, and all phases of our work made smooth and interesting. The necessity will always be rising to call upon effort to take up the fight and hold us to duty where interest has failed. And it is just here that there must be no failure, else we shall be mere creatures of circumstance, drifting with every eddy in the tide of our life, and never able to breast the current. Interest is not to supplant the necessity for stern and strenuous endeavor but rather to call forth the largest measure of endeavor of which the self is capable. It is to put at work a larger amount of power than can be secured in any other way; in place of supplanting the will, it is to give it its point of departure and render its service all the more effective.

Interest and Character: Finally, we are not to forget that bad interests have the same propulsive power as good ones, and will lead to acts just as surely. And these acts will just as readily be formed into habits. It is worth noticing that back of the act lies an interest; in the act lies the seed of a habit; ahead of the act lies behavior, which grows into conduct, this into character, and character into destiny. Bad interests should be shunned and discouraged. But even that is not enough. Good interests must be installed in the place of the bad ones from which we wish to escape, for it is through substitution rather than suppression that we are able to break from the bad and adhere to the good.

Our interests are an evolution. Out of the simple interests of the child grow the more complex interests of the man. Lacking the opportunity to develop the interests of childhood, the man will come somewhat short of the full interests of manhood. The great thing, then, in educating a child is to discover the fundamental interests, which come to him from the race and, using these as a starting point, direct them into constantly broadening and more serviceable ones. Out of the early interest in play is to come the later interest in work; out of the early interest in collecting treasure boxes full of worthless trinkets and old scraps comes the later interest in earning and retaining ownership of property; out of the interest in chums and playmates come the larger social interests; out of interest in nature comes the interest of the naturalist. And so one by one we may examine the interests, which bear the largest fruit in our adult life, and we find that they all have their roots in some early interest of childhood, which was encouraged and given a chance to grow.

6. ORDER OF DEVELOPMENT OF OUR INTERESTS

The order in which our interests develop thus becomes an important question in our education. Nor is the order an arbitrary one, as might appear on first thought; for interest follows the invariable law of attaching to the activity for which the organism is at that time ready, and which it then needs in its further growth. That we are sometimes interested in harmful things does not disprove this assertion. The interest in its fundamental aspect is good, and but needs more healthful environment or more wise direction. While space forbids a full discussion of the genetic phase of interest here, yet we may profit by a brief statement of the fundamental interests of certain well-marked periods in our development.

The Interests of Early Childhood: The interests of early childhood are chiefly connected with ministering to the wants of the organism as expressed in the appetites, and in securing control of the larger muscles. Activity is the preeminent thing—racing and romping are worth doing for their own sake alone. Imitation is strong, curiosity is rising, and imagination is building a new world. Speech is a joy, language is learned with ease, and rhyme and rhythm become second nature. The interests of this stage are still very direct and immediate. A distant end does not attract. The thing must be worth doing for the sake of the doing. Since the young child's life is so full of action, and since it is out of acts that habits grow, it is doubly desirous during this period that environment, models, and teaching should all direct his interests and activities into lines that will lead to permanent values.

The Interests of Later Childhood: In the period from second dentition to puberty there is a great widening in the scope of interests, as well as a noticeable change in their character. Activity is still the keynote; but the child is no longer interested merely in the doing, but is now able to look forward to the end sought. Interests, which are somewhat indirect, now appeal to him, and the how of things attracts his attention. He is beginning to reach outside of his own little circle, and is ready for handicraft, reading, history, and science. Spelling, writing, and arithmetic interest him partly from the activities involved, but more as a means to an end.

Interest in complex games and plays increases, but the child is not yet ready for games, which require teamwork. He has not come to the point where he is willing to sacrifice himself for the good of all. Interest in moral questions is beginning, and right and wrong are no longer things, which may or may not be done without rebuke or punishment. The great problem at this stage is to direct the interest into ways of adapting the means to ends and into willingness to work under voluntary attention for the accomplishment of the desired end.

The Interests of Adolescence: Finally, with the advent of puberty, comes the last stage in the development of interests before adult life. This period is not marked by the birth of new interests so much as by a deepening and broadening of those already begun. The end sought becomes an increasingly larger factor, whether in play or in work. Mere activity itself no longer satisfies. The youth can now play team games; for his social interests are taking shape, and he can subordinate himself for the good of the group. Interest in the opposite sex takes on a new phase, and social form and mode of dress receive attention. A new consciousness of self emerges, and the youth becomes introspective. Questions of the ultimate meaning of things press for solution, and what and who am I, demands an answer.

At this age we pass from a régime of obedience to one of self-control, from an ethics of authority to one of individualism. All the interests are now taking on a more definite and stable form, and are looking seriously toward life vocations. This is a time of big plans and strenuous activity. It is a crucial period in our life, fraught with pitfalls and dangers, with privileges and opportunities. At this strategic point in our life's voyage we may anchor ourselves with right interests to a safe manhood and a successful career; or we may, with wrong interests, bind ourselves to a broken life of discouragement and defeat.

7. PROBLEMS IN OBSERVATION AND INTROSPECTION

1. Try making a list of your most important interests in order of their strength. Suppose you had made such a list five years ago, where would it have differed from the present list? Are you ever obliged to perform any activities in which you have little or no interest, either directly or indirectly? Can you name any activities in which you once had a strong interest but which you now perform chiefly from force of habit and without much interest?

2. Have you any interests of which you are not proud? On the other hand, do you lack certain interests, which you feel that you should possess? What interests are you now trying especially to cultivate? To suppress? Have you as broad a field of interests as you can well take care of? Have you so many interests that you are slighting the development of some of the more important ones?

3. Observe several recitations for differences in the amount of interest shown. Account for these differences. Have you ever observed an enthusiastic teacher with an uninterested class? A dull, listless teacher with an interested class?

4. A father offers his son a dollar for every grade on his term report, which is above ninety; what type of interest relative to studies does this appeal to? What do you think of the advisability of giving prizes in connection with school work?

5. Most children in the elementary school are not interested in technical grammar; why not? Histories made up chiefly of dates and lists of kings or presidents are not interesting; what is the remedy? Would you call any teaching of literature, history, geography, or science successful which fails to develop an interest in the subject?

6. After careful observation, make a statement of the differences in the typical play interests of boys and girls; of children of the third grade and the eighth grade.

CHAPTER XVII
THE WILL

The fundamental fact in all ranges of life from the lowest to the highest is *activity*, *doing*. Every individual, either animal or man, is constantly meeting situations which demand response. In the lower forms of life, this response is very simple, while in the higher forms, and especially in man, it is very complex. The bird sees a nook favorable for a nest, and at once appropriates it; a man sees a house that strikes his fancy, and works and plans and saves for months to secure money with which to buy it. It is evident that the larger the possible number of responses, and the greater their diversity and complexity, the more difficult it will be to select and compel the right response to any given situation. Man therefore needs some special power of control over his acts—he requires a *will*.

1. THE NATURE OF THE WILL

There has been much discussion and not a little controversy as to the true nature of the will. Just what *is* the will, and what is the content of our mental stream when we are in the act of willing? Is there at such times a new and distinctly different content which we do not find in our processes of knowledge or emotion—such as perception, memory, judgment, interest, desire? Or do we find, when we are engaged in an act of the will, that the mental stream contains only the familiar old elements of attention, perception, judgment, desire, purpose, etc., *all organized or set for the purpose of accomplishing or preventing some act*?

The Content of the Will: We shall not attempt here to settle the controversy suggested by the foregoing questions, nor, for immediately practical purposes, do we need to settle it. It is perhaps safe to say, however, that whenever we are willing the mental content consists of elements of cognition and feeling *plus a distinct sense of effort*, with which everyone is familiar. Whether this sense of effort is a new and different element, or only a complex of old and familiar mental processes, we need not now decide.

The Function of the Will: Concerning the function of the will there can be no haziness or doubt. *Volition concerns itself wholly with acts, responses.* The will always has to do with causing or inhibiting some action, either physical or mental. We need to go to the dentist, tell some friend we were in the wrong, hold our mind to a difficult or uninteresting task, or do some other disagreeable thing from which we shirk. It is at such points that we must call upon the will.

Again, we must restrain our tongue from speaking the unkind word, keep from crying out when the dentist drills the tooth, and check some unworthy line of thought. We must here also appeal to the will. We may conclude then that the will is needed whenever the physical or mental activity must be controlled *with effort.* Some writers have called the work of the will in compelling action its *positive* function, and in inhibiting action its *negative* function.

How the Will Exerts Its Compulsion: How does the will bring its compulsion to bear? It is not a kind of mental policeman who can take us by the collar, so to speak, and say *do this*, or *do not do that*. The secret of the will's power of control lies in *attention*. It is the line of action that we hold the mind upon with an attitude of intending to perform it that we finally follow. It is the thing we keep thinking about that we finally do.

On the other hand, let us resolutely hold the mind away from some attractive but unsuitable line of action, directing our thoughts to an opposite course, or to some wholly different subject, and we have effectually blocked the wrong response. To control our acts is therefore to control our thoughts, and strength of will can be measured by our ability to direct our attention.

2. THE EXTENT OF VOLUNTARY CONTROL OVER OUR ACTS

A relatively small proportion of our acts, or responses, are controlled by volition. Nature, in her wise economy, has provided a simpler and easier method than to have all our actions performed or checked with conscious effort.

Classes of Acts or Response: Movements or acts, like other phenomena, do not just happen. They never occur without a cause back of them. Whether they are performed with a conscious end in view or without it, the fact remains the same—something must lie back of the act to account for its performance. During the last hour, each of us has performed many simple movements and more or less complex acts. These acts have varied greatly in character. Of many we were wholly unconscious. Others were consciously performed, but without feeling of effort on our part. Still others were accomplished only with effort, and after a struggle to decide which of two lines of action we should take. Some of our acts were reflex, some were chiefly instinctive, and some were volitional.

Simple Reflex Acts: First, there are going on within every living organism countless movements of which he is in large part unconscious, which he does nothing to initiate, and which he is largely powerless to prevent. Some of them are wholly, and others almost, out of the reach and power of his will. Such are the movements of the heart and vascular system, the action of the lungs in breathing, the movements of the digestive tract, the work of the various glands in their process of secretion. The entire organism is a mass of living matter, and just because it is living no part of it is at rest.

Movements of this type require no external stimulus and no direction, they are *reflex*; they take care of themselves, as long as the body is in health, without let or hindrance, continuing whether we sleep or wake, even if we are in hypnotic or anesthetic coma. With movements of reflex type we shall have no more concern, since they are almost wholly physiological, and come scarcely at all within the range of the consciousness.

Instinctive Acts: Next there are a large number of such acts as closing the eyes when they are threatened, starting back from danger, crying out from pain or alarm, frowning and striking when angry. These may roughly be classed as instinctive, and have already been discussed under that head. They differ from the former class in that they require some stimulus to set the act off. We are fully conscious of their performance, although they are performed without a conscious end in view. Winking the eyes serves an important purpose, but that is not why we wink; starting back from danger is a wise thing to do, but we do not stop to consider this before performing the act.

And so it is with a multitude of reflex and instinctive acts. They are performed immediately upon receiving an appropriate stimulus, because we possess an organism calculated to act in a definite way in response to certain stimuli. There is no need for, and indeed no place for, anything to come in between the stimulus and the act. The stimulus pulls the trigger of the ready-set nervous system, and the act follows at once. Acts of these reflex and instinctive types do not come properly within the range of volition; hence we will not consider them further.

Automatic or Spontaneous Acts: Growing out of these reflex and instinctive acts is a broad field of action which may be called *automatic* or *spontaneous*. The distinguishing feature of this type of action is that all such acts, though performed now largely without conscious purpose or intent, were at one time purposed acts, performed with effort; this is to say that they were volitional. Such acts as writing, or fingering the keyboard of a piano, were once consciously purposed, volitional acts selected from many random or reflex movements.

The effects of experience and habit are such, however, that soon the mere presence of pencil and paper, or the sight of the keyboard, is enough to set one scribbling or playing. Stated differently, certain objects and situations come to suggest certain characteristic acts or responses so strongly that the action follows immediately on the heels of the percept of the object, or the idea of the act. James calls such action *ideo-motor*. Many illustrations of this type of acts will occur to each of us: A door starts to blow shut, and we spring up and avert the slam. The memory of a neglected engagement comes to us, and we have started to our feet on the instant. A dish of nuts stands before us, and we find ourselves nibbling without intending to do so.

The Cycle from Volitional to Automatic: It is of course evident that no such acts, though they were at one time in our experience volitional, now require effort or definite intention for their performance. The law covering this point may be stated as follows: *All volitional acts, when repeated, tend, through the effects of habit, to become automatic, and thus relieve the will from the necessity of directing them.*

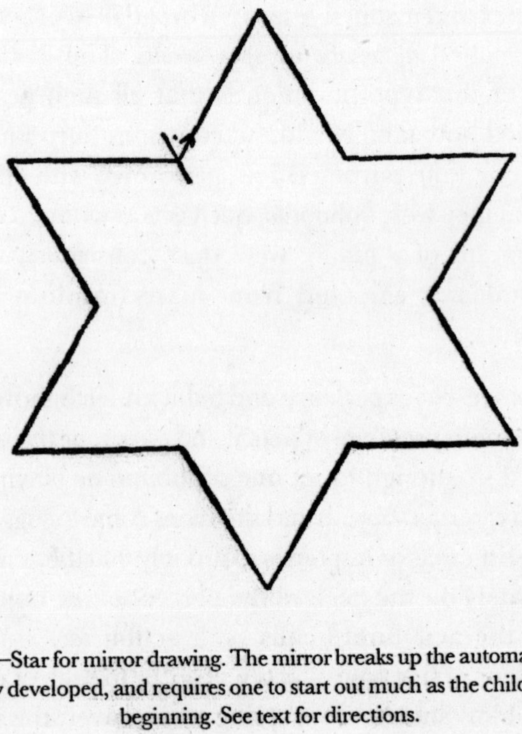

FIG. 19.—Star for mirror drawing. The mirror breaks up the automatic control previously developed, and requires one to start out much as the child does at the beginning. See text for directions.

To illustrate this law try the following experiment: Draw on a piece of cardboard a star, like figure 19, making each line segment two inches. Seat yourself at a table with the star before you, placing a mirror back of the star so that it can be seen in the mirror. Have someone hold a screen a few inches above the table so as to hide the star from your direct view, but so that you can see it in the mirror. Now reach your hand under the screen and trace with a pencil around the star from left to right, not taking your pencil off the paper until you get clear around. Keep track of how long it takes to go around and also note the irregular wanderings of your pencil. Try this experiment five times over, noting the decrease in time and effort required, and the increase in efficiency as the movements tend to become automatic.

Volitional Action: While it is obvious that the various types of action already described include a very large proportion of all our acts, yet they do not include all. For there are some acts that are neither reflex nor instinctive nor automatic, but that have to be performed under the stress of compulsion and effort. We constantly meet situations where the necessity for action or restraint runs counter to our inclinations. We daily are confronted by the necessity of making decisions in which the mind must be compelled by effort to take this direction or that direction. Conflicting motives or tendencies create frequent necessity for coercion. It is often necessary to drive our bark counter to the current of our desires or our habits, or to enter into conflict with a temptation.

Volition Acts in the Making of Decisions: Everyone knows for himself the state of inward unrest which we call indecision. A thought enters the mind which would of itself prompt an act; but before the act can occur, a contrary idea appears and the act is checked; another thought comes favoring the act, and is in turn counterbalanced by an opposing one. The impelling and inhibiting ideas we call *motives* or *reasons* for and against the proposed act. While we are balancing the motives against each other, we are said to *deliberate*. This process of deliberation must go on, if we continue to think about the matter at all, until one set of ideas has triumphed over the other and secured the attention. When this has occurred, we have *decided*, and the deliberation is at an end. We have exercised the highest function of the will and made a *choice*.

Sometimes the battle of motives is short, the decision being reached as soon as there is time to summon all the reasons on both sides of the question. At other times the conflict may go on at intervals for days or weeks, neither set of motives being strong enough to vanquish the other and dictate the decision. When the motives are somewhat evenly balanced we wisely pause in making a decision, because when one line of action is taken, the other cannot be, and we hesitate to lose either opportunity. A state of indecision is usually highly unpleasant, and no doubt more than one decision has been hastened in our lives simply that we might be done with the unpleasantness attendant on the consideration of two contrary and insistent sets of motives.

It is of the highest importance when making a decision of any consequence that we should be fair in considering all the reasons on both sides of the question, allowing each its just weight. Nor is this as easy as it might appear; for, as we saw in our study of the emotions, our feeling attitude toward any object that occupies the mind is largely responsible for the subjective value we place upon it. It is easy to be so prejudiced toward or against a line of action that the motives bearing upon it cannot get fair consideration. To be able to eliminate this personal factor to such an extent that the evidence before us on a question may be considered on its merits is a rare accomplishment.

Types of Decision: A decision may be reached in a variety of ways, the most important ones of which may now briefly be described after the general plan suggested by Professor James:

The Reasonable Type: One of the simplest types of decision is that in which the preponderance of motives is clearly seen to be on one side or the other, and the only rational thing to do is to decide in accordance with the weight of evidence. Decisions of this type are called *reasonable*. If we discover ten reasons why we should pursue a certain course of action, and only one or two reasons of equal weight why we should not, then the decision ought not to be hard to make. The points to watch in this case are (a) that we have really discovered all the important reasons on both sides of the case, and (b) that our feelings of personal interest or prejudice have not given some of the motives an undue weight in our scale of values.

Accidental type: External Motives: It is to be doubted whether as many of our decisions are made under immediate stress of volition as we think. We may be hesitating between two sets of motives, unable to decide between them, when a third factor enters which is not really related to the question at all, but which finally dictates the decision nevertheless. For example, we are considering the question whether we shall go on an excursion or stay at home and complete a piece of work. The benefits coming from the recreation, and the pleasures of the trip, are pitted against the expense, which must be incurred, and the desirability of having the work done on time. At this point, while as yet we have been unable to decide, a friend comes along, and we seek to evade the responsibility of making our own decision by appealing to him, "You tell me what to do!" How few of us have never said in effect if not in words, "I will do this or that if you will"! How few have never taken advantage of a rainy day to stay from church or shirk an undesirable engagement! How few have not allowed important questions to be decided by some trivial or accidental factor not really related to the choice in the least!

This form of decision is *accidental decision.* It does not rest on motives, which are vitally related to the case, but rather on the accident of external circumstances. The person who habitually makes his decisions in this way lacks power of will. He does not hold himself to the question until he has gathered the evidence before him, and then himself direct his attention to the best line of action and so secure its performance. He drifts with the tide, he goes with the crowd, he shirks responsibility.

Accidental Type: Subjective Motives: A second type of *accidental* decision may occur when we are hesitating between two lines of action which are seemingly about equally desirable, and no preponderating motive enters the field; when no external factor appears, and no advising friend comes to the rescue. Then, with the necessity for deciding thrust upon us, we tire of the worry and strain of deliberation and say to ourselves, "This thing must be settled one way or the other pretty soon; I am tired of the whole matter." When we have reached this point we are likely to shut our eyes to the evidence in the case, and decide largely upon the whim or mood of the moment. Very likely we regret our decision the next instant, but without any more cause for the regret than we had for the decision.

It is evident that such a decision as this does not rest on valid motives but rather on the accident of subjective conditions. Habitual decisions of this type are an evidence of a mental laziness or a mental incompetence, which renders the individual incapable of marshaling the facts bearing on a case. He cannot hold them before his mind and weigh them against each other until one side outweighs the other and dictates the decision. Of course the remedy for this weakness of decision lies in not allowing one to be pushed into a decision simply to escape the unpleasantness of a state of indecision, or the necessity of searching for further evidence, which will make the decision easier.

On the other hand, it is possible to form a habit of *indecision*, of undue hesitancy in coming to conclusions when the evidence is all before us. This gives us the mental dawdler, the person who will spend several minutes in an agony of indecision over whether to carry an umbrella on this particular trip; whether to wear black shoes or tan shoes today; whether to go calling or to stay at home and write letters this afternoon. Such a person is usually in a stew over some inconsequential matter, and consumes so much time and energy in fussing over trivial things that he is incapable of handling larger ones. If we are certain that we have all the facts in a given case before us, and have given each its due weight so far as our judgment will enable us to do, then there is nothing to be gained by delaying the decision. Nor is there any occasion to change the decision after it has once been made unless new evidence is discovered bearing on the case.

Decision Under Effort: The highest type of decision is that in which effort is the determining factor. The pressure of external circumstances and inward impulse is not enough to overcome a calm and determined *I will.* Two possible lines of action may lie open before us. Every current of our being leads toward the one; in addition, inclination, friends, honors, all beckon in the same direction. From the other course our very nature shrinks; duty alone bids us take this line, and promises no rewards except the approval of conscience. Here is the crucial point in human experience; the supreme test of the individual; the last measure of man's independence and power. Winning at this point man has exercised his highest prerogative—that of independent choice; failing here, he reverts toward the lower forms and is a creature of circumstance, no longer the master of his own destiny, but blown about by the winds of chance. And it behooves us to win in this battle. We may lose in a contest or a game and yet not fail, because we have done our best; if we fail in the conflict of motives we have planted a seed of weakness from which we shall at last harvest defeat.

Jean Valjean, the galley slave of almost a score of years, escapes and lives an honest life. He wins the respect and admiration of friends; he is elected mayor of his town, and honors are heaped on him. At the height of his prosperity he reads one day that a man has been arrested in another town for the escaped convict, Jean Valjean, and is about to be sent to the galleys. Now comes the supreme test in Jean Valjean's life. Shall he remain the honored, respected citizen and let an innocent man suffer in his stead, or shall he proclaim himself the long-sought criminal and again have the collar riveted on his neck and take his place at the oars? He spends one awful night of conflict in which contending motives make a battleground of his soul. But in the morning he has won. He has saved his manhood. His conscience yet lives—and he goes and gives himself up to the officers. Nor could he do otherwise and still remain a *man*.

3. STRONG AND WEAK WILLS

Many persons will admit that their memory or imagination or power of perception is not good, but few will confess to a weak will. Strength of will is everywhere lauded as a mark of worth and character. How can we tell whether our will is strong or weak?

Not a Will, But Wills: First of all we need to remember that, just as we do not have a memory, but a system of memories, so we do not possess a will, but many different wills. By this I mean that the will must be called upon and tested at every point of contact in experience before we have fully measured its strength. Our will may have served us reasonably well so far, but we may not yet have met any great number of hard tests because our experience and temptations have been limited.

Nor must we forget to take into account both the negative and the positive functions of the will. Many there are who think of the will chiefly in its negative use, as a kind of a check or barrier to save us *from* doing certain things. That this is an important function cannot be denied. But the positive is the higher function. There are many men and women who are able to resist evil, but able to do little good. They are good enough, but not good for much. They lack the power of effort and self-compulsion to hold them up to the high standards and stern endeavor necessary to save them from inferiority or mediocrity. It is almost certain that for most who read these words the greatest test of their will power will be in the positive instead of the negative direction.

Objective Tests a False Measure of Will Power: The actual amount of volition exercised in making a decision cannot be measured by objective results. The fact that you follow the pathway of duty, while I falter and finally drift into the byways of pleasure, is not certain evidence that you have put forth the greater power of will. In the first place, the allurements, which led me astray, may have had no charms for you. Furthermore, you may have so formed the habit of pursuing the pathway of duty when the two paths opened before you, that your well-trained feet unerringly led you into the narrow way without a struggle. Of course you are on safer ground than I, and on ground that we should all seek to attain. But, nevertheless, I, although I fell when I should have stood, may have been fighting a battle and manifesting a power of resistance of which you, under similar temptation, would have been incapable. The only point from which a conflict of motives can be safely judged is that of the soul which is engaged in the struggle.

4. VOLITIONAL TYPES

Several fairly well marked volitional types may be discovered. It is, of course, to be understood that these types all grade by insensible degrees into each other, and that extreme types are the exception rather than the rule.

The Impulsive Type: The *impulsive* type of will goes along with a nervous organism of the hair-trigger kind. The brain is in a state of highly unstable equilibrium, and a relatively slight current serves to set off the motor centers. Action follows before there is time for a counteracting current to intervene. Putting it in mental terms, we act on an idea which presents itself before an opposing one has opportunity to enter the mind. Hence *the action is largely or wholly ideo-motor and but slightly or not at all deliberate*. It is this type of will which results in the hasty word or deed, or the rash act committed on the impulse of the moment and repented of at leisure; which compels the frequent, "I didn't think, or I would not have done it!" The impulsive person may undoubtedly have credited up to him many kind words and noble deeds. In addition, he usually carries with him an air of spontaneity and whole-heartedness which goes far to atone for his faults. The fact remains, however, that he is too little the master of his acts, that he is guided too largely by external circumstances or inward caprice. He lacks balance.

Impulsive action is not to be confused with quick decision and rapid action. Many of the world's greatest and safest leaders have been noted for quickness of decision and for rapidity of action in carrying out their decisions. It must be remembered, however, that these men were making decisions in fields well known to them. They were specialists in this line of deliberation. The motives for and against certain lines of action had often been dwelt upon. All possible contingencies had been imaged many times over, and a valuation placed upon the different decisions. The various concepts had long been associated with certain definite lines of action. Deliberation under such conditions can be carried on with lightning rapidity, each motive being checked off as worth so much the instant it presents itself, and action can follow immediately when attention settles on the proper motive to govern the decision. This is not impulse, but abbreviated deliberation. These facts suggest to us that we should think much and carefully over matters in which we are required to make quick decisions.

Of course the remedy for the over-impulsive type is to cultivate deliberative action. When the impulse comes to act without consideration, pause to give the other side of the question an opportunity to be heard. Check the motor response to ideas that suggest action until you have reviewed the field to see whether there are contrary reasons to be taken into account. Form the habit of waiting for all evidence before deciding. "Think twice" before you act.

The Obstructed Will.—The opposite of the impulsive type of will is the *obstructed* or *balky* will. In this type there is too much inhibition, or else not enough impulsion. Images which should result in action are checkmated by opposing images, or do not possess vitality enough as motives to overcome the dead weight of inertia which clogs mental action. The person knows well enough what he should do, but he cannot get started. He "cannot get the consent of his will." It may be the student whose mind is tormented by thoughts of coming failure in recitation or examination, but who yet cannot force himself to the exertion necessary safely to meet the ordeal. It may be the dissolute man who tortures himself in his sober moments with remorse and the thought that he was intended for better things, but who, waking from his meditations, goes on in the same old way. It may be the child undergoing punishment, who is to be released from bondage as soon as he will promise to be good, but who cannot bring himself to say the necessary words. It not only may be, but is, man or woman anywhere who has ideals which are known to be worthy and noble, but which fail to take hold. It is anyone who is following a course of action which he knows is beneath him.

No one can doubt that the moral tragedies, the failures and the shipwrecks in life come far more from the breaking of the bonds which should bind right ideals to action than from a failure to perceive the truth. Men differ far more in their deeds than in their standards of action.

The remedy for this diseased type of will is much easier to prescribe than to apply. It is simply to refuse to attend to the contrary thoughts, which are blocking action, and to cultivate and encourage those, which lead to action of the right kind. It is seeking to vitalize our good impulses and render them effective by acting on them whenever opportunity offers. Nothing can be accomplished by moodily dwelling on the disgrace of harboring the obstructing ideas. Thus brooding over them only encourages them. What we need is to get entirely away from the line of thought in which we have met our obstruction, and approach the matter from a different direction. The child who is in a fit of sulks does not so much need a lecture on the disagreeable habit he is forming as to have his thoughts led into lines not connected with the grievance, which is causing him the trouble. The stubborn child does not need to have his will "broken," but rather to have it strengthened. He may be compelled to do what he does not want to do; but if this is accomplished through physical force instead of by leading to thoughts connected with the performance of the act, it may be doubted whether the will has in any degree been strengthened. Indeed it may rather be depended upon that the will has been weakened; for an opportunity for self-control, through which alone the will develops, has been lost. The ultimate remedy for rebellion often lies in greater freedom at the proper time. This does not mean that the child should not obey rightful authority promptly and explicitly, but that just as little external authority as possible should intervene to take from the child the opportunity for *self*-compulsion.

The Normal Will.—The golden mean between these two abnormal types of will may be called the *normal* or *balanced* will. Here there is a proper ratio between impulsion and inhibition. Ideas are not acted upon the instant they enter the mind without giving time for a survey of the field of motives, neither is action "sick lied o'er with the pale cast of thought" to such an extent that it becomes impossible. The evidence is all considered and each motive fully weighed. But this once done, decision follows. No dilatory and obstructive tactics are allowed. The fleeting impulse is not enough to persuade to action, neither is action unduly delayed after the decision is made.

5. TRAINING THE WILL

The will is to be trained as we train the other powers of the mind—through the exercise of its normal function. The function of the will is to direct or control in the actual affairs of life. Many well-meaning persons speak of training the will as if we could separate it from the interests and purposes of our daily living, and in some way put it through its paces merely for the sake of adding to its general strength. This view is all wrong. There is, as we have seen, no such thing as *general* power of will. Will is always required in specific acts and emergencies, and it is precisely upon such matters that it must be exercised if it is to be cultivated.

Will to Be Trained in Common Round of Duties: What is needed in developing the will is a deep moral interest in whatever we set out to do, and a high purpose to do it up to the limit of our powers. Without this, any artificial exercises, no matter how carefully they are devised or how heroically they are carried out, cannot but fail to fit us for the real tests of life; with it, artificial exercises are superfluous. It matters not so much what our vocation as how it is performed. The most commonplace human experience is rich in opportunities for the highest form of expression possible to the will—that of directing us into right lines of action, and of holding us to our best in the accomplishment of some dominant purpose.

There is no one set form of exercise, which alone will serve to train the will. The student pushing steadily toward his goal in spite of poverty and grinding labor; the teacher who, though unappreciated and poorly paid, yet performs every duty with conscientious thoroughness; the man who stands firm in the face of temptation; the person whom heredity or circumstance has handicapped, but who, nevertheless, courageously fights his battle; the countless men and women everywhere whose names are not known to fame, but who stand in the hard places, bearing the heat and the toil with brave, unflinching hearts—these are the ones who are developing a moral fiber and strength of will which will stand in the day of stress. Better a thousand times such training as this in the thick of life's real conflicts than any volitional calisthenics or priggish self-denials entered into solely for the training of the will!

School Work and Will Training: The work of the school offers as good an opportunity for training powers of will as of memory or reasoning. On the side of inhibition there is always the necessity for self-restraint and control so that the rights of others may not be infringed upon. Temptations to unfairness or insincerity in lessons and examinations are always to be met. The social relations of the school necessitate the development of personal poise and independence.

On the positive side the opportunities for the exercise of will power are always at hand in the school. Every lesson gives the pupil a chance to measure his strength and determination against the resistance of the task. High standards are to be built up, ideals maintained, habits rendered secure.

The great problem for the teacher in this connection is so to organize both control and instruction that the largest possible opportunity is given to pupils for the exercise of their own powers of will in all school relations.

6. FREEDOM OF THE WILL, OR THE EXTENT OF ITS CONTROL

We have seen in this discussion that will is a mode of control—control of our thoughts and, through our thoughts, of our actions. Will may be looked upon, then, as the culmination of the mental life, the highest form of directive agent within us. Beginning with the direction of the simplest movements, it goes on until it governs the current of our life in the pursuit of some distant ideal.

Limitations of the Will: Just how far the will can go in its control, just how far man is a free moral agent, has long been one of the mooted questions among the philosophers. But some few facts are clear. If the will can exercise full control over all our acts, it by this very fact determines our character; and character spells destiny. There is not the least doubt, however, that the will in thus directing us in the achievement of a destiny works under two limitations: *First*, every individual enters upon life with a large stock of *inherited tendencies*, which go far to shape his interests and aspirations. And these are important factors in the work of volition. *Second*, we all have our setting in the midst of a great *material and social environment*, which is largely beyond our power to modify, and whose influences are constantly playing upon us and molding us according to their type.

These Limitations the Conditions of Freedom: Yet there is nothing in this thought to discourage us. For these very limitations have in them our hope of a larger freedom. Man's heredity, coming to him through ages of conflict with the forces of nature, with his brother man, and with himself, has deeply instilled in him the spirit of independence and self-control. It has trained him to deliberate, to choose, to achieve. It has developed in him the power *to will*. Likewise man's environment, in which he must live and work, furnishes the problems, which his life work is to solve, and *out of whose solution will receives its only true development.*

It is through the action and interaction of these two factors, then, that man is to work out his destiny. What he *is*, coupled with what he may *do*, leads him to what he may *become*. Every man possesses in some degree a spark of divinity, a sovereign individuality, a power of independent initiative. This is all he needs to make him free—free to do his best in whatever walk of life he finds himself. If he will but do this, the doing of it will lead him into a constantly growing freedom, and he can voice the cry of every earnest heart:

Build thee more stately mansions, O my soul!

As the swift seasons roll!

Leave thy low-vaulted past!

Let each new temple, nobler than the last;

Shut thee from heaven with a dome vaster,

till thou at length art free,

leaving thine outgrown shell by life's unresting sea!

7. PROBLEMS IN OBSERVATION AND INTROSPECTION

1. Give illustrations from your own experience of the various types of action mentioned in this discussion. From your own experience of the last hour, what examples of impulsive action can you give? Would it have been better in some cases had you stopped to deliberate?

2. Are you easily influenced by prejudice or personal preference in making decisions? What recent decisions have been thus affected? Can you classify the various ones of your decisions, which you can recall under the four types mentioned in the text? Under which class does the largest number fall? Have you a tendency to drift with the crowd? Are you independent in deciding upon and following out a line of action? What is the value of advice? Ought advice to do more than to assist in getting all the evidence on a case before the one who is to decide?

3. Can you judge yourself well enough to tell to which volitional type you belong? Are you over-impulsive? Are you stubborn? What is the difference between stubbornness and firmness? Suppose you ask your instructor, or a friend, to assist you in classifying yourself as to volitional type. Are you troubled with indecision; that is, do you have hard work to decide in

trivial matters even after you know all the facts in the case? What is the cause of these states of indecision? The remedy?

4. Have you a strong power of will? Can you control your attention? Do you submit easily to temptation? Can you hold yourself up to a high degree of effort? Can you persevere? Have you ever failed in the attainment of some cherished ideal because you could not bring yourself to pay the price in the sacrifice or effort necessary?

5. Consider the class work and examinations of schools that you know. Does the system of management and control throw responsibility on the pupils in a way to develop their powers of will?

6. What motives or incentives can be used to encourage pupils to use self-compulsion to maintain high standards of excellence in their studies and conduct? Does it pay to be heroic in one's self-control?

CHAPTER XVIII
SELF-EXPRESSION AND DEVELOPMENT

We have already seen that the mind and the body are associated in a copartner ship in which each is an indispensable and active member. We have seen that the body gets its dignity and worth from its relation with the mind, and that the mind is dependent on the body for the crude material of its thought, and also for the carrying out of its mandates in securing adaptation to our environment. We have seen as a corollary of these facts that the efficiency of both mind and body is conditioned by the manner in which each carries out its share of the mutual activities. Let us see something more of this interrelation.

1. INTER-RELATION OF IMPRESSION AND EXPRESSION

No impression without corresponding expression has become a maxim in both physiology and psychology. Inner life implies self-expression in external activities. The stream of impressions pouring in upon us hourly from our environment must have means of expression if development is to follow. We cannot be passive recipients, but must be active participants in the educational process. We must not only be able to *know* and *feel*, but to *do*.

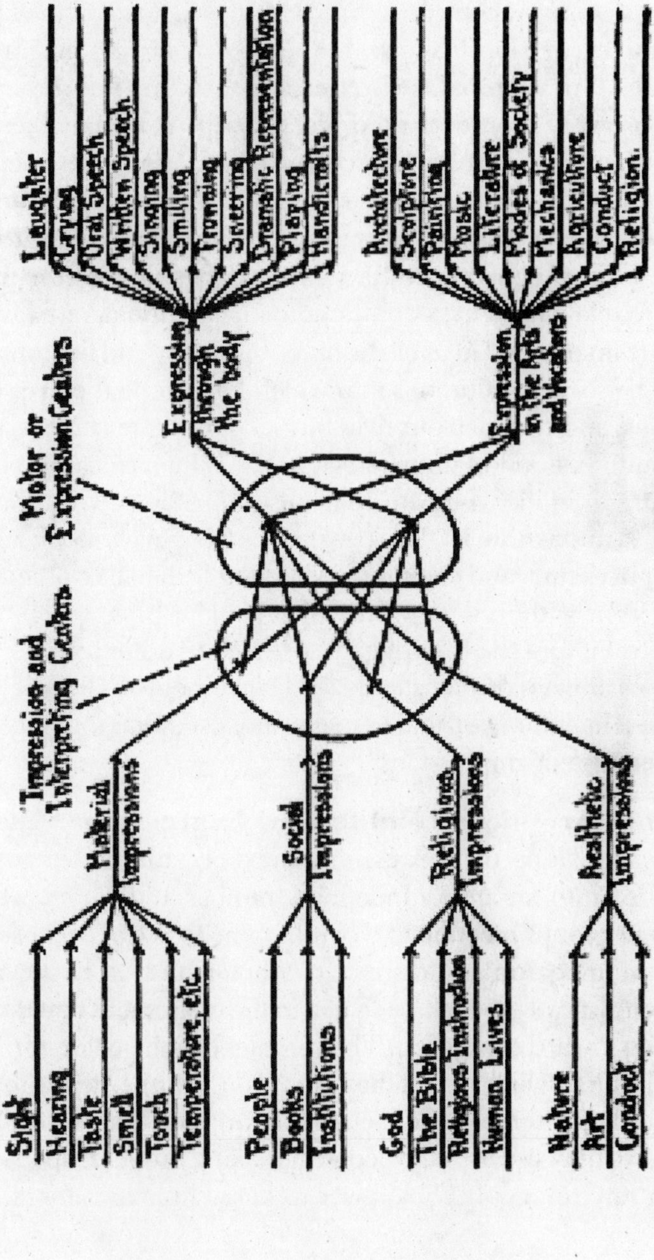
Sight
Hearing
Taste
Smell
Touch
Temperature, etc.
People
Books
Institutions
God
The Bible
Religious Instruction
Human Lives
Nature
Art
Conduct
Material Impressions
Social Impressions
Religious Impressions
Aesthetic Impressions
Impression and Interpreting Centers
Motor or Expression Centers
Expression through the body
Expression in the Arts and Vocations
Laughter
Crying
Oral Speech
Written Speech
Singing
Smiling
Frowning
Sneering
Dramatic Representation
Playing
Handicrafts
Architecture
Sculpture
Painting
Music
Literature
Modes of Society
Mechanics
Agriculture
Conduct
Religion.

FIG. 20

The Many Sources of Impressions: The nature of the impressions w come to us and how they all lead on toward ultimate expression is shown in the accompanying diagram (Fig. 20). Our material environment is thrusting impressions upon us every moment of our life; also, the material objects with which we deal have become so saturated with social values that each comes to us with a double significance, and what an object *means* often stands for more than what it *is*. From the lives of people with whom we daily mingle; from the wider circle whose lives do not immediately touch ours, but who are interpreted to us by the press, by history and literature; from the social institutions into which have gone the lives of millions, and of which our lives form a part, there come to us constantly a flood of impressions whose influence cannot be measured. So likewise with religious impressions. God is all about us and within us. He speaks to us from every nook and corner of nature, and communes with us through the still small voice from within, if we will but listen. The Bible, religious instruction, and the lives of good people are other sources of religious impressions constantly tending to mold our lives. The beautiful in nature, art, and human conduct constantly appeals to us in esthetic impressions.

All Impressions Lead toward Expression.—Each of these groups of impressions may be subdivided and extended into an almost indefinite number and variety, the different groups meeting and overlapping, it is true, yet each preserving reasonably distinct characteristics. A common characteristic of them all, as shown in the diagram, is that they all point toward expression. The varieties of light, color, form, and distance, which we get through vision, are not merely that we may know these phenomena of nature, but that, knowing them, we may use the knowledge in making proper responses to our environment. Our power to know human sympathy and love through our social impressions are not merely that we may feel these emotions, but that, feeling them, we may act in response to them.

It is impossible to classify logically in any simple scheme all the possible forms of expression. The diagram will serve, however, to call attention to some of the chief modes of bodily expression, and also to the results of the bodily expressions in the arts and vocations. Here again the process of subdivision and extension can be carried out indefinitely. The laugh can be made to tell many different stories. Crying may express bitter sorrow or uncontrollable joy. Vocal speech may be carried on in a thousand tongues. Dramatic action may be made to portray the whole range of human feelings. Plays and games are wide enough in their scope to satisfy the demands of all ages and every people. The handicrafts cover so wide a range that the material progress of civilization can be classed under them, and indeed without their development the arts and vocations would be impossible. Architecture, sculpture, painting, music, and literature have a thousand possibilities both in technique and content. Likewise the modes of society, conduct, and religion are unlimited in their forms of expression.

Limitations of Expression: While it is more blessed to give than to receive, it is somewhat harder in the doing; for more of the self is, after all, involved in expression than in impression. Expression needs to be cultivated as an art; for who can express all he thinks, or feels, or conceives? Who can do his innermost self-justice when he attempts to express it in language, in music, or in marble? The painter answers when praised for his work, "If you could but see the picture I intended to paint!" The pupil says, "I know, but I cannot tell." The friend says, "I wish I could tell you how sorry I am." The actor complains, "If I could only portray the passion as I feel it, I could bring all the world to my feet!" The body, being of grosser structure than the mind, must always lag somewhat behind in expressing the mind's states; yet, so perfect is the harmony between the two, that with a body well trained to respond to the mind's needs, comparatively little of the spiritual need be lost in its expression through the material.

2. THE PLACE OF EXPRESSION IN DEVELOPMENT

Nor are we to think that cultivation of expression results in better power of expression alone, or that lack of cultivation results only in decreased power of expression.

Intellectual Value of Expression: There is a distinct mental value in expression. An idea always assumes new clearness and wider relations when it is expressed. Michael Angelo, making his plans for the great cathedral, found his first concept of the structure expanding and growing more beautiful as he developed his plans. The sculptor, beginning to model the statue after the image which he has in his mind, finds the image growing and becoming more expressive and beautiful as the clay is molded and formed. The writer finds the scope and worth of his book growing as he proceeds with the writing. The student, beginning doubtfully on his construction in geometry, finds the truth growing clearer as he proceeds. The child with a dim and hazy notion of the meaning of the story in history or literature discovers that the meaning grows clear as he himself works out its expression in speech, in the handicrafts, or in dramatic representation.

So we may apply the test to any realm of thought whatever, and the law holds good: *It is not in its apprehension, but in its expression, that a truth finally becomes assimilated to our body of usable knowledge.* And this means that in all training of the body through its motor expression we are to remember that the mind must be behind the act; that the intellect must guide the hand; that the object is not to make skillful fingers alone, but to develop clear and intelligent thought as well.

Moral Value of Expression.—Expression also has a distinct moral value. There are many more people of good intentions than of moral character in the world. The rugged proverb tells us that the road to hell is paved with good intentions. And how easy it is to form good resolutions. Who of us has not, after some moral struggle, said, "I will break the bonds of this habit: I will enter upon that heroic line of action!" and then, satisfied for the time with having made the resolution, continued in the old path, until we were surprised later to find that we had never got beyond the resolution.

It is not in the moment of the resolve but in the moment when the resolve is carried out in action that the moral value inheres. To take a stand on a question of right and wrong means more than to show one's allegiance to the right—it clears one's own moral vision and gives him command of himself. Expression is, finally, the only true test for our morality. Lacking moral expression, we may stand in the class of those who are merely good, but we can never enter the class of those who are good for something. One cannot but wonder what would happen if all the people in the world who are morally right should give expression to their moral sentiments, not in words alone, but in deeds. Surely the millennium would speedily come, not only among the nations, but in the lives of men.

Religious Value of Expression.—True religious experience demands expression. The older conception of a religious life was to escape from the world and live a life of communion and contemplation in some secluded spot, ignoring the world thirsting without. Later religious teaching, however, recognized the fact that religion cannot consist in drinking in blessings alone, no matter how ecstatic the feeling which may accompany the process; that it is not the receiving, but this along with the giving that enriches the life. To give the cup of cold water, to visit the widow and the fatherless, to comfort and help the needy and forlorn—this is not only scriptural but it is psychological. Only as religious feeling goes out into religious expression, can we have a normal religious experience.

Social Value of Expression.—The criterion of an education once was, how much does he know? The world did not expect an educated man to *do* anything; he was to be put on a pedestal and admired from a distance. But this criterion is now obsolete. Society cares little how much we know if it does not enable us to do. People no longer admire mere knowledge, but insist that the man of education shall put his shoulder to the wheel and lend a hand wherever help is needed. Education is no longer to set men apart from their fellows, but to make them more efficient comrades and helpers in the world's work. Not the man who *knows* chemistry and botany, but he who can use this knowledge to make two blades of grass grow where but one grew before, is the true benefactor of his race. In short, the world demands services returned for opportunities afforded; it expects social expression to result from education.

And this is also best for the individual, for only through social service can we attain to a full realization of the social values in our environment. Only thus can we enter fully into the social heritage of the ages which we receive from books and institutions; only thus can we come into the truest and best relations with humanity in a common brotherhood; only thus can we live the broader and more significant life, and come to realize the largest possible social self.

3. EDUCATIONAL USE OF EXPRESSION

The educational significance of the truths illustrated in the diagram and the discussion has been somewhat slow in taking hold in our schools. This has been due not alone to the slowness of the educational world to grasp a new idea, but also to the practical difficulties connected with adapting the school exercises as well to the expression side of education as to the impression. From the fall of Athens on down to the time of Froebel the schools were constituted on the theory that pupils were to *receive* education; that they were to *drink in* knowledge that their minds were to be *stored* with facts. Children were to "be seen and not heard." Education was largely a process of gorging the memory with information.

Easier to Provide for the Impression Side of Education.—Now it is evident that it is far easier to provide for the passive side of education than for the active side. All that is needed in the former case is to have teachers and books reasonably full of information, and pupils sufficiently docile to receive it. But in the latter case, the equipment must be more extensive. If the child is to be allowed to carry out his impressions into action, if he is actually to *do* something himself, then he must be supplied with adequate equipment.

So far as the home life was concerned, the child of several generations ago was at a decided advantage over the child of today on the expression side of his education. The homes of that day were beehives of industry, in which a dozen handicrafts were taught and practiced. The buildings, the farm implements, and most of the furniture of the home were made from the native timber. The material for the clothing of the family was produced on the farm, made into cloth, and finally into garments in the home. Nearly all the supplies for the table came likewise from the farm. These industries demanded the combined efforts of the family, and each child did his or her part.

But that day is past. One-half of our people live in cities and towns, and even in the village and on the farm the handicrafts of the home have been relegated to the factory, and everything comes into the home ready for use. The telephone, the mail carrier, and the deliveryman do all the errands even, and the child in the home is deprived of responsibility and of nearly all opportunity for manual expression. This is no one's fault, for it is just one phase of a great industrial readjustment in society. Yet the fact remains that the home has lost an important element in education, which the school must supply if we are not to be the losers educationally by the change.

The School to Take Up the Handicrafts: And modern educational method is insisting precisely on this point. A few years ago the boy caught whittling in school was a fit subject for a flogging; the boy is today given bench and tools, and is instructed in their use. Then the child was punished for drawing pictures; now we aré using drawing as one of the best modes of expression. Then instruction in singing was in trusted to an occasional evening class, which only the older children could attend, and which did some itinerant singing master teach; today we make music one of our most valuable school exercises. Then all play time was so much time wasted; now we recognize play as a necessary and valuable mode of expression and development. Then dramatic representation was confined to the occasional exhibition or evening entertainment; now it has become a recognized part of our school work. Then it was a crime for pupils to communicate with each other in school; now a part of the school work is planned so that pupils work in groups, and thus receive social training. Then our schoolrooms were destitute of every vestige of beauty; today many of them are artistic and beautiful.

This statement of the case is rather over-optimistic if applied to our whole school system, however. For there are still many schools in which all forms of handicraft are unknown, and in which the only training in artistic expression is that which comes from caricaturing the teacher. Singing is still an unknown art to many teachers. The play instinct is yet looked upon with suspicion and distrust in some quarters. A large number of our schoolrooms are as barren and ugly today as ever, and contain an atmosphere as stifling to all forms of natural expression. We can only comfort ourselves with Holmes's maxim, that it matters not so much where we stand as in what direction we are moving. And we certainly are moving toward a larger development and greater efficiency in expression on the part of those who pass through our schools.

Expression and Character: Finally, all that has been said in this discussion has direct reference to what we call character—that mysterious something which we so often hear eulogized and so seldom analyzed. Character has two distinct phases, which may be called the *subjective* phase and the *social* phase; or, stating it differently, character is both what we *are* and what we *do*. The first of these has to do with the nature of the real, innermost self; and the last, with the modes in which this self finds expression. And it is fair to say that those about us are concerned with what we are chiefly from its relation to what we do.

Character is not a thing, but a process; it is the succession of our thoughts and acts from hour to hour. It is not something which we can hoard and protect and polish unto a more perfect day, but it is the everyday self in the process of living. And the only way in which it can be made or marred is through the nature of this stream of thoughts and acts which constitute the day's life—is through *being* or *doing* well or ill.

Two Lines of Development: The cultivation of character must, then, ignore neither of these two lines. To neglect the first is to forget that it is out of the abundance of the heart that the mouth speaks; that a corrupt tree cannot bring forth good fruit; that the act is the true index of the soul. To omit the second is to leave the character half formed, the will weak, and the life inefficient and barren of results. The mind must be supplied with noble ideas and high ideals, with right emotions and worthy ambitions. On the other hand, the proper connection must be established between these mental states and appropriate acts. And the acts must finally grow into habits, so that we naturally and inevitably translate our ideas and ideals, our emotions and ambitions into deeds. Our character must be strong not in thought and feeling alone, but also in the power to return to the world its finished product in the form of service.

4. PROBLEMS IN INTROSPECTION AND OBSERVATION

1. Do you find that you understand better some difficult point or problem after you have succeeded in stating it? Do you remember better what you have expressed?

2. In which particular ones of your studies do you think you could have done better if you had been given more opportunity for expression? Explain the psychology of the maxim; we learn to do by doing.

3. Observe various schools at work for the purpose of determining whether opportunities for expression in the recitations are adequate. Have you ever seen a class when listless from listening liven up when they were given something to *do* themselves?

4. Make a study of the types of laughter you hear. Why is some laughter much more pleasant than other laughter? What did a noted sculptor mean when he said that a smile at the eyes cannot be depended upon as can one at the mouth?

5. What examples have you observed in children's plays showing their love for dramatic representation? What handicrafts are the most suitable for children of primary grades? For the grammar school? for the high school?

6. Do you number those among your acquaintance who seem bright enough, so far as learning is concerned, but who cannot get anything accomplished? Is the trouble on the expression side of their character? What are you doing about your own powers of expression? Are you seeking to cultivate expression in new lines? Is there danger in attempting too many lines?

INDEX